Adobe® GoLive® CS TIPS and TRICKS

THE 200 BEST

Adam Pratt
Lynn Grillo

Adobe Press

Adobe GoLive CS Tips and Tricks
The 200 Best

Adam Pratt
Lynn Grillo

Adobe Press books are published by Peachpit Press
Peachpit Press
1249 Eighth Street
Berkeley, CA 94710
510/524-2178
800/283-9444
510/524-2221 (fax)

Peachpit Press is a division of Pearson Education

To report errors, please send a note to errata@peachpit.com

For the latest on Adobe books, go to www.adobepress.com

Editor: Corbin Collins
Production Editor: Becky Winter
Copyeditor: Liz Welch
Compositors: David Van Ness, Danielle Foster
Indexer: FireCrystal Communications
Cover design: Maureen Forys
Interior design: Maureen Forys

This book was designed and laid out in Adobe InDesign.

ISBN 0-321-27877-1

9 8 7 6 5 4 3 2

Printed and bound in the United States of America

To Cindy, Drew, and Katie.
Now that the book's done,
let's go to the park!

—Adam

For my favorite guys,
Joe and Nicco

—Lynn

Acknowledgements

A few special thanks are in order to people who helped make this project successful. First, a big *thank you* to Jeffrey Warnock of Adobe Press. Without his help, this book would not even have been started, let alone finished. Thank you also to Terry White, Technical Resources Manager at Adobe Systems, for his support.

We are indebted to designer Chris Converse, who graciously supplied samples of his designs for us to use in the screen captures for this book. Chris's work can been seen in Chapters Three and Four, where files from the InDesign User Group Web site which Chris designed are used extensively. He also supplied SmartObject examples, collection samples, and even regex patterns. Thank you, Chris! Visit Chris's Web site at http://www.ChrisConverse.com.

We'd be remiss not to mention the editorial and development team at Peachpit, but most especially Corbin Collins and Liz Welch, whose sharp eyes and fine crafting of the English language gave polish to these pages. Many thanks to the third-party developers who gave us access to their software and assistance during our testing. Finally, we owe a huge debt of gratitude to the GoLive engineering and product teams for building such cool software.

Contents

Foreword

Over the years, I have had the pleasure of working alongside two of Adobe's greatest enthusiasts, evangelists, and educators: Lynn Grillo and Adam Pratt. Through their ubiquitous presence online and their behind-the-scenes work in various GoLive alpha and beta forums, they have shown an unwavering commitment to helping individuals around the world become more productive with Adobe GoLive and the rest of the Adobe Creative Suite.

The evolution of Web and interactive design disciplines continues to take shape around the separation of structure and presentation, and Adobe GoLive CS is at the forefront of this remarkable transformation in communication. The book you hold in your hands offers much insight into a very feature-rich, deep, and powerful design and development application.

And it's not just their masterful expertise on the material itself that is so valuable here—how they have applied and presented it is also worthy of admiration. Adam and Lynn have included helpful screenshots for each of their 200 tips (for one example) and have even dedicated a whole chapter to incredibly useful third-party actions and extensions (for another). All-in-all, this book promises to save thousands of designers and webmasters untold amounts of time.

All of us at Adobe hope you will use this rewarding reference alongside Adobe GoLive CS as we do: dog-earing especially helpful pages and highlighting content that proves useful time and time again. GoLive fans rejoice: *Adobe GoLive CS Tips and Tricks* is a treasure trove of information. Happy mining!

George Arriola
Adobe GoLive Senior Product Manager

CHAPTER ONE

Getting Started

Adobe's new Creative Suite Premium—which includes Photoshop CS, Illustrator CS, InDesign CS, GoLive CS, and Acrobat 6.0 Professional—has significantly changed the graphic-design software industry. For the first time, designers are able to purchase the software they need for print, Web, and PDF publishing, all in one box. While there are hundreds of thousands of GoLive users around the world, many new users are being introduced to GoLive for the first time through the Creative Suite. GoLive is an incredibly powerful and fun Web-authoring application. On its own it's pretty impressive, but combining GoLive with the rest of the Creative Suite is truly sweet!

We've done our best to write a tips-and-tricks book that teaches beginners the basics and shows seasoned users some special hints. We'll wow even the most experienced among you with power tips that will save you time and enable you to be more creative as you build sites with GoLive.

This first chapter introduces you to the interface, shows you how to optimize GoLive for optimum performance and productivity, and teaches even the pros a few new tricks. Let's get started!

TIP 1 Getting Started with the Welcome Screen

To kick things off, launch GoLive. You'll see a Welcome screen, similar to the Welcome screens in the other Creative Suite applications. This screen gives you several easy ways to get started with the software (**Figure 1**).

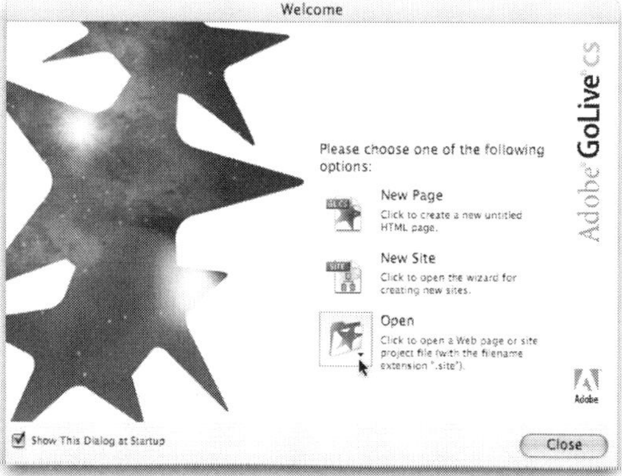

Figure 1 The Welcome screen opens when you launch GoLive and helps get you going with common tasks.

When you click the New Page icon, GoLive creates a new blank Web page. This can be a good place to start if you just want to tinker around and check out the rest of the interface.

It might be tempting to begin with a new page, but we strongly recommend you start with the New Site icon instead. The real power of GoLive is revealed when you use its amazing Site window and site-management features. It's possible to edit individual Web pages in GoLive without the Site window, but unless you're really savvy you'll probably end up with broken links and missing images. Clicking the New Site icon opens the Site Wizard (explained in detail in Tip 11).

If you click the Open icon in the Welcome screen, you'll see a standard Open dialog where you can open any GoLive file for editing. If you've already used GoLive to edit Web sites or pages, the most recent files are listed in the pull-down menu that appears when you click and hold the Open icon. This is a handy shortcut to sites and pages you edit frequently.

Picking Up Where You Left Off

To open all the sites and pages that were open the last time you quit GoLive, press the Shift key and click the Close button in the Welcome screen. Voilà!

Accessing the Welcome Screen and Its Commands Again

After you select an option in the Welcome screen, the only way to open that screen again is to relaunch GoLive. However, the File menu includes New Page, New Site, Open, and Open Recent commands, all of which correspond to options in the Welcome screen.

Turn It Off!

You'll probably like the Welcome screen at first, but after a while it might start to annoy you. If you want to turn it off, just deselect the Show This Dialog at Startup option in the bottom-left corner.

TIP 2 Customizing Keyboard Shortcuts

We strongly believe that software should be flexible and allow you to customize as much as possible. One practical way that GoLive lets you adapt the software to how you work is through customizable keyboard shortcuts. If there's an obscure menu command you use frequently, there's no need to send a feature request to Adobe to change it. Open the Keyboard Shortcuts Editor (from the application menu on the Mac or from the bottom of the Edit menu on Windows) to assign a custom keyboard shortcut (**Figure 2**).

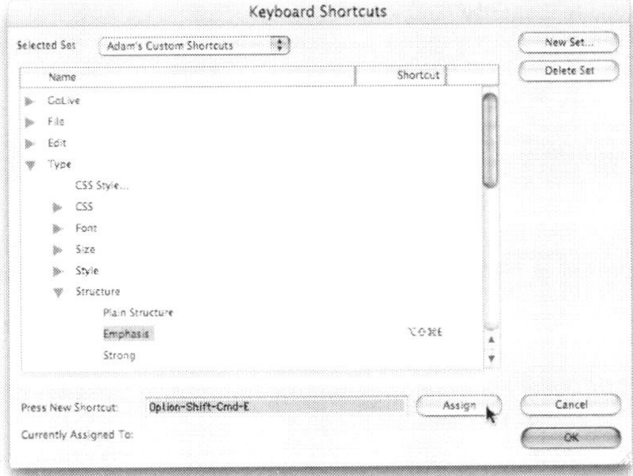

Figure 2 The Keyboard Shortcuts editor lets you add, remove, and reassign custom keyboard shortcuts for the menu commands you use most often.

Notice at the very top of the dialog there are already two sets of keyboard shortcuts in the Selected Set menu: GoLive Factory Default and the GoLive 5 Set. To create your own set, click the New Set button, name the set, and click OK.

Now select the command in the menu listing that you want to customize and type the new shortcut in the Press New Shortcut field at the bottom of the dialog. If you assign a menu command a keyboard shortcut that is already assigned to another command, a warning at the bottom of the dialog tells you what the shortcut is currently assigned to. Find a unique shortcut that isn't already taken, or if you want to make the change anyway click the Assign button, and the shortcut is removed from the old command and assigned to the new command.

Switching from Default to Custom Shortcuts

If friends or coworkers need to use GoLive on your computer, and your custom keyboard shortcuts are confusing them, just temporarily switch back to the GoLive Factory Default set. You can always return to your custom set.

Sharing Shortcuts

If you create a great set of keyboard shortcuts, you'll want to make them the same on every computer you work on—and maybe even share them with coworkers. Copy the shortcuts setting file (from User/Library/Preferences/Adobe/GoLive/Settings7/Shortcuts on the Mac or Documents and Settings\User\Application Data\Adobe\Adobe GoLive/Settings7\Shortcuts on Windows) to the same location on the other machine.

TIP 3 Setting Preferences

Understanding Modules

To understand what a module does, select it in the list under the Modules pane, then click the triangle next to the Show Item Information option at the bottom of the window.

Before you start working in GoLive CS, we recommend you familiarize yourself with the application preferences. You'll only change a few things now, but when you need to make further adjustments in the future you'll know where to look. Open the preferences by selecting Adobe GoLive > Preferences on the Mac or Edit > Preferences in Windows (**Figure 3**).

Figure 3 The application preferences are a good place to start customizing the software to meet your needs.

Start in the General section and look at the At Launch options. You could have GoLive create a new blank page every time you launch the application, but you'll probably just want to set it to Do Nothing and open the sites you need to work on. In case you turned off the Welcome screen as described in Tip 1, you can turn it back on here.

Another handy set of preferences appears under the Modules section in the left-hand pane. You can enable and disable GoLive features by clicking the On/Off check box and restarting GoLive. Disabling features can speed up launch times and reduce the amount of RAM required.

The last settings to edit are the preview browser options. Select Browsers on the left, click the Find All button, and GoLive scours your entire hard drive for Web browsers. If GoLive isn't picking up one of your browsers, or the browser is installed somewhere unusual, click Add to choose it manually. All the browsers listed in the preferences are also added to the File > Preview In menu.

TIP 4

Using the Objects Palette

Though the Objects palette resembles Photoshop's toolbar, it works differently. This palette is where all the objects that you might add to a Web page or Web site are stored. The icons in the top section of the Objects palette represent the different categories of objects. When you choose a category at the top, all the objects in that category are displayed at the bottom.

To place one of the objects, just drag it from the Objects palette to a Web page or Web site. The default Objects palette sections are shown in **Figure 4**.

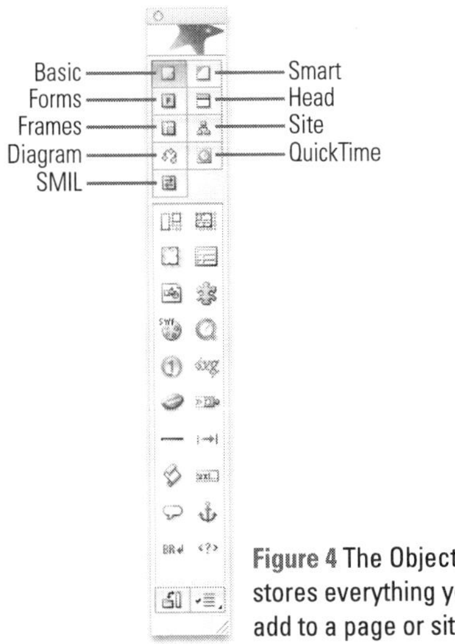

Figure 4 The Objects palette stores everything you might add to a page or site.

Basic Basic page elements such as tables, images, and multimedia files (see Chapter 3).

Smart Advanced page elements such as native Adobe image file formats (see Chapter 7) and JavaScript Actions (see Chapter 8).

Forms All the form elements you'll ever need (see Tip 156).

Head Web page head items such as keywords and other metatags (see Tip 26).

Palette or Toolbar?

The Objects palette in GoLive CS looks more like a toolbar. If you prefer the way it looked in previous versions of GoLive, just click the Toggle Orientation button in the bottom-left corner of the palette.

Configuring for Compliance

If you need to target a specific W3C code specification, such as HTML 3.2, HTML 4 Strict, or XHTML 1.1, use the Configure submenu in the bottom-right corner of the Objects palette to limit the available objects so that your source code is compliant.

Frames iFrames, frames, and prebuilt framesets are stored here (see Tips 64 and 65).

Site Objects you'd add to the Site window such as blank pages, email addresses, and folders for organization (see Chapter 2).

Diagram Dozens of different objects you might use to create a site map with the Diagram feature (see Tip 164).

QuickTime Twenty multimedia formats you can use to create interactive QuickTime movies (see Tip 158).

SMIL (Synchronized Multimedia Integration Language) Objects used to create interactive, multimedia presentations. SMIL is beyond the scope of this book, but to learn more you can download *Adobe GoLive CS Multimedia Authoring* from http://media.studio.adobe.com/tips/media/en/glv7multimedia/pdfs/glv7multimedia.pdf.

TIP 5 Inspector Palette

The Inspector palette in GoLive is where you edit and customize selected objects (**Figure 5**). The cool thing about the Inspector palette is that it's context-sensitive and changes depending on what is selected. For example, if you select an HTML table you'll see options for adjusting rows, columns, and borders—but if you select a page in the Site window, you'll see options for adjusting the filename and page title.

Grabbing Lost Palettes

If you ever have a palette that's stuck and you can't move it, try pressing the Control/Option (Mac) or Ctrl/Alt (Windows) keys to grab it with a hand cursor.

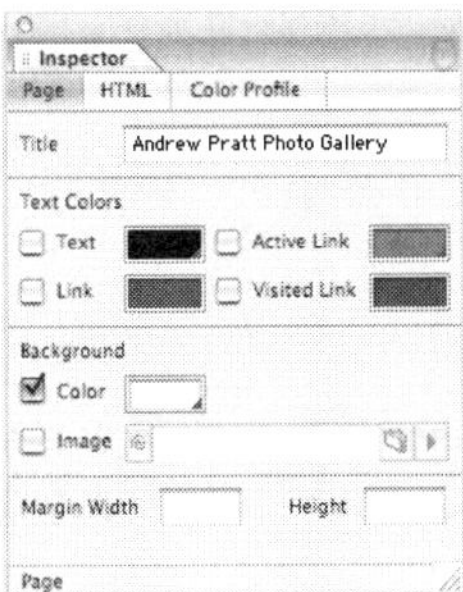

Figure 5 The context-sensitive Inspector palette lets you adjust any selected object.

When there are too many options to fit in the Inspector palette, the settings are distributed across multiple tabs in the palette, as shown in Figure 5. If you're looking for a setting in the Inspector but can't find it, be sure to check the other tabs. If you're not sure you're inspecting the right object, just look in the bottom-left corner of the palette where it shows the name of the Inspector, such as Image, Text, or Table.

TIP 6 Managing Palettes

GoLive CS has improved the way you can stash palettes on the left and right edges of your monitor. We really like the Adobe palettes, but let's face it—you want to look at *documents*, not a clutter of palettes. To stash a palette, grab its tab and drag it to the left or right edge of the monitor (**Figure 6a**).

Figure 6a Palettes can be neatly stashed on the right or left edges of your computer screen.

Click the tab of a stashed palette, and it slides into view. Click the tab again, and it slides back to its docked position. To stash more than one palette together in a group, just drag another palette by its tab into a stashed palette. To adjust the height of a stashed palette, click its bottom edge and slide it up or down (**Figure 6b**).

Figure 6b When your mouse pointer turns into a two-sided arrow, you can drag the edge of a stashed palette to lengthen or shorten it. That's great when you want to stash several palettes together.

Note

Mac OS X users should note that it's not possible to stash palettes on the same monitor edge as the OS X dock.

Stashing and Unstashing All Palettes

No doubt you'll really like the way GoLive CS stashes palettes to maximize your usable screen real estate. But opening and closing lots of palettes can still be tedious. A cool power user trick is to Option/Alt-click on a stashed palette to open or close all stashed palettes simultaneously.

GoLive CS now has docked palettes that match the behavior of other Adobe applications, including Photoshop, Illustrator, and InDesign. To dock a palette, grab its tab and hold it over the bottom edge of another palette until you see a blue line appear, and then let go (**Figure 6c**). Now when you move the top palette, any palettes docked along with it will move, too.

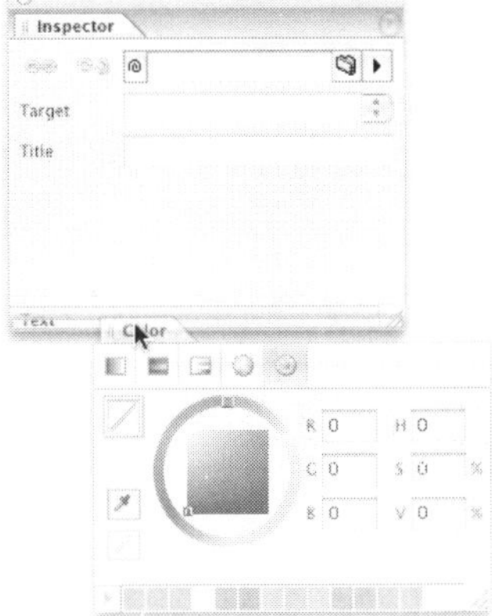

Figure 6c A blue highlight appears when the palettes overlap. If you let go, the palettes will be docked together.

Docking groups of palettes top to bottom is a great way to manage your palettes, and it makes it easy to move them all around at one time. The problem with docking palettes is that if you dock too many tall ones, the lower ones can get lost off the bottom of the screen. To remedy that problem, click the triangle to the left of the palette names to twirl open or close a palette set (**Figure 6d**).

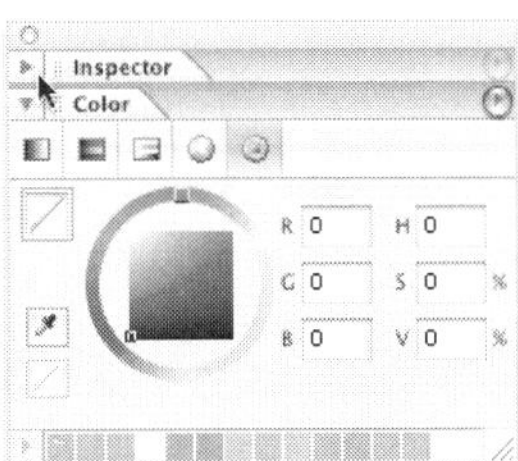

Figure 6d Click the handy-dandy arrow button on the upper left of a palette group to collapse the entire group.

Rearranging Palette Tabs

This might not seem like a big deal, but if you've used Adobe applications as long as we have, you'll appreciate the following attention to detail: GoLive is the first Adobe application that lets you rearrange palettes that are grouped together without having to ungroup them first! That's correct—you can just grab a palette tab and move it to the left or right of any other tab in the group until you have them situated just how you like them.

TIP 7 Finding Palettes

Alphabetized Order

The Window menu in GoLive CS is now sorted alphabetically like the rest of the Creative Suite applications. The only exception is that toolbars are listed at the top and open document and site windows are listed at the bottom. This alphabetical listing makes it so much easier to find those missing palettes and seldom-used features.

We've shown how to take charge of your palettes by stashing, docking, and twirling them, but let's not forget an even more fundamental function: finding them. Where are the rest of the palettes hiding? They're in the Window menu, of course. Simply choose Window and then select the name of the palette you want to open from the list (**Figure 7a**).

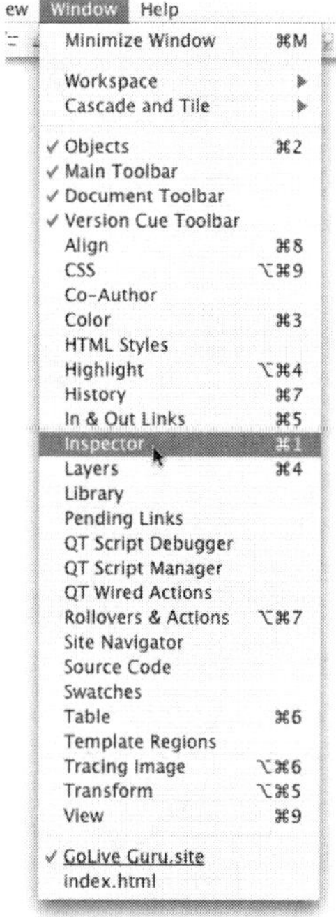

Figure 7a There's a plethora of palettes in the Window menu.

Notice that plenty of palettes have keyboard shortcuts associated with them, so when you become familiar with which palettes are used for which tasks, you'll be able to invoke your favorite palette by pressing its keyboard shortcut.

Also nested in the Window menu are options for Workspace (see Tip 8) and for Cascade and Tile. Choosing Window > Cascade and Tile > Cascade places all of the open Windows in a neat stack (**Figure 7b**), whereas choosing Window > Cascade and Tile > Tile Horizontally (or Vertically) lines all of the open windows up next to one another (**Figure 7c**).

Figure 7b Can't find one of your windows? Use Cascade to stack them up neatly one on top of the other.

Figure 7c Tiling windows lets you see them all at once.

Customizing the Workspace

After you have set up your GoLive palettes exactly as you like, you can save the workspace so that you may revert to it at any time. This is extremely helpful if you find that after a work session you've got palettes strewn all over the place. Choose Window > Workspace > Save Workspace and then give your workspace a name (**Figure 8a**).

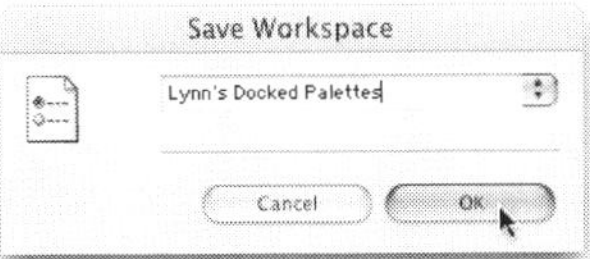

Figure 8a By using workspaces, you can always have your favorite palettes just where you want them. Simply give your workspace a name.

Go ahead and get as messy as you'd like with your palettes. To tidy up the workspace again, simply choose Window > Workspace, select the name of your saved workspace from the list, and then watch as all the palettes jump back into position (**Figure 8b**).

Figure 8b Choose a workspace name from the workspace submenu to put palettes back where they belong. If only our real desks were this easy to straighten up.

There's more to workspaces than simply creating or using one. To go back to the default palette location, choose Window > Workspace > Default Workspace. To manage a workspace, choose Window > Workspace > Manage Workspaces and then you can create, delete, or rename a workspace.

TIP 9 Helping Yourself

Every now and again you may be unsure about how to accomplish a specific task in GoLive CS. Fortunately, GoLive's Help menu comes to the rescue. Just like all the applications in the Adobe Creative Suite, GoLive CS includes a fully searchable User Guide that is installed by default and accessible from the Help menu. Choose Help > GoLive Help (**Figure 9a**), and the User Guide is launched into your Web browser (**Figure 9b**).

Figure 9a Help is always at your fingertips: simply choose Help, then GoLive Help.

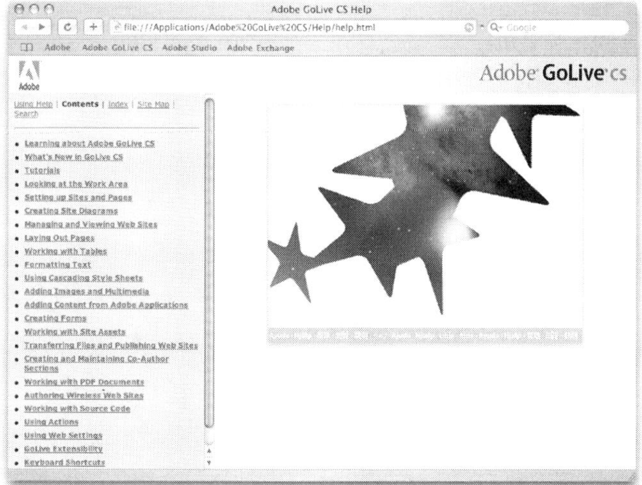

Figure 9b The HTML Help files automatically launch in your default Web browser.

A common misconception is that you need to be online in order to access the Help files, but that's not true. The files themselves are HTML files that are sitting in a folder called Help, right inside your GoLive application folder.

PDF User Guides

What if you'd like to print a part or even all of the User Guide? Your best bet would be to print from the included PDF version of the User Guide. This PDF file can be found on the installation CD in a folder called Documentation. If you installed GoLive CS as part of the Adobe Creative Suite, the PDF version of the User Guide is on Disk One of the Resources and Extras disks inside the Documentation folder.

Click the Index link to go to a specific term or use the Search link to look for all instances of a term. Type your search term into the input field, then click the Search button (**Figure 9c**).

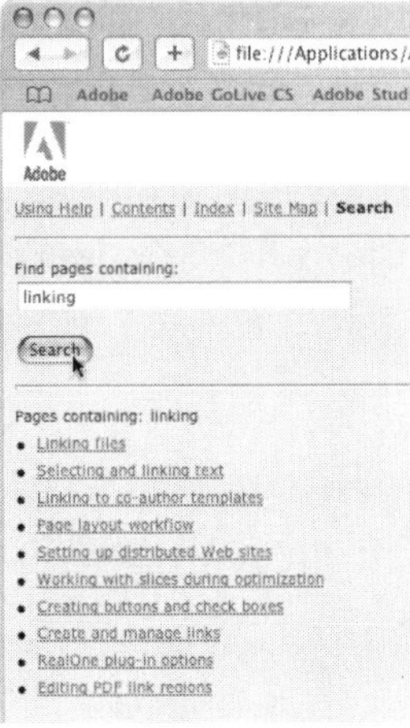

Figure 9c Use the Search feature to quickly find all the help files related to a specific topic.

The results of a search are displayed as clickable links on the left, each of which loads information into the area on the right. Use the navigation links at the top or bottom of each page to go to the next or previous related topic (**Figure 9d**).

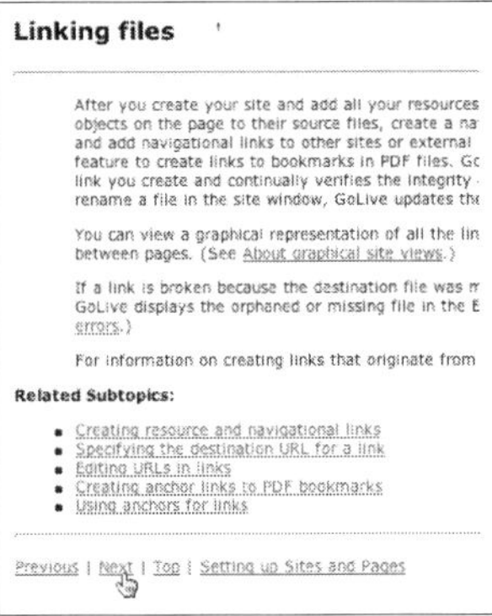

Figure 9d The Help file includes navigational links that take you to related topics.

TIP 10 Updating Software Automatically

Since its initial release, GoLive CS has had two updates. As of this writing, the current version of GoLive CS is 7.0.2. To ensure that you have the most recent update that includes many bug fixes, use the Update feature built into the Help menu (**Figure 10a**).

Figure 10a From the Help menu, choose Updates to check for any new releases.

If your version is current, GoLive will show a dialog stating that there are no updates available. If you do need the update, you'll get a dialog showing the name of the update and asking if you'd like to download it. You can then download and install the update (**Figure 10b**).

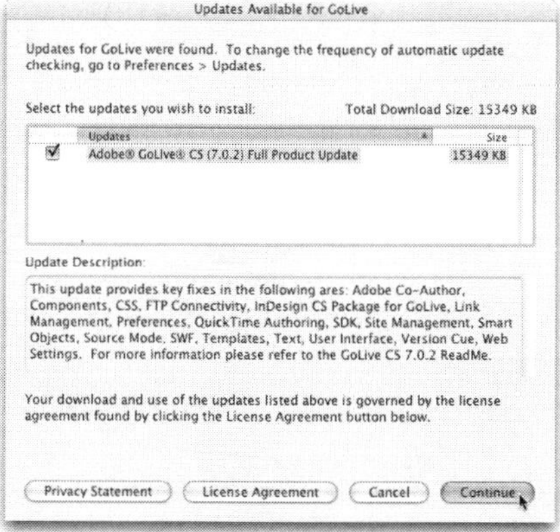

Figure 10b Use the Update Manager to download and install new GoLive updates.

If you're not sure what version of GoLive you're using, just select Help > About GoLive on Windows or GoLive > About GoLive on the

Updating Manager Preferences

You can set GoLive to automatically check for updates in the application preferences. Choose GoLive > Preferences (Edit > Preferences on Windows) and then click Update Manager in the bottom of the list on the left. From there you can choose to check for preferences at certain intervals or only when manually invoked.

Mac, and the exact version of GoLive will appear in the upper-left portion of the About screen (**Figure 10c**).

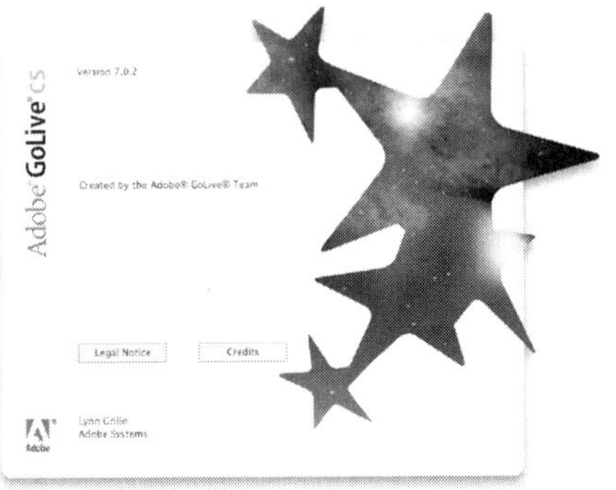

Figure 10c The About screen shows which version of GoLive is being used.

CHAPTER TWO

Working with Sites

GoLive is not merely an application for building Web pages, but an unstoppable powerhouse of site management. Let's face it: you build Web sites with tons of pages and images and links, not individual Web pages. Without reliable site management you can forget the idea of a hyperlinked "web" of files.

Using GoLive without the Site window makes about as much sense as driving a car without wheels—you could try it, but why make your work so hard? Site management is an area where GoLive really shines, and understanding the Site window will help you get the most out of the software.

Once you grasp how the Site window works, you'll see why GoLive makes it nearly impossible to have missing images or broken links in your Web site. You'll marvel at the three site-mapping modes. Your heart will race at the thought of multiple undos!

Learn the ways of the Site window. Trust the Site window. Be one with the Site window. Oh yeah, and save yourself tons of time and frustration, too. All right, let's get going.

TIP 11 Creating New Sites with the Site Wizard

Start the GoLive Site Wizard by selecting File > New Site and you'll see the first of four screens (**Figure 11a**) that will walk you through the process of creating a new site in GoLive. If you need to collaborate with other GoLive users on the same site or need a version control system, choose the Version Cue Project option. Otherwise, choose Single User and click the Next button.

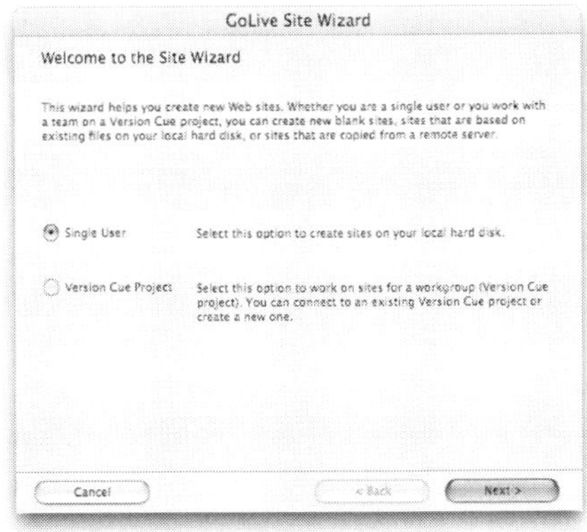

Figure 11a Decide whether you'll work on your own or collaborate with others.

Note

For an explanation of Version Cue, see Tip 135.

When you select Single User, the second screen gives you four more options to pick from (**Figure 11b**). If you're starting from scratch, choose Blank Site. If you already have some files or an old site on your hard drive that you want to start managing with GoLive, select Import from Folder. If you've inherited an existing site that's on a server somewhere but you don't have a copy of the files, choose the Import from Server option and you can download the files via FTP (File Transfer Protocol) or HTTP (Hypertext Transfer Protocol). You can also create site templates (for projects that will share certain elements) and use them later by selecting the Copy from Template option at the bottom.

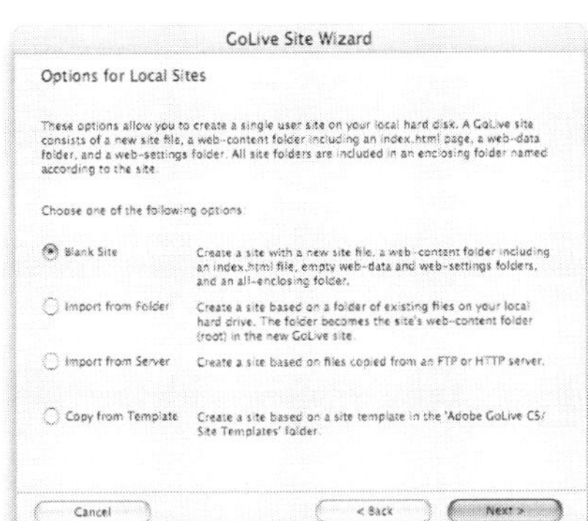

Figure 11b Select Blank Site to start a new Web site from scratch.

When you create a new blank site, the next screen asks you to name it, as seen in **Figure 11c**.

Figure 11c Name your site in the Site Name field.

Note

The Site Name you enter doesn't have to match the domain name of the site.

The last of the four screens (**Figure 11d**) lets you choose where to store the new site file. You can store your sites anywhere you want, but we recommend you keep them in a consistent location such as your Documents folder or a Projects folder. When you're done, click Finish, and your new Site window will open.

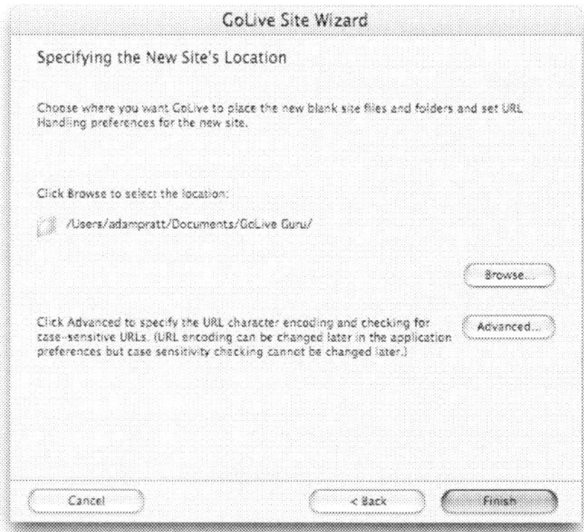

Figure 11d Decide where you want to save the site on your hard drive and click Finish.

Switching to GoLive

If you already have a Web site that was created in another application such as Macromedia Dreamweaver or Microsoft FrontPage, select the Import from Folder option on the second wizard screen, and you can easily migrate those existing sites to GoLive.

TIP 12 Understanding the Site File Structure

GoLive has a specific way of organizing directories so that every item can be tracked via the built-in site-management tools. Let's define what each folder is called and what each one does.

In this example, the Web site being built is called working_with_sites. All of the documents that make up the site, both those that get uploaded to the server and those that stay on the local computer, are housed inside an enclosing folder named working_with_sites.

Inside the working_with_sites folder you will find the following:

- The Root folder (named web-content)—These are the HTML pages, images, multimedia files, and so on that make up your Web site. These items get uploaded to your server.
- The Data folder (named web-data)—Inside are items you work with to create your Web site, such as components, stationeries, templates, Smart Objects, InDesign Packages, Site Trash, and so forth. These items do not get uploaded to the server. They are for you to work with locally on your computer.
- The Settings folder (named web-settings)—GoLive stores settings files in this folder. There is no need for you to access them, though. GoLive will use them when necessary.
- The Site file (working_with_sites.site)—This is the workhorse of GoLive. It is the brain that keeps track of all the things in all of the folders listed above. It manages your links, your URLs, your FTP settings, your site colors; it also tracks errors and does much more. When you open the Site file, it becomes the Site window.

With the Site file opened up as the Site window, the contents of the Root folder (web-content) are listed in the left pane under Files. The contents of the Data folder (web-data) are listed in the right pane (**Figure 12**).

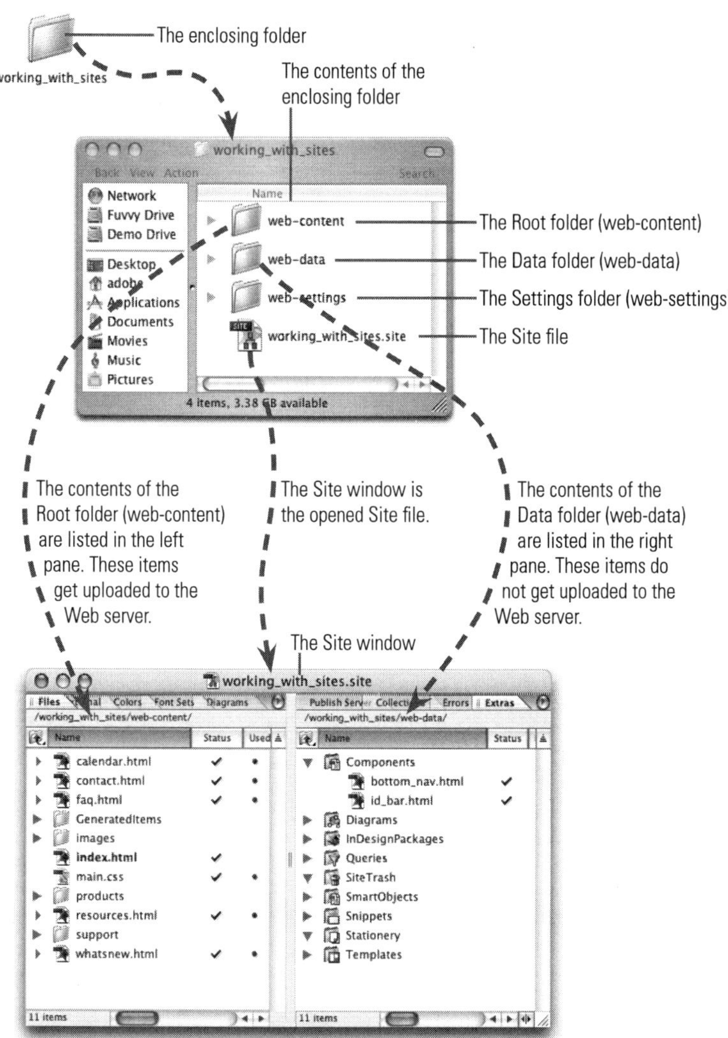

Figure 12 The enclosing folder holds the web-content, web-data, and web-settings folders, as well as the Site file. The Site file, when opened, shows a window separated into two panes, and it lists the items inside the web-content (left side) and web-data (right side) folders.

The Site File Backup

The Site file backup is created when you open a site. It is, very simply, a backup of the Site file. When you close the site, the backup goes away. If you crash, it will probably stay in the folder. If you crash a lot, you might find a whole bunch of them in there.

We suggest that you open the Site file from the original whenever possible. If the original has been corrupted, then try the backup.

You can turn off the preference that creates a backup file by choosing GoLive > Preferences > Site (Mac) or Edit > Preferences > Site (Windows), and then deselecting "Automatic backup of site file."

TIP 13 Adding Files to a Site

Creating a new site in GoLive is a great place to start, but soon you'll need to add other files such as images, Portable Document Format (PDF) files, and other documents to your Web site. GoLive offers the following three easy ways to add existing files to a Web site. Pick the method you like best.

Drag and Drop

Lazy people like us prefer the drag-and-drop method because it's definitely the easiest. Just select the files in the operating system (using Finder on the Mac or My Computer on Windows) and drag them into the Files tab of the Site window (**Figure 13a**). If you see a dialog asking you to confirm the copy, just click Yes. Notice that dragging and dropping *copies* the files into the site rather than moving them, which means you end up with two copies of the files.

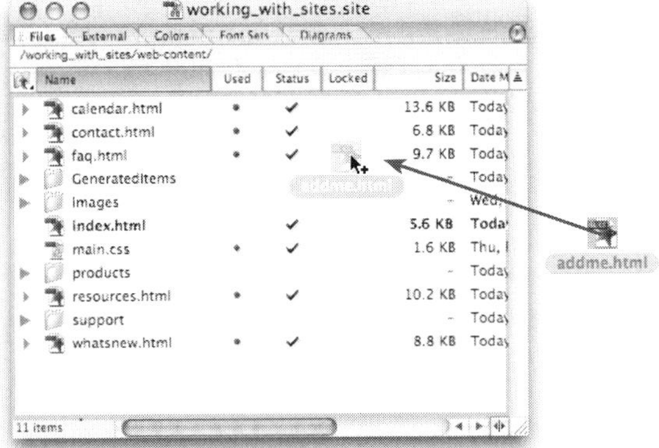

Figure 13a Drag and drop files to add them to your site.

Import Files

If you prefer to work with the menus, then make sure the Files tab of the Site window is active and select File > Import > Files to Site. Select the files you want to add (Shift-click to select multiple files at once) and click OK. The selected files are copied to the site, and the originals are still where you found them.

Save and Refresh View

The third option is to just save the files into the Root (web-content) folder and then refresh the Site View. For example, say you use Photoshop to create a Web Photo Gallery and you save the results in the site's Root folder. When you switch to GoLive, you won't see the new files appear in the Files tab until you choose Site > Refresh View or click the Refresh icon in the toolbar (**Figure 13b**).

Figure 13b Click the Refresh icon in the toolbar to see new files in the Site window.

TIP 14 Moving, Renaming, and Deleting Files

If you move a file to a new place on your hard drive outside of Go-Live, you'll end up with broken links, missing images, and heartburn. Instead, manage all the assets in your Web site from the Files tab of the Site window, and GoLive will handle all the dirty work for you. As long as you manage the files from the Site window, GoLive will update all the hyperlinks and references inside HTML, Cascading Style Sheets (CSS), JavaScript Actions, PDF, QuickTime, and Shock-wave Flash (SWF) for you. This even works with third-party actions and extensions.

Navigating the Site Window

If you've opened a subfolder in your site and want to get back to the top of your site, click the up arrow button in the top-left corner.

Moving

To move a file, just drag it into the folder where you want to put it. To move a file up a level in the file structure, drag the file on top of another file at the same level you want to move to, as seen in **Figure 14a**.

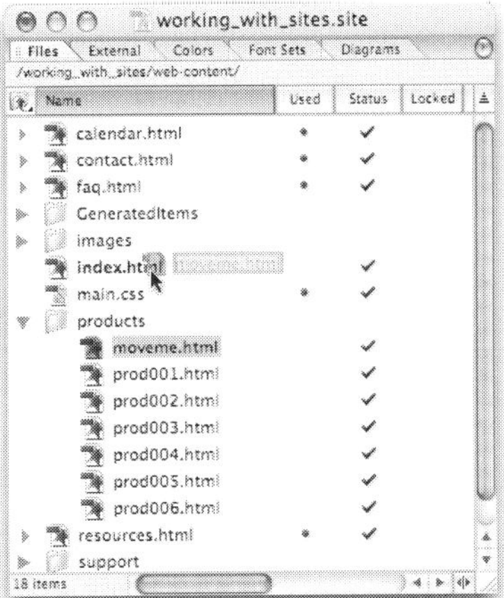

Figure 14a Drag a file over another file to move it to that level.

You can also use the Edit > Copy and the Edit > Paste commands to copy and paste files from one folder to another.

Renaming

To rename a file in the Files tab of the Site window, click on the filename, wait a second, and then click again until the filename (but not the extension) is highlighted. Now just type the new filename and press Return or Enter. Notice you can also rename files and folders in the Name field of the Inspector.

When you move or rename a file or folder that is referenced by another file in the site, you'll see a confirmation dialog (**Figure 14b**). When you're ready to confirm the change, click OK and watch GoLive automagically update your entire site for you.

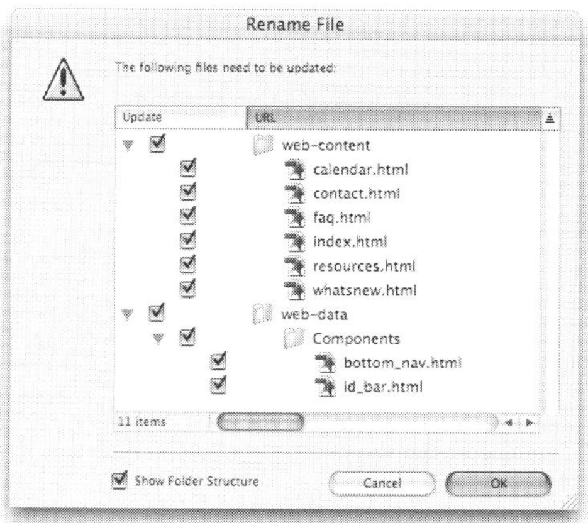

Figure 14b When you move or rename a file or folder, GoLive makes sure all your links are correct.

Deleting

To delete a file or folder in the Files tab, just select it and click the trashcan icon in the toolbar (**Figure 14c**). You can also delete selected files with the keyboard by pressing Command-Delete on the Mac or Delete in Windows. When you delete files, you'll see a dialog asking you to confirm the change. Even after you delete the files, you can always retrieve them from the Site Trash over in the Extras tab of the Site window.

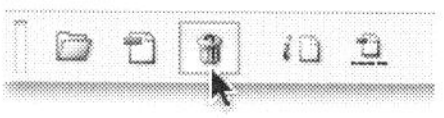

Figure 14c Click the trashcan icon in the toolbar to delete selected files.

Make a Mistake?

Have you ever moved a file into the wrong folder? Made a typo? Accidentally deleted a file? If so, you'll love the fact that GoLive's Site window gives you 20 levels of undo. Just hit Command-Z (Mac) or Ctrl-Z (Windows), and GoLive will undo the most recent file manipulation *and* all the site management to make sure everything's back in order.

TIP 15 Changing File View Modes

Helpful Icon View

If you forget what the folders in the Extras tab of the Site window are for, change the view to Icons in the Extras tab. Now the big beautiful icons will make it easier to remember the different features.

The default view in the Site window shows files in a simple list view (called Details on Windows), but GoLive CS introduces three helpful new options: icons, thumbnails, and tiles. Access these view options with the Site > View menu or with a Control-click (Mac) or right-click (Windows) in the Files or Extras tab of the Site window (**Figure 15**).

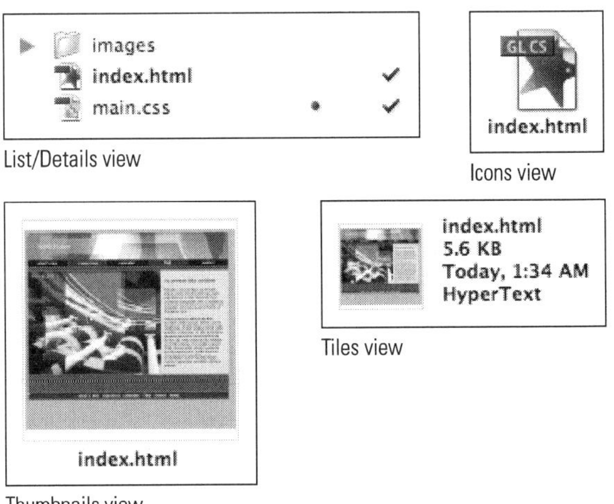

Figure 15 Choose from one of four available view modes in the Site window.

These new view modes make GoLive work more like the Photoshop File Browser, and they even reveal helpful metadata about your files. Just hold your cursor over a file, and you'll see a tool tip pop up with information such as name, file size, date modified, and file status.

TIP 16 Understanding the Site Window Tabs

Before we get much further into our exploration of GoLive, let's do a quick rundown of all the tabs in the Site window. We'll begin on the left side and work our way across (**Figure 16a**).

Figure 16a The left side of the Site window is where you'll perform most of your day-to-day site-management tasks.

- Files—Think of this tab as the root folder of your Web site. Everything that you upload to your Web server needs to be stored here (see Tips 12 through 14).
- External—Store all the email addresses and Web site addresses you'll link to in here (see Tip 21).
- Colors—To keep the colors throughout a site consistent, store frequently used color swatches here (see Tip 59).
- Font Sets—Whether you use font tags or Cascading Style Sheets (CSS), this is where you store your favorite font groupings for Web-friendly type (see Tip 93).
- Diagrams—GoLive includes integrated site-mapping tools, and this is where you store those diagrams (see Tip 164).

Simplifying the Site Window

You can hide and reveal the right side of the Site window by clicking the Toggle Split View icon in the bottom-right corner of the window.

The right side of the Site window is also important; it's responsible for behind-the-scenes tasks such as storing templates, tracking errors, and saving settings files (**Figure 16b**). You'll definitely use these tabs, but less frequently than the ones on the left.

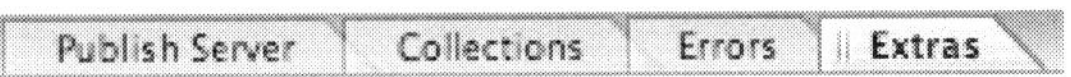

Figure 16b The right side of the Site window is where you'll upload files to a server, fix errors, and store library items.

- Publish Server—Use this tab to upload and download files to your Web server right within the Site window (see Tips 172–176).
- Collections—Store aliases (or shortcuts) to frequently used files here (see Tip 163).
- Errors—The real-time error checking in GoLive instantly flags any broken links, missing images, or orphaned files and displays the errors here (see Tip 166).
- Extras—The assets available in the Library palette (templates, components, snippets, and so on) are stored here in the Site window (see Tip 107).

TIP 17 Managing the Site Window Tabs

Considering how many tabs there are in the Site window, it should relieve you to know they're completely customizable. For starters, you can rearrange the order of the tabs and even move them from the left to right, and vice versa. If you want to move the Extras tab next to Files, just drag the tab to the left side of the window and then drag it between the Files and External tabs (**Figure 17a**).

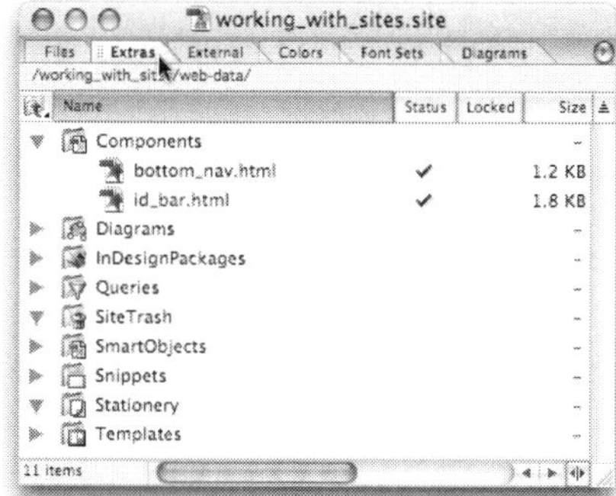

Figure 17a Customize the Site window for maximum productivity.

If you have multiple displays or a huge LCD attached to your computer, then you might have enough screen real estate to pull some tabs out of the Site window so you can see them all at the same time. Just drag one of the tabs out of the Site window until it separates into its own window. If the tab is a feature you don't use often, then you can even "tear it out" and then close it to get it out of your way.

In case you tear off or close a tab and then need it back again, select the name of the tab from the flyout menu in the top-right corner of the Site window (**Figure 17b**). You can also use this flyout menu to open the Navigation and Links views for site mapping and link tracking.

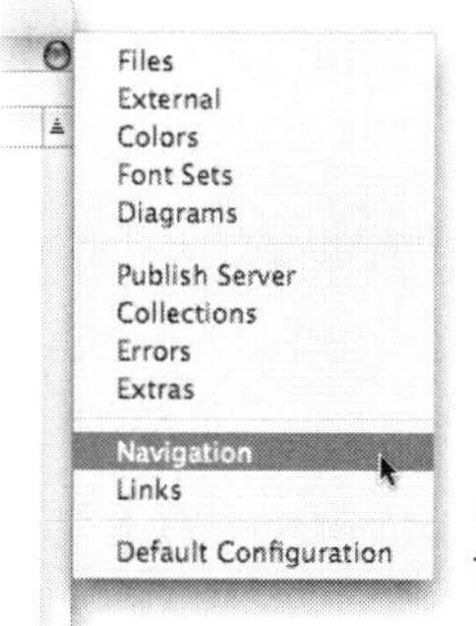

Figure 17b Reopen closed tabs with the flyout menu.

Resetting the Site Window

To reset the tabs in the Site window to their default locations and thus restore that factory-fresh scent, select the Default Configuration option at the bottom of the Site window flyout menu.

TIP 18 Selecting Multiple Files

To make it as easy as possible to learn and use GoLive, the brilliant GoLive engineering team has made the Site window look and behave just like your operating system. That means that while the features are identical between the Mac and Windows versions, GoLive behaves like a Mac on a Mac and like Windows on a Windows PC.

For example, to select multiple contiguous files in the Site window, you select the first file, press and hold the Shift key, and then click on the last file in the sequence. This is new behavior for many Mac users, but it works exactly like the new Finder in Mac OS X (**Figure 18**).

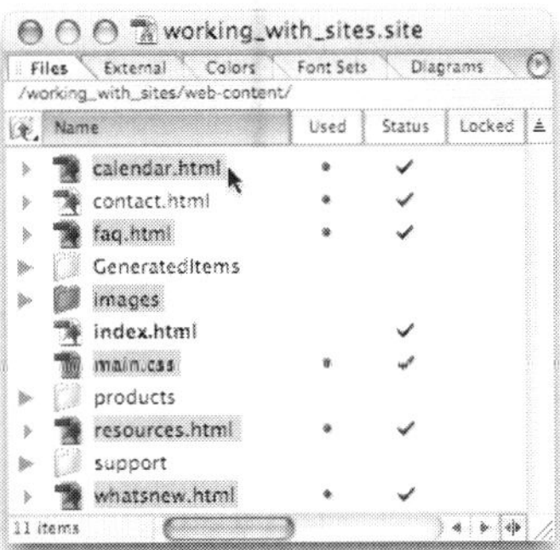

Figure 18 Command-click (Mac) or Ctrl-click (Windows) to select multiple noncontiguous files. Shift-clicking will select all the files in the range.

To select multiple noncontiguous files in the Site window, Command-click (Mac) or Ctrl-click (Windows) on the files.

Opening Files with Shortcuts

To open a file with your keyboard from the Site window on a Mac, just press Command-down arrow. The Windows equivalent, which matches the Windows behavior, is to select the file and press the Enter key.

TIP 19 Viewing Content in the Inspector

You can see your files in the Site window, but to see a nice preview without opening the files, look in the Content tab of the File Inspector. You can view just about any file format, including GIF, JPEG, HTML, QuickTime, Photoshop, Illustrator, and PDF.

If you have a large image like the one in **Figure 19a**, you'll be able to see only a small portion of the file. Notice the numbers in the bottom-left corner of the Inspector—those numbers tell you this file is 398 pixels wide by 600 pixels high.

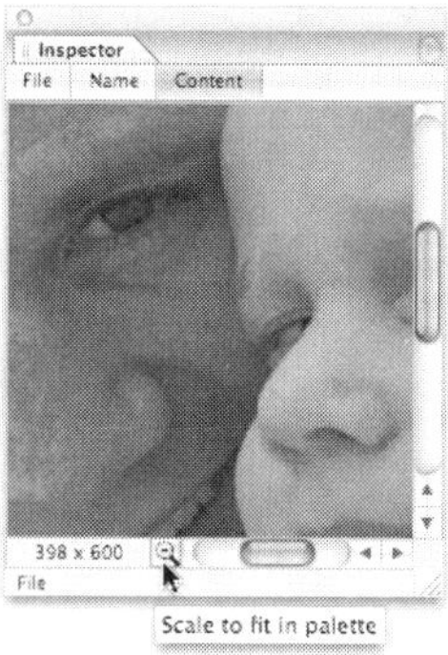

Figure 19a You can preview Web pages and graphics in the Content tab of the Inspector.

The scale-to-fit icon in the bottom-left corner of the Inspector makes it easy to see all of a large image at once. Just click this icon, and GoLive changes the preview dimensions (but not the actual image size) so that it fits perfectly in the Inspector (**Figure 19b**).

Figure 19b The scale-to-fit option lets you see the entire image at once.

When you're sure that you've located the right file, just drag and drop it from the Inspector into your Web page to place the image.

Customizing the Columns

If you want to reorder the columns (Status, Used, Size, Kind, and so on) in the Files tab of the Site window, just drag (Command-drag on Mac) the column headers to move them. To disable a column, Control-click (Mac) or right-click (Windows) and uncheck the one you want to hide.

TIP 20 Counting File Usage

Have you ever wondered how many times a page, graphic, or PDF file is referenced throughout a site? If you look in the Used column in the Files tab of the Site window, you can see a little tick mark if the file is referenced. For more detailed reporting, just widen the Used column by dragging the column header dividers with your mouse pointer, and you'll see that GoLive actually keeps a running tally of how many times a file is referenced throughout the site (**Figure 20**). This is just one more reason GoLive users rave about the awesome site-management capabilities.

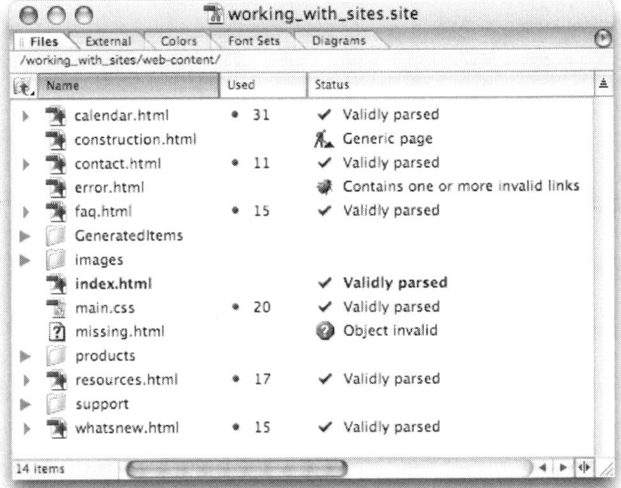

Figure 20 Widen the Used column in the Site window to get more detailed information.

While we're tinkering around in the Site window, try widening the Status column in the Files tab. You'll see nicely written explanations of what the various status icons mean.

TIP 21 Managing URLs and Email Addresses

GoLive does an amazing job of managing files in a Web site, and it's also adept at managing external references such as email and Web site addresses. To add an external reference to your site, make sure the External tab is active. Then click the Create New Address or Create New URL icon in the toolbar or drag the Address or URL object from the Site section of the Objects palette. Customize the external reference in the Inspector so that it looks something like **Figure 21.**

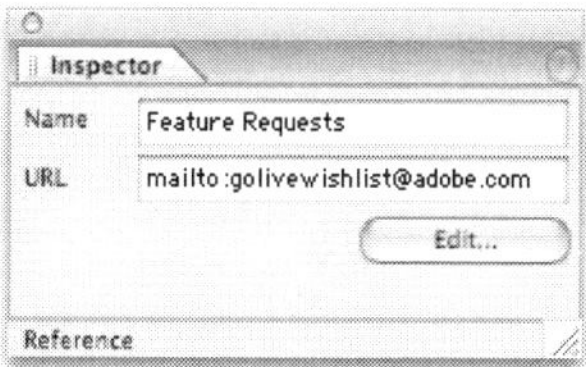

Figure 21 Edit external references in the Inspector palette.

To apply an external reference as a hyperlink, just drag it from the Site window onto a selected image or text in a Web page in GoLive's Layout Editor. (See Tip 29 for more information on linking.)

If you have an existing site in GoLive and you want to see what email addresses and external URLs are hyperlinked throughout the site, choose Site > Get References Used. All the detected references are added to the External tab of the Site window, where you can organize and update them.

To update every instance of an email address throughout a site, just select it in the External tab and make the change in the Inspector. For example, if the Big Shot gets a promotion, you can change his email address from bigshot@company.com to biggershot@company.com in one central location instead of in each instance.

Checking External Links

Instead of verifying every external link individually by hand, select the External tab and choose Site > Check External Links. Check marks in the Status column are good. If you see a red bug you should double-check the address.

Importing Favorites as Externals

If you have favorites from Internet Explorer that you want to use as links in a Web site, choose File > Import > Favorites as Site Externals and select your favorites.html file. If you use a different browser (such as Safari or Opera), you can drag and drop URLs from the address bar or the bookmarks list directly into the External tab in GoLive.

CHAPTER THREE

Working with Pages

We remember the early days of the Web when we had to walk to work in four feet of snow in our bare feet, uphill both ways, and type all of our source code by hand. Back then, the two biggest competitors in the Web-design software market were SimpleText and Notepad. Fortunately, Web-design software such as GoLive has come a long way and makes the process of building interactive, visually compelling Web sites easier than ever.

You can still write code in GoLive, but it's usually much more efficient to work in GoLive's Layout Editor and let the software write all the HTML for you. GoLive offers six different ways to edit and preview your Web pages, but many users will spend most of their time in the Layout Editor. The accurate layout of this visual authoring environment makes it easy for anybody to build Web sites with the ease of drag and drop.

Because you, too, will spend most of your time in the Layout Editor, we decided to make this the longest chapter in the book. We start by covering some basic layout tools such as zooming, panning, guides, and rulers. We also cover different layout techniques, including layout grids, tables, and layers. Toward the end, we cover the use of color in GoLive and sharing color swatches and settings between all the Creative Suite applications.

TIP 22 Touring the Six Document Modes

When you open a Web page in GoLive you see six tabs across the top of the document window (**Figure 22**). Each tab offers a different way to edit or view your page. To change modes, click on the document tabs. Let's start on the left side and work our way across.

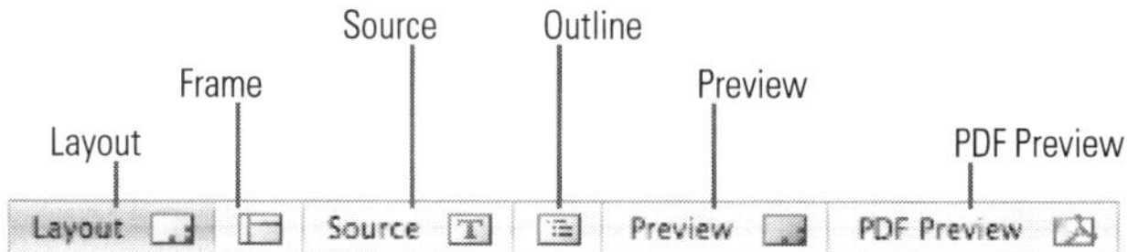

Figure 22 There are six powerful ways to edit and preview your Web pages in GoLive.

Layout Editor Most visual designers spend most of their time using GoLive's friendly Layout Editor. When you add objects and edit your layout in this mode, GoLive writes all the source code for you. Learning HTML really isn't that hard, but there's no sense in typing it all out if you don't have to (see Tips 22–54).

Frame Editor HTML frames are not nearly as popular as they used to be, but if you need to create frames pages this is the mode you work in (see Tips 64–65).

Source Code Editor If you want to get some dirt under your fingernails and dig into the code, you're going to love the new Source Code Editor in GoLive CS. It was just rewritten from the ground up and is chock-full of timesaving features (see Tips 66–73).

Outline Editor The Outline Editor is often overlooked, but it's one of our favorite features in the entire application. Newbies and experts alike love this unique outline view of the structure of a page (see Tips 74–80).

Layout Preview To see an accurate preview of how your Web pages will look in a browser, switch to this preview mode. The GoLive preview engine for Windows users is Internet Explorer; on the Mac it's Opera (see Tips 72–74).

PDF Preview GoLive CS now includes one-click conversion of any Web page to an Adobe PDF (Portable Document Format) file (see Tips 84–92).

Changing the Default Mode

The default document mode is the Layout Editor, and, like so many other things in GoLive, you can customize it. In the General section of the application preferences, select your favorite option from the Default Mode pull-down menu.

TIP 23 Using the Document Window Icons

Changing Page Titles

Search the Web for the phrase "Welcome to Adobe GoLive" and you'll discover hundreds of thousands of pages where GoLive users forgot to give their pages good titles. Make sure you're not guilty of this crime!

Several small enhancements have been made to the document bar at the top of every Web page window in GoLive. For starters, the head section (see Tip 24) of a Web page is now clearly labeled at the left edge of the document (**Figure 23**). To reveal the head section, just click the triangle next to the Head label.

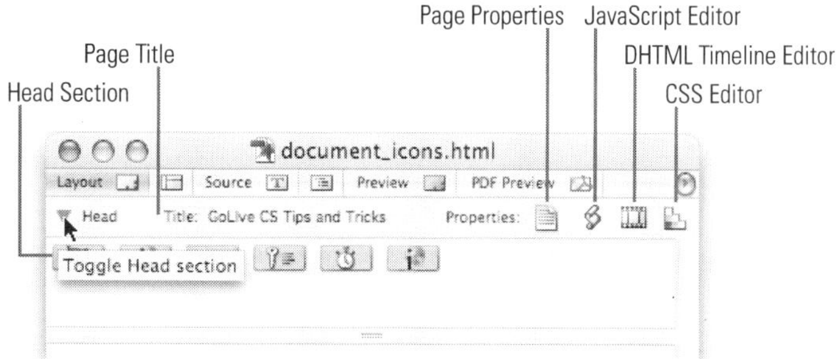

Figure 23 The icons at the top of each document window allow you to customize the page and open other editing environments.

Next is the page's Title field, which is a clearly labeled text box. The page title appears along the very top of the browser window when visitors view your site. The page title is also used when visitors add the page to their bookmarks or favorites, so it's important to give each page a useful and accurate title.

The Page Properties icon is now grouped with the JavaScript Editor, DHTML Timeline Editor, and CSS Editor icons at the upper-right end of the document window. Select the Page Properties icon to change page attributes such as page title, link colors, margins, and background image in the Page Inspector.

To open the JavaScript Editor, DHTML Timeline Editor, or CSS Editor for the page, just click the corresponding icon at the top right of the document window. If you'd rather use menu commands or keyboard shortcuts for these options, you'll find a Page Properties command in the Special menu and the three editors in the View menu.

TIP 24 Understanding the Head and Body of a Web Page

If you've taken the time to learn the basics of HTML, you'll remember that every page is divided into two main areas: the head and the body. The head section is at the beginning of the page and is invisible to users unless they view the source code. The head is where you place things like metatags for search engine optimization and certain kinds of JavaScript Actions.

Click the triangle in the upper-left corner of the document window to reveal the head section (**Figure 24**). Place objects such as metatags in the head of the page by dragging and dropping them from the head section of the Objects palette.

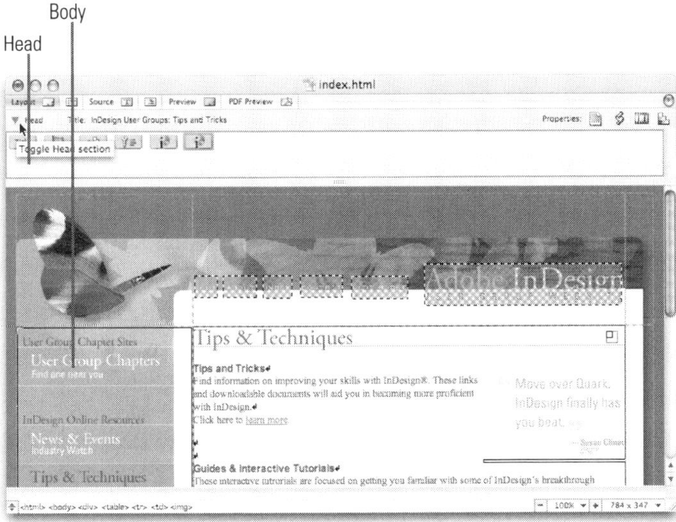

Figure 24 Put your metatags in the head section.

The body is the visible area of the page where you place all the content your Web site visitors will see. Everything below the head section is called the body, and this is where you'll place tables, layers, text, images, and so on.

Head Objects Snap to Head Section

GoLive is so smart that if you try to place head objects such as metatags or refresh tags in the body of the Web pages, they will automagically be moved to the head section of the page.

TIP 25 Inserting Objects in a Page

Objects from Contextual Menus

Control-click (Mac) or right-click (Windows) in the Layout Editor and choose an object from the Insert Object menu. After you've used this feature a few times, GoLive will show the ten objects you've inserted most recently at the top of the list.

As you start to build your site in GoLive you'll add a variety of objects such as tables, CSS layers, images, and multimedia to the pages. If you can drag and drop, you can build Web pages—it's really that easy. Just drag and drop the items you need from the Objects palette into the Layout Editor or double-click the object in the Objects palette, and it will be inserted in the page at the location of your cursor.

After the object has been added to the page, you can adjust its settings in the context-sensitive Inspector palette. For example, if you select an image in the Layout Editor, the Inspector lets you control attributes such as width, height, and alignment. If you have a table selected, the Inspector lets you adjust such things as the number of rows and columns and the borders and spacing in the table (**Figure 25**).

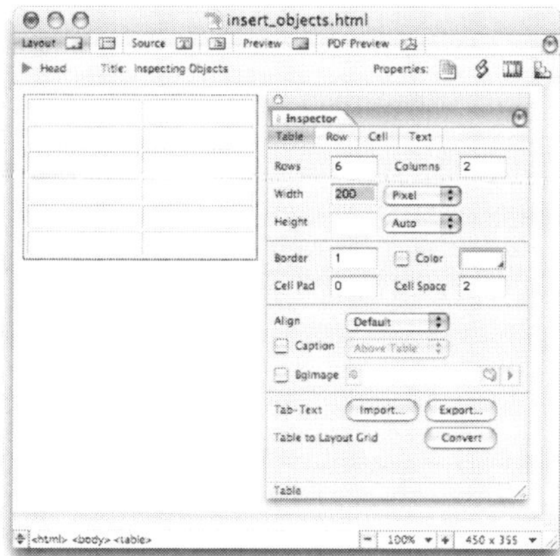

Figure 25 Drag and drop page items from the Objects palette and change their settings in the Inspector palette.

Notice that not all the objects in the Objects palette can be added to the Layout Editor. For example, Site and Diagram objects only work in the Site window and Diagram windows. Similarly, the QuickTime and SMIL objects only work in the QuickTime and SMIL editors.

TIP 26 Using Metatags

There are many metatags you can use in your Web pages, and each has a specific function. In this tip we take a look at two particular kinds: keywords and description. Search engines still depend on these two tags to help them determine if your site meets the criteria of a person's search. This makes it important to include keywords and description tags, especially on your home page and other important entry pages, and to know the best way to set their attributes.

Keywords are a listing of words that exemplify the content of the page or site. If the site is all about custom window treatments, for example, you might include keywords such as *fabric*, *draperies*, *sashes*, and *blinds*. You could also include keywords that indicate where your business is located (*Princeton*, *Trenton*, *New Jersey*, and so on) or other pertinent information (*swatches*, *phone ordering*, *next day service*) that a customer might use in a search.

To create a keyword metatag, drag and drop the Keyword object from the Head portion of the Objects palette into the page (**Figure 26a**).

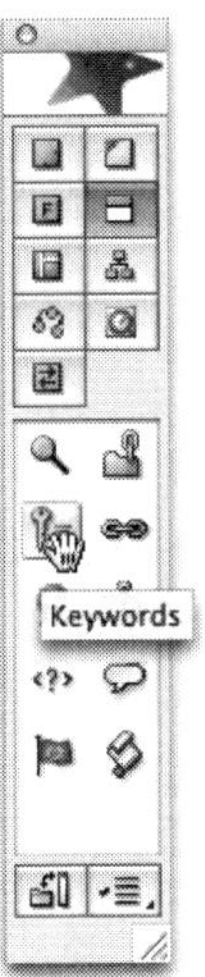

Figure 26a The Keyword object has a little key on it.

Keyword Magic

If there is a word in the text on your page that you'd like to include in your keyword list, select the word and then press Shift-Command-A (Mac) or Shift-Ctrl-A (Windows), and it will automatically be added as a keyword.

GoLive automatically opens the head section and drops the object in. Select the Keyword icon in the head section and then in the Inspector palette type a keyword into the input field. Press Return or Enter to add it to the list. Repeat as needed to complete your list (**Figure 26b**).

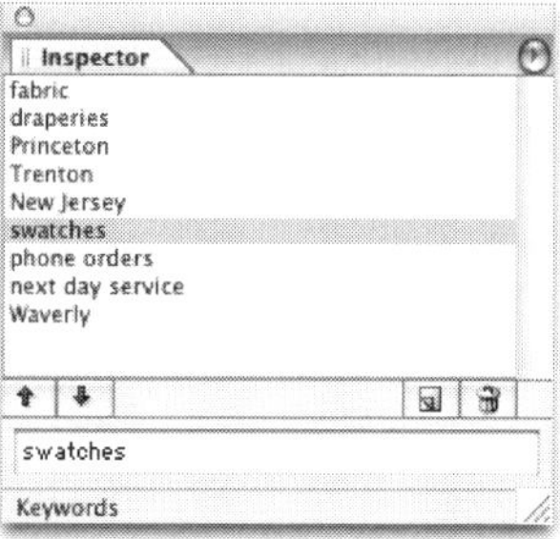

Figure 26b Add, edit, or delete keywords via the Keyword Inspector.

Note

Do not use bogus keywords with the intention of directing more traffic to your site. It's rude. Plus most search engines will catch on to your deception when they index the site and realize there is no content on that topic anywhere in it.

The description metatag gives the browser a bit of descriptive text to use when a search has been run and the site meets the criteria. So if a person runs a search on "*custom draperies, New Jersey*," the search engine returns a link to the site followed by a description, if included. If there is no description, the search engine will use text on the page. To insert a description metatag, open the Head portion of the page, double-click the Meta object, and then in the meta Inspector select description from the pull-down menu (**Figure 26c**). In the text input field, type the description of your Web site. If possible, include keywords in your descriptive text for the best results.

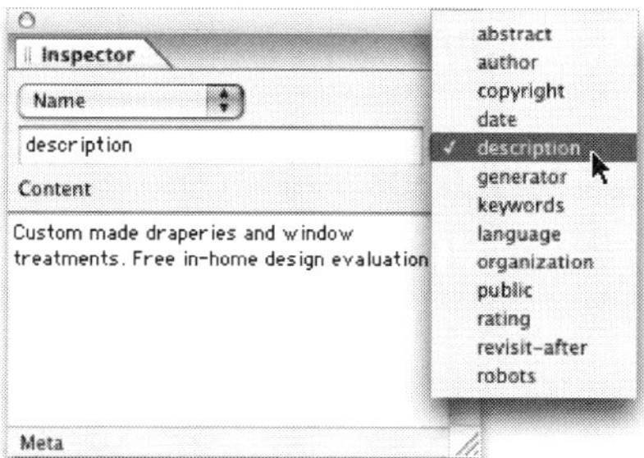

Figure 26c Choose description from the pull-down menu and enter the description.

TIP 27 Viewing Page Rulers

Here's a small but useful tip. To show rulers on your page in the Layout Editor, simply choose View > Show Rulers or press Command-R (Mac) or Ctrl-R (Windows) on your keyboard (**Figure 27**). To put them away, choose the command a second time. If you zoom in on the page, the rulers get larger, too (see Tip 45).

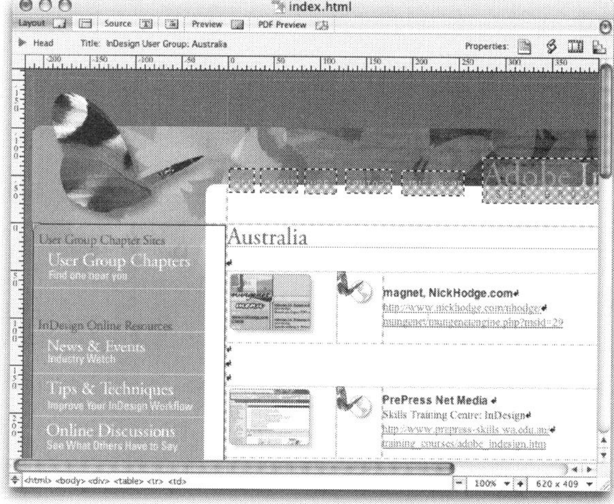

Figure 27 Page rulers help you line up objects on a page.

When an object on the page is selected, look carefully at the rulers and you'll see a darker band of gray indicating where the top and left edges of the object line up to the ruler.

Ruler Swooshing

When you turn the rulers on or off on a Mac, they swoosh in or out of the page as an animation with sound. On Windows they just... well, they just turn on and off.

Rotating the Split Source View

Hold Option (Mac) or Alt (Windows) when you click the Split Source icon to rotate the orientation of the two views.

TIP 28 Viewing Split Source

GoLive includes several ways to edit your pages, including the visual Layout Editor and a Source Code Editor. You may prefer one or the other, but a handy trick is to combine both the Layout Editor and the Source Code Editor at the same time with the Split Source mode. You can work in either mode and watch the results update in real time in the other mode.

To turn on Split Source View and edit your layout and source code simultaneously, click the show/hide icon ≑ in the bottom-left corner of the document window. You can also choose View > Show Split Source or press Command-Y (Mac) or Ctrl-Y (Windows) to toggle Split Source View (**Figure 28**).

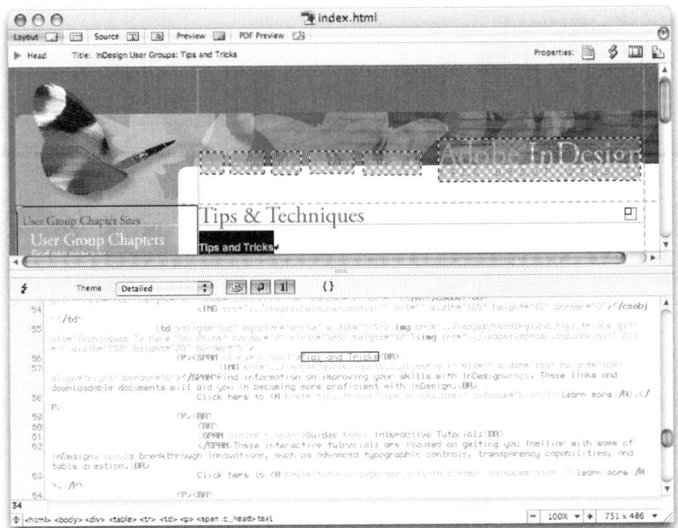

Figure 28 Split Source View lets you edit layout and source code simultaneously.

One more power tip is to open a document in Outline mode and turn on the Split Source View for a powerful editing environment coders will love. Another way to view the visual layout and source code at the same time is to work in the Layout Editor and open the Source Code palette from the Window menu.

TIP 29 Creating Links

Probably the most fundamental feature of a Web page is a hyperlink, often simply called a link. The idea behind the Web, of course, is that you look at a page and click links that take you to additional information on other pages. Hyperlinks can be created on both text and images, and GoLive offers a number of ways to create links. Let's start with text links.

To make a link out of text, first select the text and then choose one of the following:

- Type the URL into the Link field of the Inspector palette.
- Use the Fetch URL tool in the Inspector palette and point and shoot at a page in your files list or at the Page Properties icon (see Tip 23) of another open page. When the page icon is highlighted, let go of the mouse button and you'll have created linked text (**Figure 29a**).

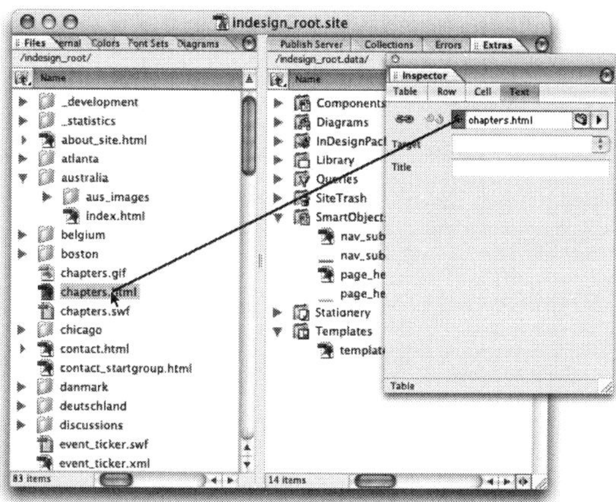

Figure 29a Use GoLive's Fetch URL tool to create links.

- Click the browse button at the right end of the link field and navigate to a document. Select the document to create the link.

(continued on next page)

Linking to the Site Window

If you've ever wanted to create a link but can't see your files list because the Site window is behind the other pages, try this: Use the Fetch URL tool and point to the Select Window icon in the toolbar. The Site window will pop to the front, and then you can finish your link. This trick works equally well for popping open folders in the files list, or for bringing forward tabs in the Site window.

- Choose a file from the list in the pull-down menu at the right end of the link field to select from recently used files (**Figure 29b**).

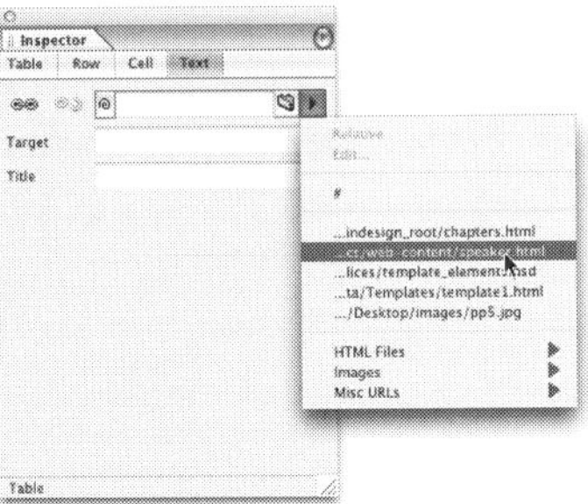

Figure 29b Use this handy list to create a link.

- Hold down the Command key (Mac) or the Ctrl key (Windows) and point and shoot directly from the selected text to a file in the Files tab of the Site window (**Figure 29c**).

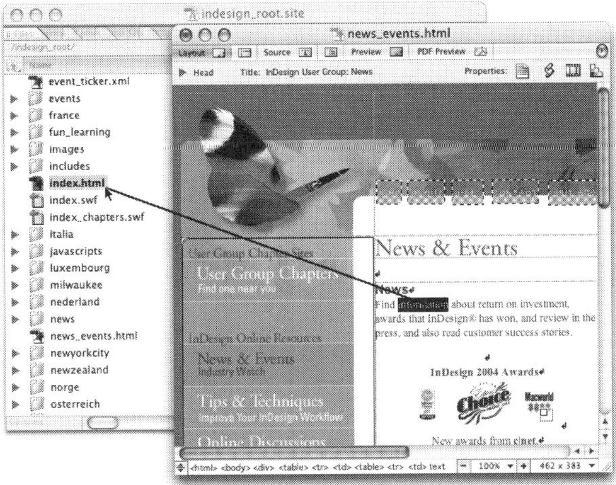

Figure 29c No need to go to the Inspector—you can link directly from the selected text.

Creating links from a selected image can be done using the first three of the four ways listed above. Just remember to click the Link tab of the Inspector before making the link.

Yet another method of linking to a document is dragging and dropping a file from the Site window into an opened page. This automatically creates a link to that page using the filename as the link text. (The exception is PDF—take a look at Tip 128 to see what happens there!)

TIP 30 Autocompleting http and mailto Links

Most external hyperlinks point to Web sites or email addresses and consistently include `http://` or `mailto:` at the beginning of the link. Did you know that GoLive automatically adds these parts of hyperlinks in the link field of the Inspector palette? For example, if you assign a link and type `www.adobe.com` in the Inspector, GoLive completes the address to a fully valid URL of `http://www.adobe.com` when you press Return/Enter (**Figure 30**).

Figure 30 GoLive intelligently autocompletes http and mailto links in the Inspector.

It's a handy little tip that'll save you unnecessary and error-prone typing time. When you need to type the address to servers using other protocols such as ftp:// or https://, GoLive is smart enough to leave those alone and not append the http:// protocol.

This works for email addresses, too. If you type `email@domain.com` into the link field of the Inspector palette and press Return/Enter, GoLive automatically completes the link as `mailto:email@domain.com`.

Viewing Link Warnings

If you have a bad link on a page, GoLive lets you know by putting a little red bug in the status column of the files list.

To easily locate the bug on the page, use the Link Warnings icon on the toolbar. To make things super easy for you, the icon in the toolbar uses the same bug icon as the one in the status column (**Figure 31**).

Figure 31 The Link Warnings icon on the toolbar.

First, open the page with the bug and then click the Link Warnings icon. The error on the page will be highlighted in red. If you don't see anything highlighted in red, remember to look in the head portion of the page. The error could be there. Select the highlighted area and relink it via the Inspector palette.

I'm Warning You!

The Link Warnings feature is not exclusive to the Layout Editor. You can use it in the Source Code and Outline Editors, too. In fact, we think the Outline Editor is the easiest place to find errors since the highlight color really pops off the page. If you don't feel comfortable fixing errors in the Outline Editor, just select the highlighted tag and switch back to Layout Mode. The troublesome link should still be selected and you can then fix it as usual.

TIP 32 Adding Document Encodings to Pages with Errors

Document encoding is a little piece of HTML syntax that tells the browser which character set (charset) to use when displaying a Web page. *Charset* refers to the set of characters used in a particular language (English, French, and so on). If you open a page that was created without a document encoding assigned, GoLive will offer options for correcting the omission. Use one of the following methods to assign a document encoding to a page. If you open a file missing the document encoding, a dialog opens. Selecting the first radio button and then clicking Open opens the page while temporarily using the encoding selected in the pull-down menu, but the code is not added to the page. To add the code permanently to the page, click the second radio button and choose the preferred encoding from the pull-down (**Figure 32a**). GoLive writes the necessary code, and you won't get the dialog the next time you open the page.

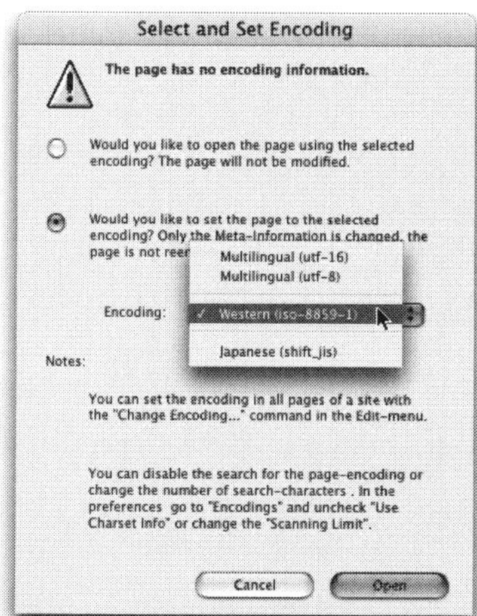

Figure 32a Select the character set from the pull-down menu and click the appropriate radio button.

Where's My Language?

The last option in the File > Document Encoding submenu is Edit. Edit lets you enable additional character sets, such as Greek, Cyrillic, and Korean, among others.

Once a page is open, you can still change the character encoding by choosing File > Document Encoding and then choosing from the list in the submenu (**Figure 32b**).

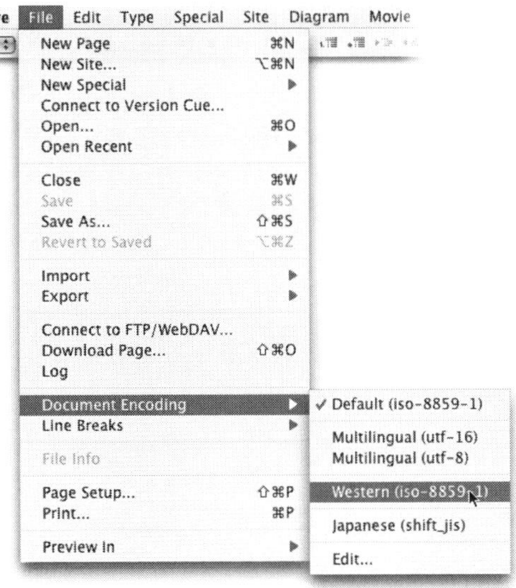

Figure 32b You can add or change the document encoding type from the File menu.

TIP 33 Designing with Layout Grids and Layout Text Boxes

Have you ever wished there was an easy way to put images and text exactly where you want them on a Web page? Would you like to be able to group several images and move them all at once? Would you like to nudge several images tightly up against one another so no space shows in between? Well, the GoLive layout grid is the answer to your prayers.

The Layout Grid object is found in the Basic set of the Objects palette. To use one on a page, either drag and drop from the Objects palette or double-click the object to insert it at the point of your cursor. You can also insert one by using the contextual menu and choosing Insert Object > Basic > Layout Grid.

Resize the grid by dragging one of its three blue resize handles or by typing pixel dimensions into the width and height fields of the layout grid Inspector. Then it's a simple matter of putting other objects onto the grid. Move objects on the grid by dragging or by pressing the arrow keys to nudge right, left, up, or down.

You can drag images and movies directly onto the grid, but text needs to go inside a layout text box. If you drag and drop text onto a grid, GoLive automatically creates a layout text box at the default size of 32x32 pixels, so you'll most likely need to resize it. To do so, drag any one of its eight resize handles. Of course, you could create the layout text box first and then paste or drag text into it. Drag a layout text box from the Objects palette and drop it onto the grid, then resize as needed (**Figure 33**).

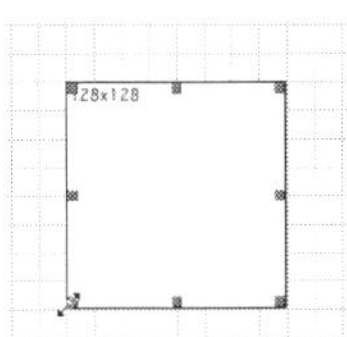

Figure 33 Resize a layout text box by dragging any one of its eight handles.

You can select multiple objects on a layout grid by dragging across them or Shift-clicking them and then moving them all at once. If you want, you can use the Group and Ungroup icons on the toolbar to keep them together or break them apart, or open the Align palette from the Window menu and line them up however you'd like. Look in the Grid Inspector for additional options such as coloring the grid or setting a background image.

Targeting Grid Locations

Click once at the intersection of two lines on the layout grid and look closely. You'll see a little blinking cursor indicating that you've just set a target. If you then double-click an object in the Objects palette, that object will land precisely in the spot you've targeted.

TIP 34 Converting Layout Grids to Tables

Two-Way Street

Not only can you convert a layout grid to a table, but you can also convert a table to a layout grid. Simply select your table and then in the Table Inspector click the Convert button next to Table to Layout Grid. See Tip 36 for more info on using tables.

What you might not know about GoLive's layout grids is that they are nothing more than tables when displayed by a browser. GoLive uses a special syntax to make the table display as a grid in GoLive and offers you the option of changing your grid into a standard HTML table. To do so, select your layout grid and then choose Layout Grid to Table from the Special menu (**Figure 34**).

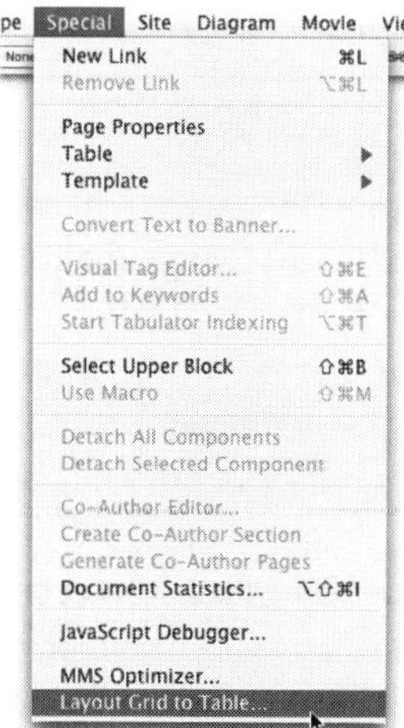

Figure 34 You can easily convert a layout grid into a standard table.

When the dialog appears, you can set options to strip the control row, which is selected by default, or to both strip the control row and replace any spacer tags with a transparent GIF. If you don't want to do either of those things, don't select either option.

TIP 35 Designing with Layers

Layout grids are fantastic for quickly designing Web pages, but a more modern approach is to use layers. Layers offer even more flexibility than layout grids when it comes to placing objects on a page, because you can overlap layers, stack them, turn them on and off, and even animate them.

Note

In GoLive CyberStudio 3 and Adobe GoLive 4, 5, and 6, layers were called floating boxes. Enough people were bewildered by that odd name that the GoLive team finally changed it.

It's easy to put a layer on the page. As with the other objects in the Basic set of objects, either drag and drop a layer onto a page or double-click to insert one. You can also add new layers from the Layers palette, which can be opened from the Window menu.

Notice that a layer has two parts: a black rectangle indicating the layer's border and a tiny square yellow marker (**Figure 35a**). Clicking the yellow marker brings the Layer Inspector into focus; clicking the black rectangle not only focuses the Inspector, but also selects the layer itself, allowing you to move it. If you move the yellow marker, you are actually moving the syntax for the layer in the HTML source code, whereas if you move the rectangle, you are repositioning the layer on the page.

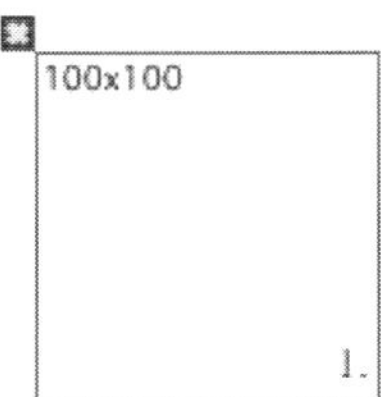

Figure 35a A layer has two parts, the black rectangle and the small square marker.

Tip

If you would like two layers to always move together, put the yellow marker for one inside of the other.

Styling Layers in the CSS Editor

Layers are written as <div> tags with unique IDs in the HTML syntax and as such can be completely styled in the CSS Editor. Use CSS to adjust positioning or size; to add borders, padding, or margins to a layer; and much more!

You can put other objects such as an image, a table, text, or even a layout grid into a layer. It's a good idea to give a descriptive name to your layers. Although GoLive automatically assigns a name to each layer, it's hard to tell which is which unless they are named properly. You'll also want to assign each layer a Z-index, which indicates the order in which they are stacked. Use the Inspector palette to accomplish both those tasks (**Figure 35b**).

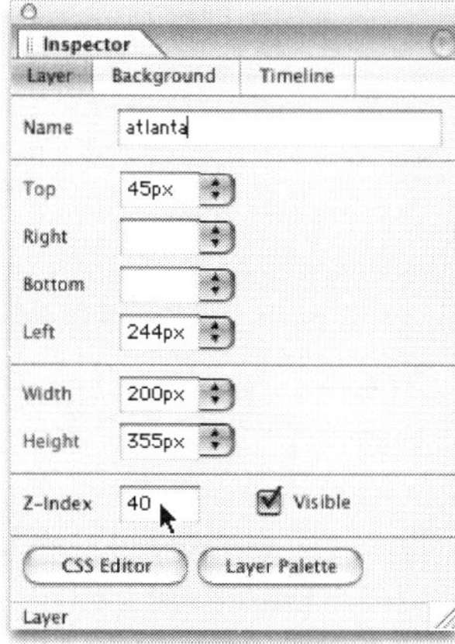

Figure 35b Set a layer's attributes, such as name and Z-index, in the Inspector palette.

Although you can move layers by dragging them, you can also position them using the fields in the Inspector. You'll also notice a check box for Visible in the Inspector. This turns a layer on or off in the browser and is often used in conjunction with a link or action to show and hide layers.

Go to the Background area in the Layer Inspector to assign a color or background image to a layer. The Timeline portion of the Layer Inspector has a nifty way of letting you create a quick animation. Select a layer and click the record button, then move the layer around the page. GoLive automatically sets time markers as it records the movement. To fine-tune your animation, click the Open Timeline Editor button and work directly in the Timeline Editor itself.

Another way to select a layer is to click its name in the Layers palette. The Layers palette also sports Create New Layer and Delete Selected Layers buttons (**Figure 35c**).

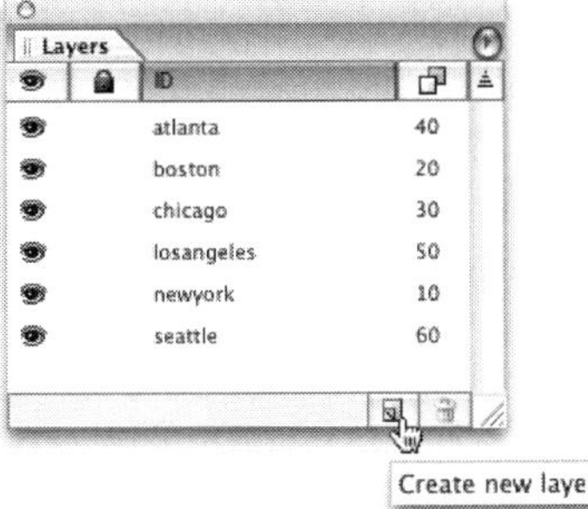

Figure 35c Create or delete layers, give layers a name, or select layers in the Layers palette.

If you'd like to able to move layer names in the list, choose Hierarchic from the Layers palette menu and then simply drag the layer names up or down. The Hierarchic mode also gives a nice visual representation of nested layers. The little eyeball icon to the left of a layer in the Layers palette turns the layer on or off as you are editing, but it does not affect the visibility of the layer in the browser. For that you need to use the Visibility option in the Inspector.

Jumping from the Inspector

A handy new feature in GoLive CS is the addition of two new buttons in the Layer Inspector: the CSS Editor and the Layer palette. One easy click and you have instant access to the tools you need to work with layers.

TIP 36 Designing with Tables

In the beginning, text on an HTML page ran clear across the window with nary a column in sight, and tables were only used as a way to cohesively present tabular data in a Web browser. Designers quickly realized that they could create more complex layouts by housing them in a table. With the recent improvements in CSS, table-less designs now are all the rage, but there are still times when tables are the only logical option. GoLive handles tables very gracefully, with some unique features such as the Table palette, so let's take a look.

GoLive has three important tools for building tables effectively: the Table object, the Table Inspector, and the Table palette (**Figure 36a**).

Command-Dragging to Create Tables

If you press the Command (Mac) or the Ctrl (Windows) key as you drag the Table object in the Objects palette, a small dynamic preview appears, allowing you to drag out a table with the exact number of rows and columns you want. Release the modifier key when you've got the size you want and finish the drag-and-drop operation into the Layout Editor. The next time you use the Table object, it contains the number of rows and columns you used last.

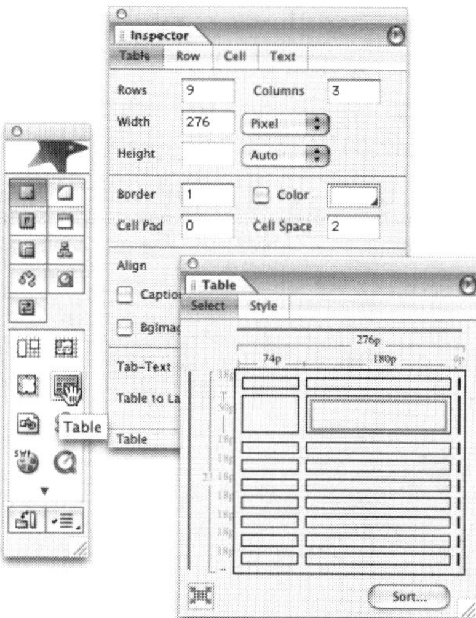

Figure 36a Use these tools for building tables: the Table object, the Table Inspector, and the Table palette.

The Table object is found in the Basic set of the Objects palette. Drag and drop one onto a page or double-click to insert one and then use the Inspector to set its attributes, such as the number of rows and columns. Across the top of the Table Inspector are buttons called Table, Row, Cell, and Text, where you will find options for setting specific table attributes. What's cool is that if you select a row in your table, GoLive automatically brings the Row tools into focus; if you select a cell, the Cell tab comes forward, and so on.

When defining a table, row, or cell's width or height, you can use the pull-down menu to choose Pixel, Percent, or Auto. Pixel sets a specific size in pixels, but Percent and Auto work differently. If you set your overall table size as 80 percent, then the table will expand or contract to take up 80 percent of the page it's on. If you use Auto, then the table will expand or contract according to the content inside it. When setting size options for individual cells, you can achieve various effects by combining Pixel or Percent in a column with Auto in the adjacent column. For example, if you create a table with two columns (two cells) and set the first cell at 125 pixels and the second cell to Auto, the first column will always remain 125 pixels while the second will expand or contract. If you instead set the first cell at 25 percent and the second at 75 percent, the two columns will always remain proportionate whether or not the table itself expands.

The Inspector is also where you set the table border, cell padding, and cell spacing, as well as where you assign color to the table, a row, or even an individual cell. Here's a quick explanation of these settings in the Inspector (**Figure 36b**):

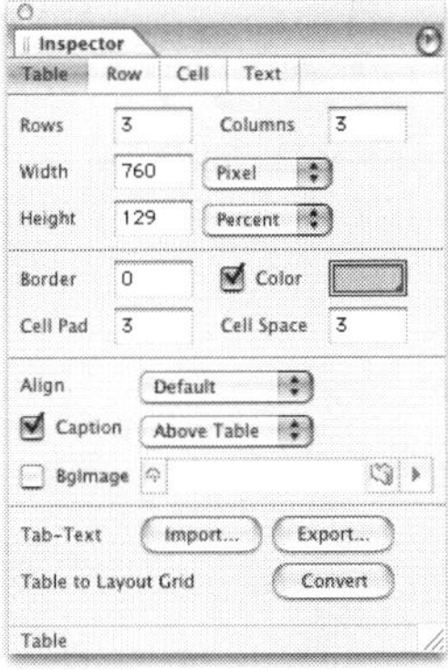

Figure 36b The Table Inspector.

- Border—Defines the size of the border around the outside of the whole table.
- Cell Pad—Puts padding between the contents of a cell and its border and applies to all cells in the table.
- Cell Space—Puts spacing in between cells and applies to all cells in the table.

(continued on next page)

Merging Mania

A neat trick for merging cells is to select one, hold down the Shift key, and press the right arrow key to merge right or the down arrow key to merge down. Be careful, though. While the content in the first cell is not affected, the content in the merged cells will be deleted. Move content into the first cell before merging a cell with other cells.

- Align—Left or Right allows other content to wrap around the table. Center aligns the table to the middle. Default puts the table on the left, but with no wrap.
- Caption—Puts a space either above or below the table suitable for a caption.
- BgImage—Allows you to define a background image for the table. Background images set this way will tile, so using CSS to define a background is often more suitable.
- Tab-Text—Import brings delimited text into a GoLive table, whereas Export extracts data from a GoLive table to a delimited text format.
- Table to Layout Grid—Turns a table into a GoLive layout grid.

Note

You can copy a range of cells from a Microsoft Excel spreadsheet and paste it directly into a GoLive table. GoLive will automatically create the correct number of rows and columns needed for the data (see Tip 38).

To add rows or columns, choose one of the following methods:

- Select a cell and then in the Table portion of the Inspector palette type in the number of rows and columns you desire.
- Select a cell and then in the Cell portion of the Inspector palette use the Add Row/Column or Delete Row/Column button.
- Select a cell, choose Special > Table, and insert a column or row.
- Select a cell, use the contextual menu to choose Insert or Remove, and then insert a column or row.
- Put your cursor inside the last cell of a table and press Tab to create a new bottom row.
- Press the Command key and then drag the bottom or right side of the table (Mac only).

You combine cells—for example, turn a row of four cells into one long cell—by merging them. To merge cells, select a range of cells, Control-click/right-click them, and choose Merge Cells or select Special > Tables > Merge Cells from the menu (see Tip 37).

A table cell can hold any content that you can put on a page, such as text, images, or even another table, and data can be both imported into and exported from GoLive tables (see Tip 38).

TIP 37 Selecting Tables

Table handling is very elegant in GoLive, and in this tip we show you a bunch of handy table-selection tricks that make daily production tasks easy. When a row, column, or cell is selected, you'll notice a thick black stroke around the selection.

Vendor	Part #	Description	Cost
Itto	36593	Muffler	$89.00
Imagine	96782	Upholstery	$329.00
Enviro	16677	Xeon Lamps	$589.00
Moshler	90427	LED Visor	$499.00
Itto	56341	Aluminum Wheels	$719.00
Enviro	18592	Carbon Frame	$1204.00
Imagine	23675	Tinted Glass	$118.00

Figure 37a Select an entire table by clicking the top or left edge.

- Selecting tables with the mouse pointer—To select an entire table, single-click the top or left edge of the table (**Figure 37a**).
- Selecting tables with the markup tree—If the cursor is already inserted inside the table you want to select, click the <table> tag in the markup tree at the bottom of the document window. If you have nested tables, make sure you select the correct table.

Vendor	Part #	Description	Cost
Itto	36593	Muffler	$89.00
Imagine	96782	Upholstery	$329.00
Enviro	16677	Xeon Lamps	$589.00
Moshler	90427	LED Visor	$499.00
Itto	56341	Aluminum Wheels	$719.00
Enviro	18592	Carbon Frame	$1204.00
Imagine	23675	Tinted Glass	$118.00

Figure 37b Select a cell by clicking its bottom or right edge.

- Selecting a table cell with the mouse pointer—To select an individual table cell, single-click the bottom or right edge of the cell (**Figure 37b**).
- Selecting a table cell with the markup tree—If the cursor is already inserted inside the table cell you want to select, click the <td> tag in the markup tree at the bottom of the document window.

(continued on next page)

Using the Table Palette

All of these table-selection tips work in the Table palette just as they do in the Layout Editor. Open the Table palette in the Window menu and resize it so it's easier to select tiny table cells.

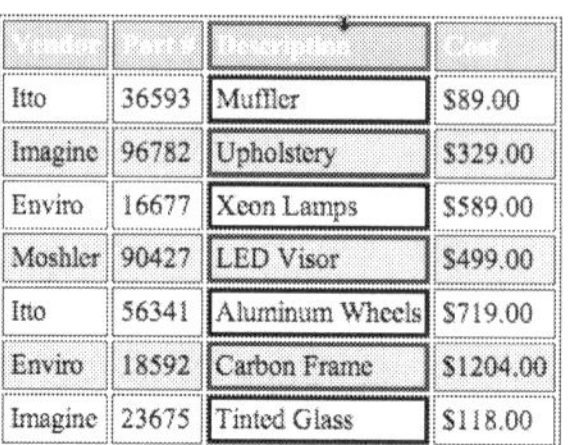

Vendor	Part #	Description	Cost
Itto	36593	Muffler	$89.00
Imagine	96782	Upholstery	$329.00
Enviro	16677	Xeon Lamps	$589.00
Moshler	90427	LED Visor	$499.00
Itto	56341	Aluminum Wheels	$719.00
Enviro	18592	Carbon Frame	$1204.00
Imagine	23675	Tinted Glass	$118.00

Figure 37c Selecting entire rows and columns is easy.

- Selecting table columns—To select an entire table column, move your cursor near the top of the column and single-click with the down-facing arrow mouse pointer (**Figure 37c**). To select multiple adjacent columns, click near the top of one column and drag horizontally. To add multiple noncontiguous columns to the selection, Shift-click the tops of other columns. To subtract a column from a selection, Shift-click the top of the column.

- Selecting table rows—To select an entire table row, move your mouse pointer near the left edge of the row and single-click with the right-facing arrow mouse pointer. To select multiple adjacent rows, click near the left edge of one row and drag vertically. To select multiple noncontiguous rows, Shift-click the left edges of other rows. To subtract a row from a selection, Shift-click the left edge of the row.

Vendor	Part #	Description	Cost
Itto	36593	Muffler	$89.00
Imagine	96782	Upholstery	$329.00
Enviro	16677	Xeon Lamps	$589.00
Moshler	90427	LED Visor	$499.00
Itto	56341	Aluminum Wheels	$719.00
Enviro	18592	Carbon Frame	$1204.00
Imagine	23675	Tinted Glass	$118.00

Figure 37d Add and subtract cells from your selection by holding the Shift key.

- Selecting multiple table cells—To select a region of adjacent table cells, simply click and drag over the cells.

- Selecting noncontiguous table cells—To select noncontiguous table cells, start with at least one cell selected and then Shift-click the other cells (**Figure 37d**). To subtract a table cell from a multicell selection, just Shift-click the table cells.

- Selecting tables and table cells with the keyboard—Press Control-Return (Mac) or Ctrl-Enter (Windows) to navigate up through your table structure. For example, if you have table cell content selected and you invoke this shortcut, you select the containing table cell. If you have a table cell selected and use this shortcut, you select the entire table. If you use this shortcut on a nested table, you select the parent table cell.

- Selecting table cell contents—When you have a table cell selected and want to edit the contents of the cell and not the cell itself, press Return/Enter or switch to the Text tab of the Table Inspector.

TIP 38 Importing Data into Tables

Importing text into tables works seamlessly with several applications, including Microsoft Excel, Microsoft Word, AppleWorks, Lotus 123, and Lotus Word Pro. Just follow these three easy steps:

1. Select the cells and choose Edit > Copy to copy the text from the original file, such as a Microsoft Excel spreadsheet or a Microsoft Word table.
2. Switch to GoLive and select a cell in an empty table. Note that the empty table in GoLive does not need to have the correct number of rows or columns because GoLive will automagically adjust the size of the table to accommodate the content.
3. Choose Edit > Paste to paste the contents into the selected table. That's all there is to it! Just paste the contents of the Clipboard into the empty table, and GoLive does the conversion for you.

If you need to import a plain-text file into a table, choose Special > Table > Import Tab-Delimited Text and select the text file. You can also export tab-delimited text from HTML tables in GoLive (**Figure 38**). Just select the table in the Layout Editor and choose Special > Table > Export Tab-Delimited Text to save out a text file.

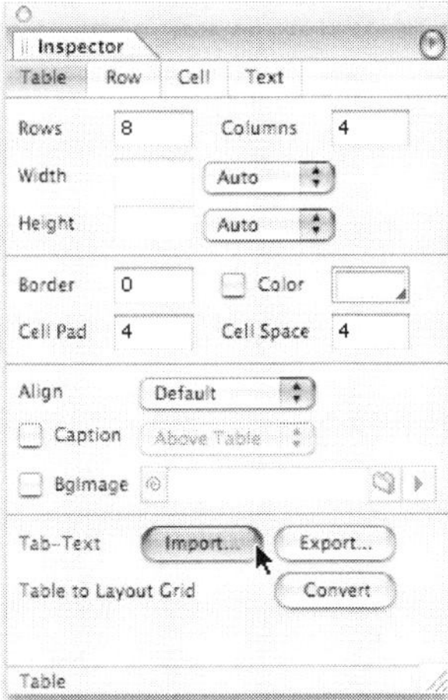

Figure 38 You can copy and paste, use the Special > Table command, or click these buttons in the Table Inspector to import and export table data.

Importing Partial Tables

The cell you select in the table determines the upper-left starting point for the imported text. This means that if you already have other content in your table, such as column headers, you can select the leftmost cell in the second row and you'll end up with everything intact when you paste.

TIP 39 Fixing Table Widths

The power of GoLive's table handling means it's typical for Web designers to experiment with several design options when they're working with tables. One of the pitfalls of this flexibility is that you can end up with some funky math for the widths of your tables and table cells. Specifically, the sum of the table cell widths might not equal the overall width of the table.

GoLive flags the problem by displaying any mathematical errors in red in the Select tab of the Table palette. Place your mouse pointer over these red table measurements (320p in **Figure 39a**) and you'll see the arrow mouse pointer change to a checkmark.

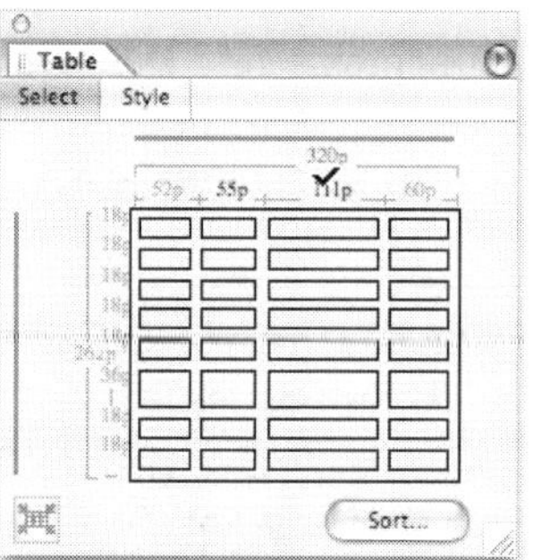

Figure 39a Click the red table measurements with the checkmark mouse pointer to correct the table math.

Click the red numbers with the checkmark mouse pointer, and GoLive instantly calculates the correct math and fixes your source code so that the table will render more reliably across different browsers and platforms (**Figure 39b**).

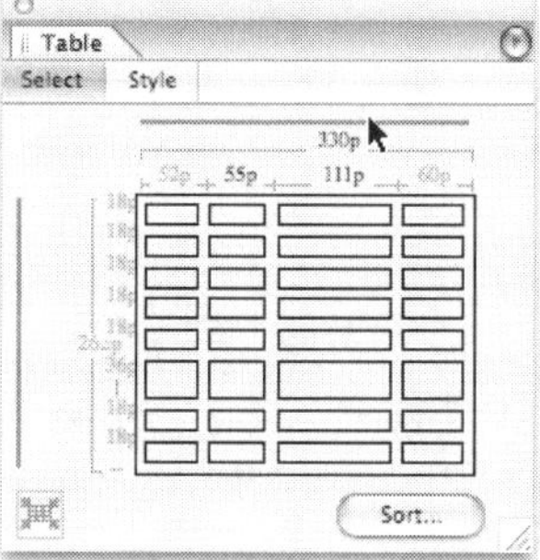

Figure 39b After fixing the math in this example, the table width is 330 pixels instead of 320 pixels.

TIP 40 Sorting Table Data

Sometimes the data you place in an HTML table is perfectly formatted and ordered, but occasionally you need to re-sort it. For example, you might need to sort a table according to part number or price. The good news is that sorting table data in GoLive is really easy.

Select the table you want to sort (see Tip 37) and open the Table palette from the Window menu. Next, click the Sort button in the bottom-right corner of the Table palette to see the Sort Table dialog (**Figure 40**).

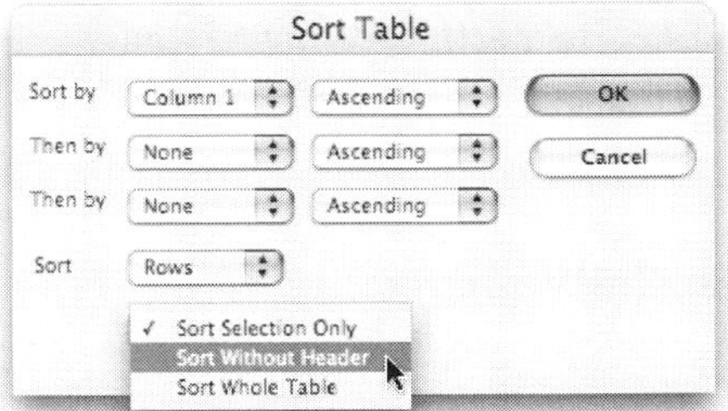

Figure 40 The Sort Table dialog offers several ways to reorder your table data.

The sort options include:

- Sort by—You can choose which row or column you want to sort by. You can even designate secondary and tertiary sort criteria with the Then by options.
- Ascending or Descending—You can sort alphanumerically in ascending or descending order. For example, if you want the item with the lowest price listed first, choose Ascending, but if you want the highest price listed first, choose Descending.
- Sort Rows or Columns—If you want to sort top to bottom, which is the most common, choose Rows. If you want to sort left to right, choose Columns.
- Sort Selection Only—Sorts only the cells you had selected when you opened the Sort Table dialog and ignores unselected cells.
- Sort Without Header—Sorts the entire table except the first row or column—that is reserved as a header for text labels.
- Sort Whole Table—Sorts the entire table even if only part of the table is selected.

Sorting Just the Selection

If you want to sort only part of the entire table, select the cells that you want to sort before you open the Sort Table dialog.

TIP 41 Rearranging Tables

Sorting table data alphabetically or numerically is a big time-saver, but sometimes you just need to rearrange entire sections of a table. For example, you might want to move the price column to the far right of a table or the part number column to the far left.

To rearrange table columns or table rows, just select them and drag them by the small black handle in the upper-left corner of the selection. The key to rearranging table content is seeing the thick black lines between rows or columns that indicates the drag location (**Figure 41**). You can also rearrange multiple rows and columns after you select them (see Tip 37). This feature even works on multiple cells as long as they are adjacent.

Vendor	Part #	Description	Cost
Itto	36593	Muffler	$89.00
Imagine	96782	Upholstery	$329.00
Enviro	16677	Xeon Lamps	$589.00
Moshler	90427	LED Visor	$499.00
Itto	56341	Aluminum Wheels	$719.00
Enviro	18592	Carbon Frame	$1204.00
Imagine	23675	Tinted Glass	$118.00

Figure 41 Rearranging tables is as easy as drag and drop.

To make a copy of your selection, just drag it to a different area of the page outside the table. This drag-and-drop technique works in the Table palette just as it does in the Layout Editor.

TIP 42 Styling Tables

Importing, sorting, and rearranging table data in GoLive helps you organize the content, but styling the rows and columns helps give the data the visual clarity you need to communicate effectively. Select a table, open the Table palette from the Window menu, and switch to the Style tab of the palette (**Figure 42**) to style the table.

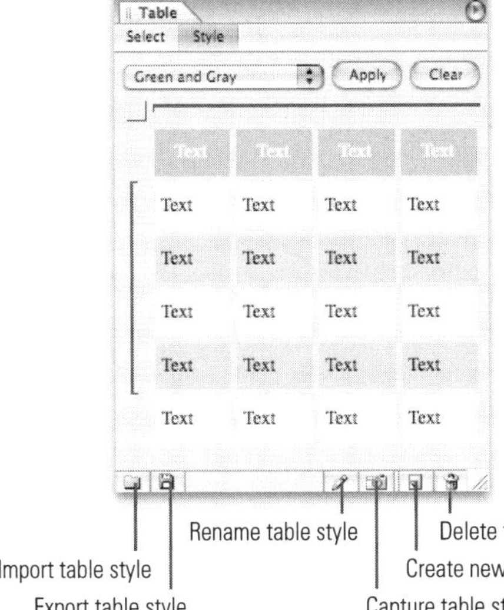

Figure 42 The Style tab of the Table palette gives you all the tools you need to style your tables.

To style a table selected in the Layout Editor, select a table style from the pull-down menu at the top of the Table palette and click Apply. If the table style doesn't look like you expected, click the Clear button in the Table palette and try a different style.

The default table styles give you a place to start, but you'll probably want to design your own. You can apply formatting to a table—including font, font size, font color, table color, row color, cell color, borders, padding, spacing, and alignment—and click the Create new table style icon at the bottom of the palette. Give the new table style a name and click OK. Now you can use the same style in other pages and sites and guarantee visual consistency.

Sharing Table Styles

If you create table styles you want to share with others, select Export Table Styles from the flyout menu in the Table palette. The table styles are saved as an XML file that you can share with others. To import tables styles from another GoLive user, choose Import Table Styles from the flyout menu in the Table palette. This is an easy way to ensure visual consistency when you have several designers contributing to the same project.

If you make some changes to a table and want to update the table style, select the table in the Layout Editor and the table style in the Table palette and then click the Capture icon at the bottom of the Table palette. This will update the existing table style instead of creating a new one.

To rename a table style, select it in the pull-down menu, click the Rename icon, and give the style a new name. If the Table palette contains styles you know you'll never use, you can select them in the palette and click the Delete icon to permanently delete them.

Bonus Tip

Experiment with the blue borders on the top-left edge of the table style preview in the Table palette. This will affect how frequently the pattern repeats and will be most obvious when applied to larger tables.

TIP 43 Zooming in Nested Tables

Selecting nested tables can be really tricky, so GoLive has a table zooming feature that makes it easy to select nested parent and child tables. It's just like zooming in and out of multiple tables—but without the dizziness.

Select a table in the Layout Editor or insert your cursor in a table cell and open the Table palette from the Window menu. To select the parent table the current table is nested inside of, click the Select Parent Table icon in the bottom-left corner of the Table palette (**Figure 43a**). If you have multiple nested tables, you can keep clicking this icon to select the next parent table, the next parent table, and so on.

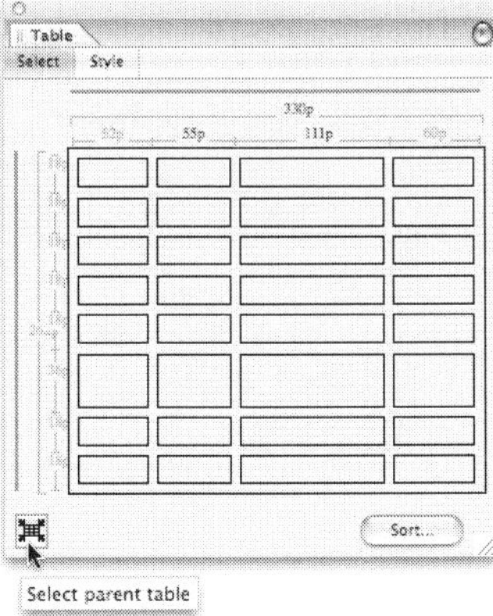

Figure 43a Click the Select Parent Table icon in the Table palette to zoom out of nested tables.

To select a table nested inside another table, click the gray outline of the nested table in the Table palette (**Figure 43b**).

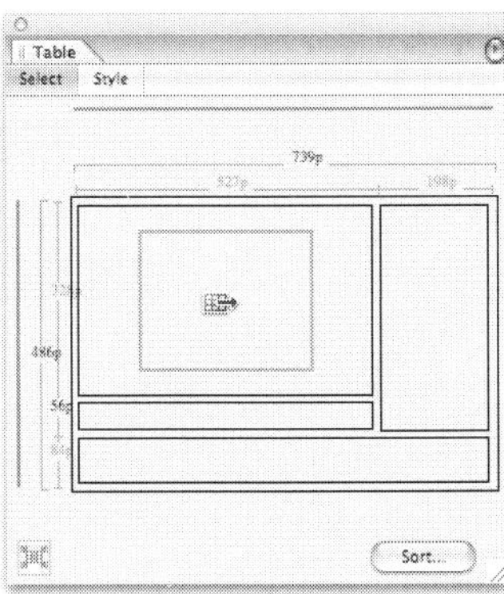

Figure 43b Click the gray outline of the nested table to zoom in.

TIP 44 Selecting Tiny Images in Tables

Many users find it challenging to select small images, such as single-pixel GIFs, inside table cells. The new zooming feature can help (see Tip 45), but sometimes there are even easier ways. For example, the markup tree in the status bar, located at the bottom of the document window, makes this delicate task very easy.

First, select the table cell where the tiny image is positioned. Next, click and hold on the <td> tag in the markup tree and select the <img> tag to select the image (**Figure 44a**).

Figure 44a Select tiny images with the markup tree in the status bar.

When the tiny image is selected, you'll see its attributes in the Inspector palette (**Figure 44b**). Now you can change its dimensions in the Inspector or delete the image.

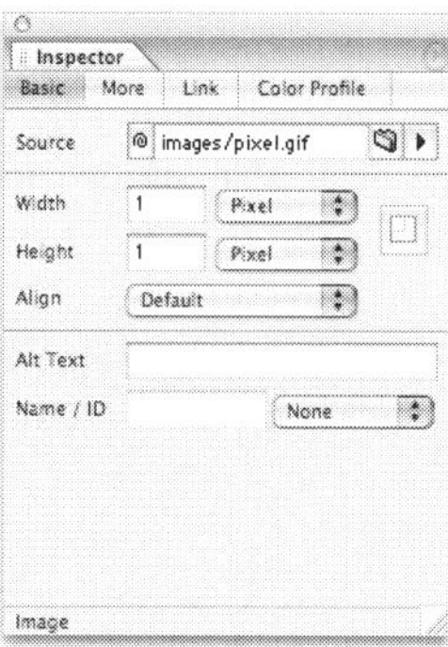

Figure 44b Change the dimensions of the tiny image in the Inspector.

New in GoLive CS

When you place a single-pixel image in the Layout Editor, the dimensions are 32x32 pixels instead of 1x1. This makes it easy to select and resize the image. If you want to force the single-pixel image to use its 1x1 dimensions, click the Set to original size icon ☐ in the Inspector.

Select Upper Block

GoLive has a convenient feature that allows you to easily select the element or tag that encloses your current selection in the page you are editing. Invoke the Select Upper Block command by choosing it in the Special menu or press Command-Shift-B (Mac) or Ctrl-Shift-B (Windows).

This handy command works in Layout, Source, and Outline modes and makes page editing much easier. Some practical uses include selecting nested tables, entire paragraphs, or stylized text.

TIP 45 Zooming in Layout

GoLive CS has an amazing new zoom control in the visual authoring environment of the Layout Editor. Zooming in can be helpful for such tasks as selecting or aligning small objects, and zooming out can help you get a visual overview of a really long page. You can now zoom from 1% to 1600% using the Zoom Value menu in the bottom-right corner of the document window (**Figure 45**). Zooming has been one of the most frequent feature requests over the years and the GoLive engineering team has pulled it off with style.

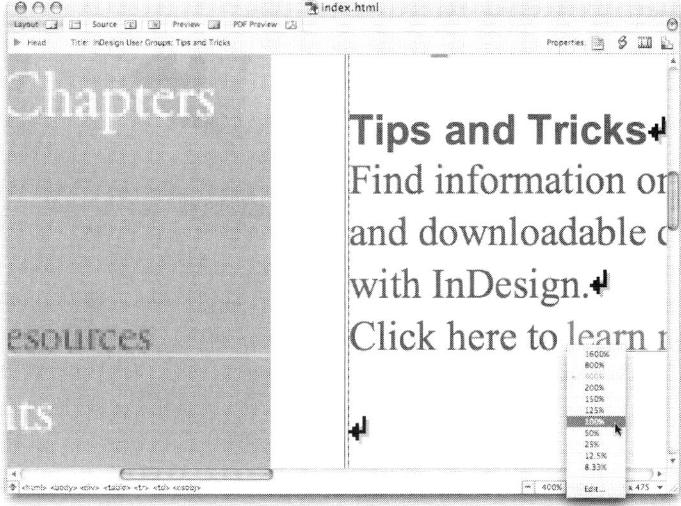

Figure 45 GoLive has the ability to zoom in and out of pages, just like the rest of the applications in the Creative Suite.

You can easily select preset zoom values in the pull-down menu or you can just click the minus button to zoom out and the plus button to zoom in. If you want to set a zoom value that isn't listed, select Edit at the bottom of the list and type in a number.

Zoom Toggle

Zooming is a really nice addition to GoLive CS, but our favorite zoom tip is to simply click on the zoom value at the bottom of the document window. This toggles back and forth between 100% and the previous setting. For example, if you need to zoom out from 100% to 50% to see the overall page composition, just click the zoom value to instantly switch back to 100% again.

TIP 46 Customizing Window Sizes

Both the Site window and documents themselves can be resized by dragging the lower-right corner, but did you know that you can tell GoLive what page size you prefer and in what position you'd like new pages and new sites to open on your screen?

Open a page and then look in the lower-right corner. You'll see a page size listed there in pixels. As you resize the page, those dimensions update. Click and hold the small down arrow to see the Window Size pull-down list, which offers additional page sizes that you can choose from (**Figure 46a**).

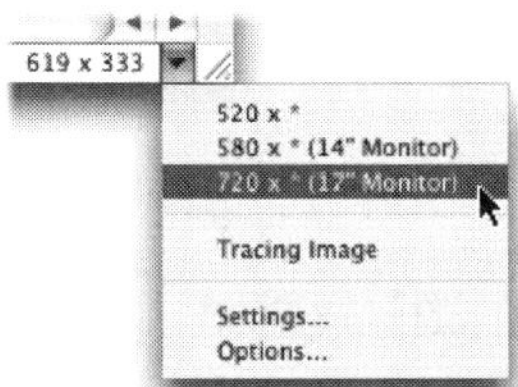

Figure 46a The Window Size pull-down.

Choose Options from the pull-down list. In the dialog that opens, you can edit the default page sizes, delete them, or add your own (**Figure 46b**). Use the buttons in the lower right to add or delete new window configurations. Reorder the list by selecting an item and clicking the arrows on the lower left to move it up or down.

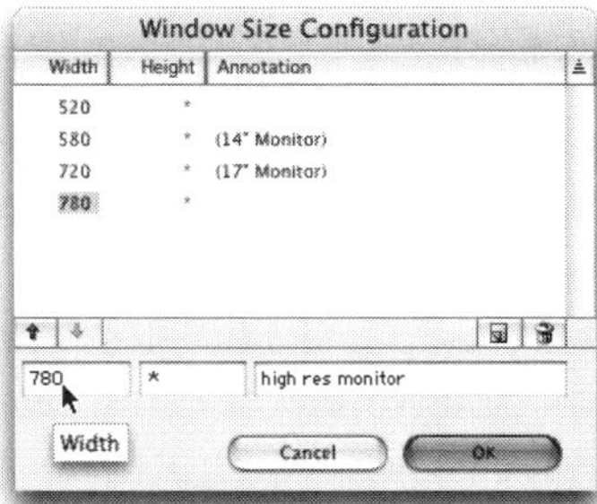

Figure 46b The Window Options dialog.

Once you've got your window size options set, you may have one that you'd like to use for all new documents that are created. Set the front window to the desired size and then choose Settings from the pull-down. In the dialog that opens, enable the Markup Document Windows and/or Site Windows options (**Figure 46c**). Doing so records both the size of the windows and their position on the screen. Click OK.

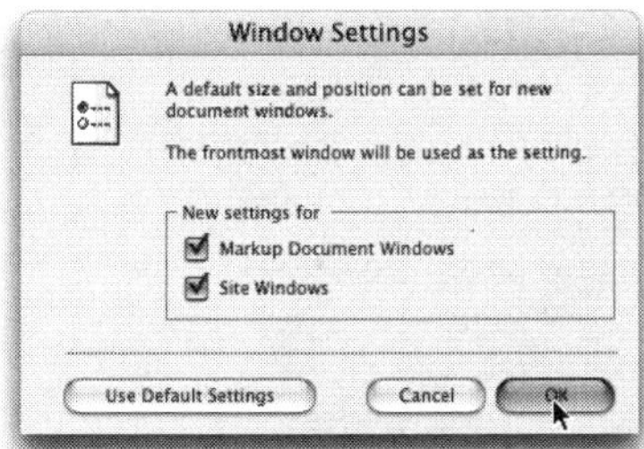

Figure 46c The Window Settings dialog.

From then on, any new documents or sites you create will open in the size and position you set in the Window Settings dialog.

Back to the Beginning

You can always go back to the default window configuration by choosing Settings from the Window Size pull-down list and then clicking the Use Default Settings button.

Panning with the Hand Tool

In many of the other Creative Suite applications you can move a page around by using the Hand tool. GoLive CS does not have such a tool that you choose from a toolbox, but we know a trick to finding it anyway.

On a Mac, hold down the Control and Option keys (Ctrl-Alt on Windows) to invoke the Hand tool (**Figure 47**). Now you can use it as you would in Photoshop, Illustrator, InDesign, or Acrobat by dragging the contents of a window up, down, to the right, or to the left.

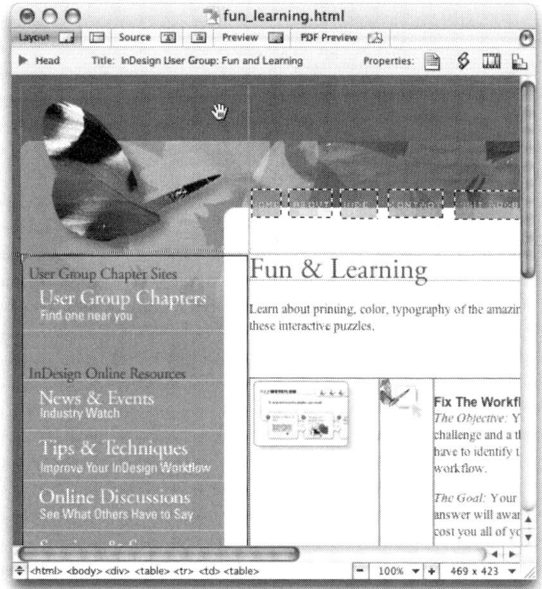

Figure 47 Invoke the Hand tool by pressing the special combination of keys on your keyboard.

Remember, if all the content on the page fits into the visible area of the window, nothing will pan, so only use this feature when the content exceeds the boundaries of the document window or when you are zoomed into the page.

TIP 48 Designing with Smart Guides

The GoLive engineers know a good thing when they see it. That's why they thanked the Illustrator team and then proceeded to put Smart Guides, which originated in Illustrator, into GoLive CS. What are Smart Guides, exactly? They are guides that automatically become visible as you are moving objects around a page. When the edge of one object lines up with the edge of another object, the guide magically appears, which gives you an easy way to line up objects with incredible precision and speed (**Figure 48**).

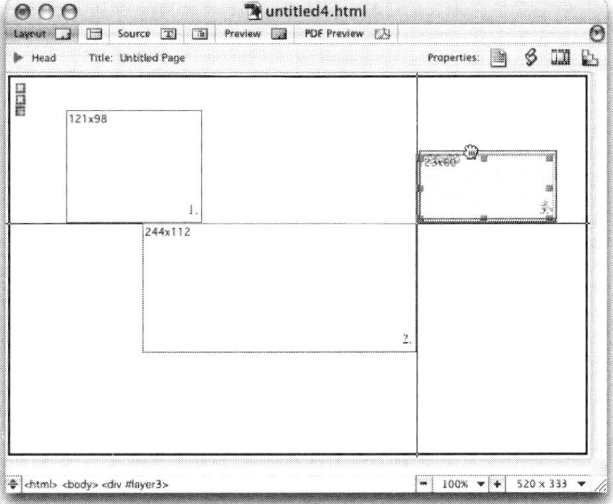

Figure 48 Smart Guides automatically appear when one object encounters the edge of another object.

Smart Guides can be found in the following areas of GoLive:

- When you're moving objects on a layout grid.
- When you're working with multiple layers.
- In the QuickTime Editor.
- In the SMIL Editor.

Don't Be Too Smart!

If you prefer not to use Smart Guides, you can turn them off by deselecting Smart Guides from the View menu.

TIP 49 Changing View Profiles

The View palette in GoLive offers a plethora of options that many users don't know about. Using the View palette, you can simulate what your page will look like in a number of browsers or based on a specific profile.

Start by opening the View palette from the Window menu and opening a page. Notice that there are pull-down menus labeled Basic Profile and User Profiles. Nested in the list are subcategories. Choose a browser profile from the Basic Profiles list, and your page will simulate that browser. Recently used profiles are listed at the top of the menu (**Figure 49a**).

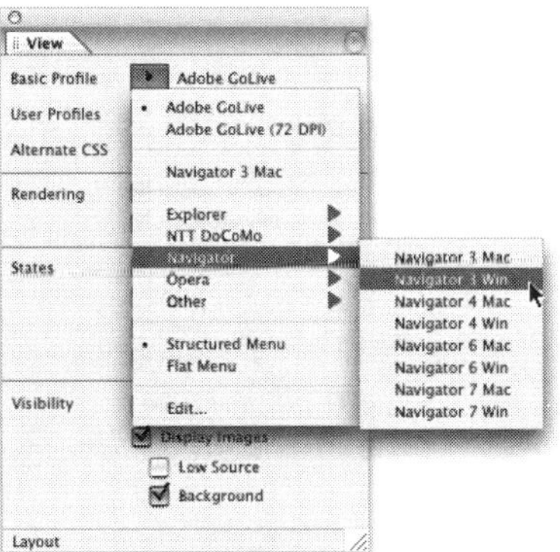

Figure 49a Choose from the options in the Basic Profile menu to simulate how your page will look in various browsers or devices.

This is helpful if you want to see how a page will look in a very old browser, such as those that don't support CSS, or how the page will look in a device such as a mobile phone.

Choose an option from the User Profiles list to view the page in a particular way—for instance, to see how your page will appear at a particular size or with no images. We find the Plain Text Only option valuable when we need to edit text and don't want a lot of other clutter in the way. Again, recently used options will be listed at the top of the menu (**Figure 49b**). You can have multiple User Profiles enabled at a time.

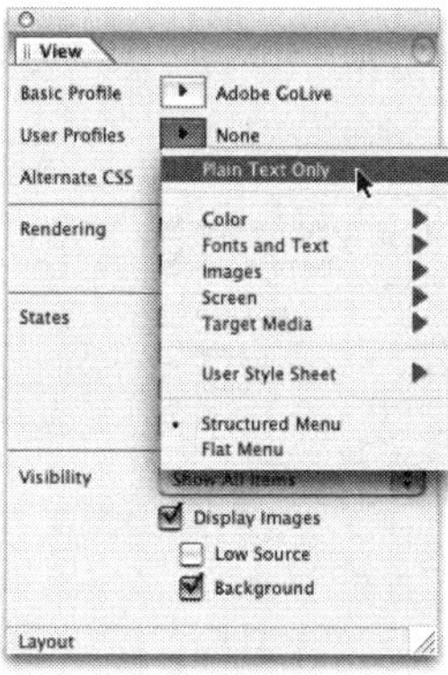

Figure 49b The User Profiles offer a number of helpful views, including a quick way to see only the text on your page.

Flat Menu Option

If you prefer, you can change the way the profile menu appears by selecting Flat Menu from either the Basic or User Profiles menu. You'll get all the same options as in the structured menu, but they'll be in one long list instead of in submenus.

Note

The view options are not a replacement for testing your pages with real browsers. They're great in a pinch, but don't get lazy. Test, test, test on multiple browsers and across platforms.

TIP 50 Turning Invisible Elements On and Off

GoLive has an incredible level of control when it comes to showing and hiding invisible elements such as form containers, image map areas, and table borders. Look in the General > Invisible Elements section of the application preferences and you'll see that you can create multiple sets of invisible item options. To create a new set, click the Create New Set button, give the set a name, and select the options on the right. In the example shown in **Figure 50a**, GoLive will hide all invisible elements *except* layer and table borders, a helpful arrangement when you want to hide unnecessary elements but still see the layout structure of the page.

Editing Visibility Sets

You can quickly go to the Invisible Elements preferences by choosing Edit Set from the Visibility pull-down menu in the View palette.

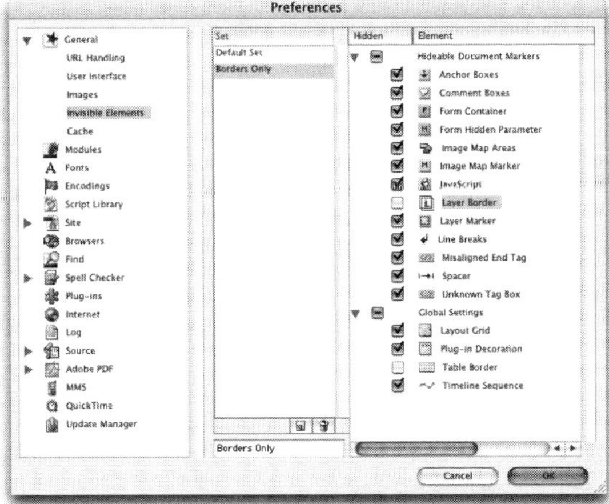

Figure 50a Create new sets of invisible elements in GoLive's preferences.

To use a custom visibility set, simply open a page in Layout mode and select the set in the Visibility pull-down menu in the View palette (**Figure 50b**).

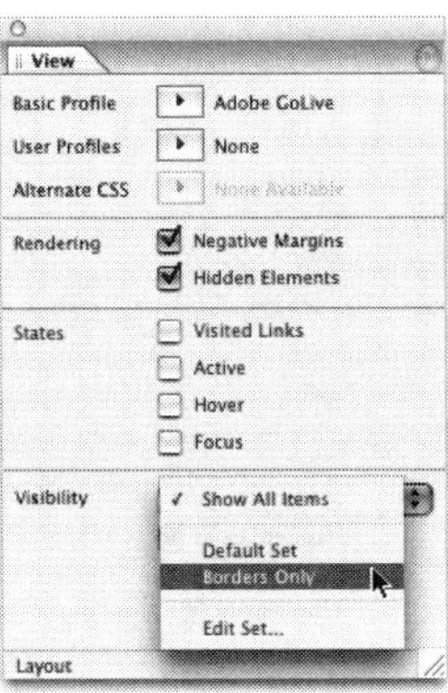

Figure 50b Choose a Visibility set in the View palette.

TIP 51 Visual Tag Editor

If you've ever wanted to edit an HTML element but didn't want to switch out of Layout mode or give up part of the window to the Split View, then the Visual Tag Editor is the solution for you. Using the Visual Tag Editor, you can edit a piece of code or insert a new tag.

To open the Visual Tag Editor, choose Special > Visual Tag Editor. If you select text in the page and invoke the Visual Tag Editor, the Wrap option will be enabled, meaning that the tag you add will be wrapped around your selection. If you select a tag in the markup tree of the document (see the following tip) and then invoke the Visual Tag Editor, the selected tag will appear in the window, and the Edit option will be enabled so that you can edit the current tag. If you position your cursor in the Layout Editor where you'd like a new tag to be added and then invoke the Visual Tag Editor, the Insert option will be enabled.

To add a tag or attribute, either type into the field at the top of the window or double-click in the list on the left. Once a tag has been added, press the spacebar to continue. Notice that as soon as you type a space, attributes of the tag you are editing appear in the list. You can also use the built-in markup tree to navigate through the code and find a particular tag to edit (**Figure 51**).

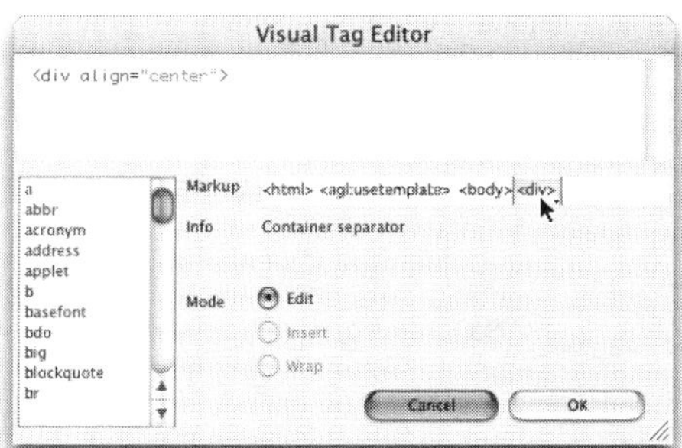

Figure 51 The Visual Tag Editor.

Note

If the tag or attribute you want is not visible in the list, scroll down to find it—or press its first letter on your keyboard, and GoLive will jump to the entries that begin with that letter. Descriptive information is shown in the Info field when a tag or attribute is selected in the list.

There are so many ways that the Visual Tag Editor can come in handy, but here's an example that's pretty basic. Open the Visual Tag Editor, use its markup tree to select a <div> tag, and then add an ID. Easy, quick, precise.

Syntax Tool Tip

Hold down Option-Shift (Mac) or Alt-Shift (Windows) and hover your mouse pointer over any object in the Layout Editor. After you pause for a second, you'll see a helpful tool tip showing you the source code for the closest object under the cursor.

TIP 52 Navigating the Markup Tree

A great feature that was introduced in GoLive 6 is the markup tree in the bottom of the document window for documents that use structured markup, such as HTML, XHTML, and PHP pages. There are many timesaving ways to use the Markup Tree bar, but we focus on two particular benefits: selecting child and parent elements of the current selection.

The markup tree can be used to select child elements of the currently selected object. For example, select a table in the Layout Editor and then click and hold on the <table> tag in the Markup Tree bar to select a <tr> tag (table row), as shown in **Figure 52**.

Figure 52 Drill down to child elements of a selected tag using the markup tree.

You can also use the Markup Tree bar to select parent elements. For example, to make sure you've selected an entire text hyperlink, select the linked text in Layout mode and then click the <a> tag in the Markup Tree bar. The Markup Tree feature is also available in the Visual Tag Editor dialog (see Tip 50).

Removing Elements and Content

If you Control-click (Mac) or right-click (Windows) on an element in the markup tree, you'll see two very powerful options: Replace Element by Its Content and Remove Element's Content. These options come in handy when you want to do some fancy maneuvering of the HTML syntax without actually touching the code. For example, if you have a piece of text enclosed in a <font> tag and want to remove the font tag, simply select the <font> tag in the markup tree and then choose Replace Element by Its Content from the contextual menu.

TIP 53 Calculating Document Statistics

Do you ever wonder how long it will take for a certain page to download over a 56k connection? An ISDN line? A T1 connection? Open a Web page in GoLive and choose Special > Document Statistics to get a helpful estimate of download times at various connection speeds (**Figure 53**).

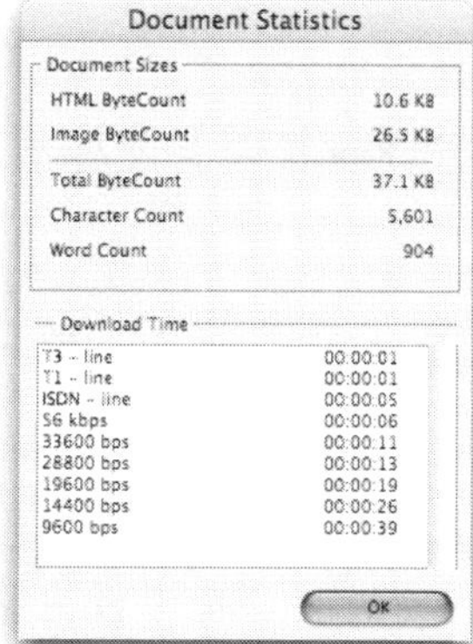

Figure 53 Document Statistics can help you decide if your pages need to go on a diet.

The Document Statistics dialog shows you the size of your source code, your images, and the overall page size. Copy editors will appreciate the ability to get character and word count information for the selected page. At the bottom of the dialog is a list of estimated download times at different connection speeds. Lots of factors such as server load and Internet traffic can affect real-world performance, but these numbers should give you a good estimate.

TIP 54 Adding and Changing DOCTYPEs

A DOCTYPE—short for document type declaration—should be included at the beginning of every page you create (**Figure 54a**). The DOCTYPE tells your visitors' Web browsers what flavor of HTML or XHTML you used to create your page and helps render the page accurately.

Figure 54a Every page should have a DOCTYPE in the beginning of the source code.

Click the flyout menu in the upper-right corner of the document window and select the appropriate DOCTYPE from the Doctype menu (**Figure 54b**). If your page uses HTML, you can only select an HTML DOCTYPE; if it uses XHTML, you can only select an XHTML DOCTYPE.

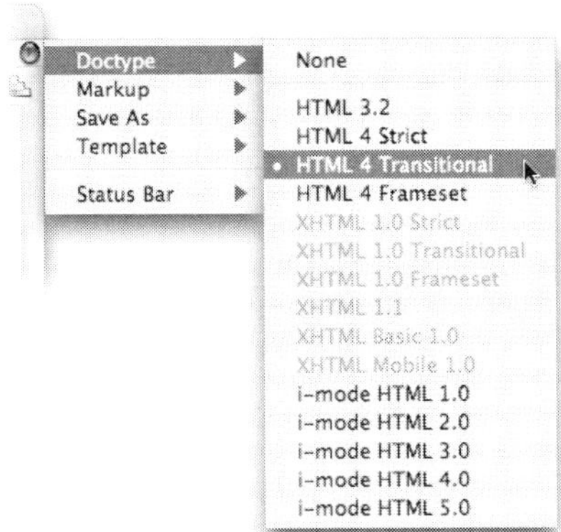

Figure 54b Choose the appropriate DOCTYPE from the document flyout menu. Notice you can also convert the markup of a page between HTML and XHTML using the document flyout menu. Choose Markup > Convert to HTML or Markup > Convert to XHTML as needed, and GoLive does the dirty work for you.

Short vs. Long DOCTYPEs

By default, GoLive writes a short version of the DOCTYPE for HTML pages. It writes the short version because a long DOCTYPE (with the URL of the DTD) can cause problems in some browsers.

To switch from the short to the long version of a DOCTYPE, hold the Option (Mac) or Alt (Windows) key and choose the DOCTYPE from the document flyout menu. To switch from the long version to the short version, choose the DOCTYPE in the document flyout menu with no modifier keys.

TIP 55 Managing Color with the Swatches and Color Palettes

GoLive CS includes a brand-new Swatches palette that is similar to the Swatches palettes you may be already familiar with in Photoshop, Illustrator, and InDesign (**Figure 55a**). This means it's that much easier to learn GoLive and work with color in familiar ways. The Swatches palette should be open by default, but if you can't find it or you've accidentally closed it, just open it from the Window menu.

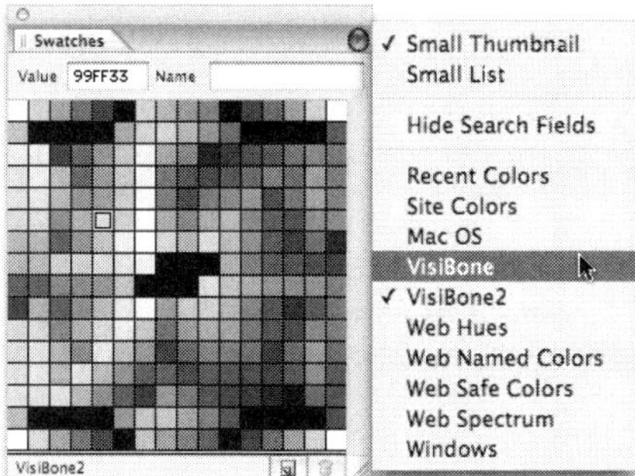

Figure 55a The Swatches palette in GoLive works like other Adobe applications.

To change between different swatch sets, use the palette menu in the upper-right corner and select the one you want to use. The VisiBone swatch layouts are some of our favorites. To create a new swatch, mix a new color in the Color palette and click the New Swatch icon at the bottom of the Swatches palette.

If you use other Adobe applications, you might prefer the list view for your swatches so you can see a color swatch and a text description of the swatch. The good news is that GoLive CS offers you this same familiar way to manage your swatches for Web design. Just use the Swatches palette menu and select Small List instead of Small Thumbnail.

Sharing Swatches with Photoshop

Not only does GoLive CS have a new Swatches palette, but it also uses the same swatches file format as Adobe Photoshop. This means it's easy to create graphics and swatches in Photoshop and then share those swatches with GoLive to ensure consistency throughout your workflow. Just create the swatches in Photoshop, save them with the Save Swatches command in the Photoshop Swatches palette menu, and then place the .aco file in the GoLive/Settings/Color Swatches folder. The next time you launch GoLive, your new swatches will be available in the Swatches palette.

Note that GoLive can only import RGB, CYMK, and grayscale swatches. Other color values such as LAB and HSB are reset to default values.

Searching Swatches

Searching for specific values or names of swatches is easy in GoLive CS. Just turn on the Show Search Fields option in the Swatches palette menu, and color value and color name fields will appear at the top of the palette. Now to locate a specific color within your active swatches, just enter a search value and press Return/Enter. Note that this handy features works in both thumbnail and list views.

The Color palette in GoLive also works like other Adobe applications and includes color pickers for grayscale, RGB, CMYK, HSB, and HSV. Switch between the different color pickers by clicking the icons at the top of the Color palette or choose from the flyout menu. Select a color field in any palette or toolbar and mix the color in the Color palette to see the changes in real time (**Figure 55b**).

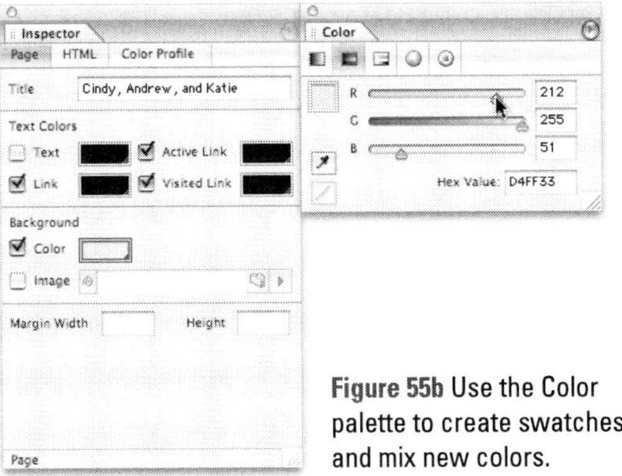

Figure 55b Use the Color palette to create swatches and mix new colors.

TIP 56 Picking Web-Safe Colors

If picking Web-safe colors is important to you, GoLive makes it very easy to do just that. The simplest way is to choose colors from the VisiBone, VisiBone2, Web Hues, Web Safe, or Web Spectrum swatch sets in the Swatches palette (**Figure 56a**).

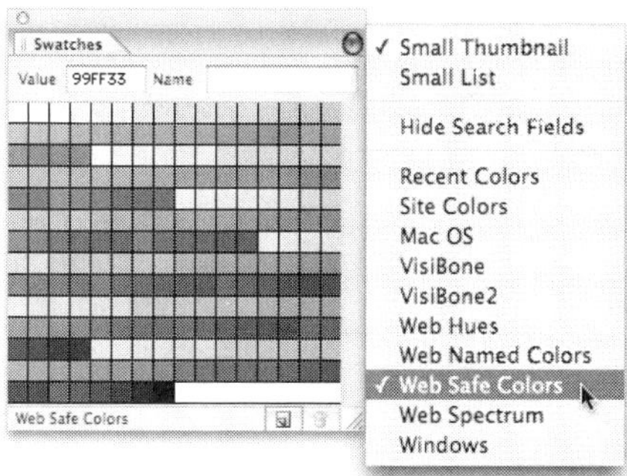

Figure 56a Several of the swatch sets show you only Web-safe colors.

Another way to make sure you select a Web-safe color swatch is to turn on the Small List View option in the Swatches palette and select only colors with the small cube icon next to them (**Figure 56b**). Lastly, you can turn on the Web Colors Only option in the Color palette menu and you can mix colors with any of the familiar color mixers and be confident you'll get only Web-safe colors.

Figure 56b Several of the swatch sets show you only Web-safe colors.

Are Web-Safe Colors Necessary?

In the early days of the Web, most computer monitors could display only 256 colors. This meant Web designers tried to limit their color usage to the 216 Web-safe colors so they wouldn't have any unexpected dithering in their graphics. Computer monitors and graphics cards have come a long way over the years and now usually display thousands or millions of colors. This means it's probably not necessary to limit your color palette to Web-safe colors anymore.

Using the Eyedropper Tool

Removing Color

We've shown you several ways to manage and apply color, but what about removing color? Select the text or color field you want to change and click the remove color icon (the empty white box with a red line through it) on the left edge of the Color palette. You can achieve the same result by selecting the Type > Remove Color command for selected text.

The Eyedropper tool in the Color palette allows you to quickly sample color from anywhere on your monitor. It even works in other windows and other applications that might be open in the background. For example, the Eyedropper allows you to match the color of text selected in your Web page with a color in an open Photoshop document or Illustrator logo.

Select the Eyedropper tool in the Color palette and place your mouse pointer over the color you want to sample (**Figure 57**). When you see a preview of the sampled color in the top-left corner of the Color palette, click to sample the color and apply it to your selection.

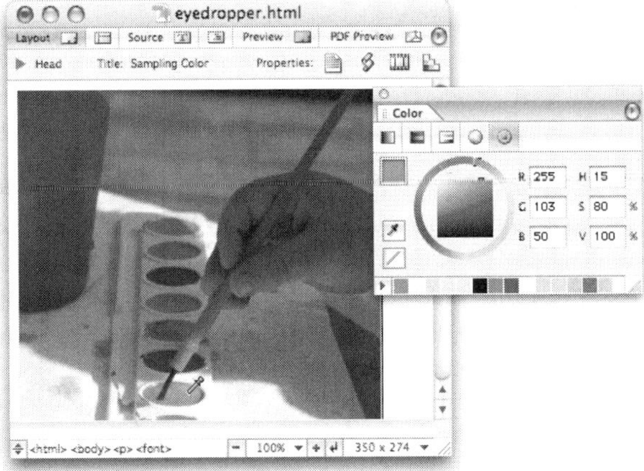

Figure 57 Use the Eyedropper to sample color anywhere on your screen.

TIP 58 Using Color Shortcut Menus

Normally, you apply a color to something by selecting the object, selecting the color field that corresponds to the selected object, and then picking a swatch from the Swatches palette or mixing a color in the Color palette. This works fine, but you might have noticed that there's a small black triangle in the bottom-right corner of every color field throughout GoLive. When you click and hold on the black corner triangles, you get access to a convenient pop-up swatch picker where you can make instant color changes (**Figure 58a**). You can also Control-click (Mac) or right-click (Windows) anywhere in the color field to open the swatch shortcut menus.

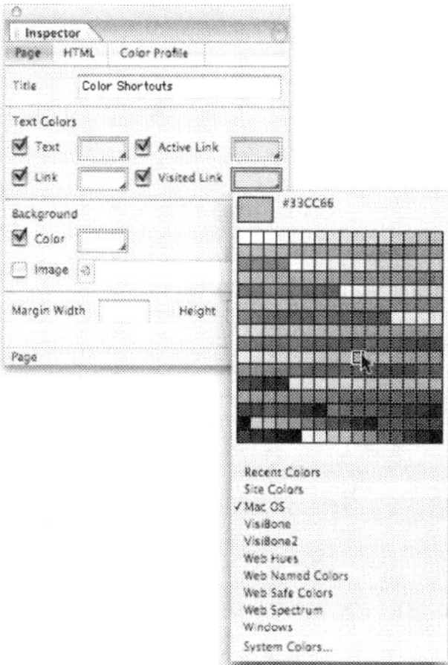

Figure 58a Pick colors quickly from the swatch shortcut menus in every color field.

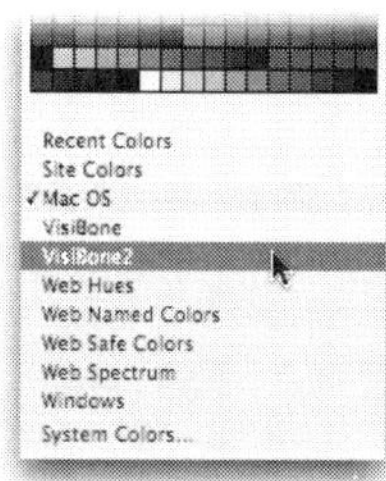

Figure 58b You can customize the swatch set that is available in the color fields.

That's handy, but what makes these hidden menus really powerful is that you can choose which set of swatches is shown when you open it. You can select any of the installed color swatches, including the popular VisiBone swatches, from the bottom of the pull-down menu (**Figure 58b**).

Color fields exist in many different parts of GoLive, including the toolbar, the CSS Editor, the Highlight palettes, and several Inspectors. This means there are lots of places to put this trick to good use.

TIP 59 Remembering Recently Used Colors

When you plan a site or start designing a Web page, a major consideration is the consistent use of color. If you mix a color you want to remember, just click the small triangle in the bottom-left corner of the Color palette to add it to the list of recently used colors (**Figure 59a**). Colors you apply to objects are added automatically to the row. This is an efficient way to store colors and compare your options. If you don't see the row of recent color swatches at the bottom of the Color palette, make sure the Show Recent Colors Option is checked in the palette menu.

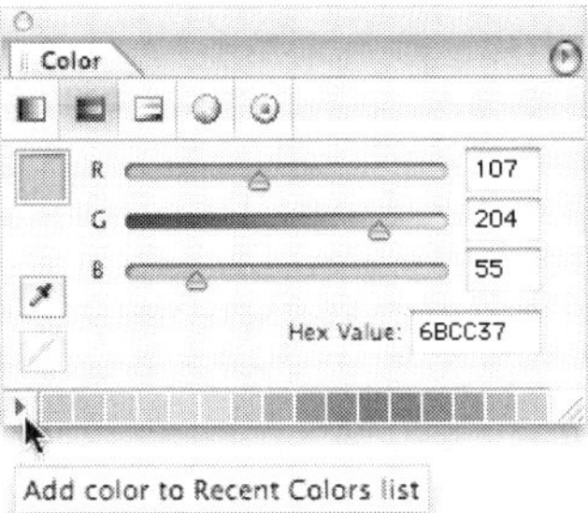

Figure 59a The bottom row of the Color palette stores recently used colors for easy access.

To see more of your recently used colors, make the Color palette wider. For an exhaustive history of colors you've used, open the Swatches palette, switch to the Recent Colors swatch set, and set the view to Small List in the palette menu. GoLive keeps track of all the colors you use and even records the date and time the swatch was remembered (**Figure 59b**).

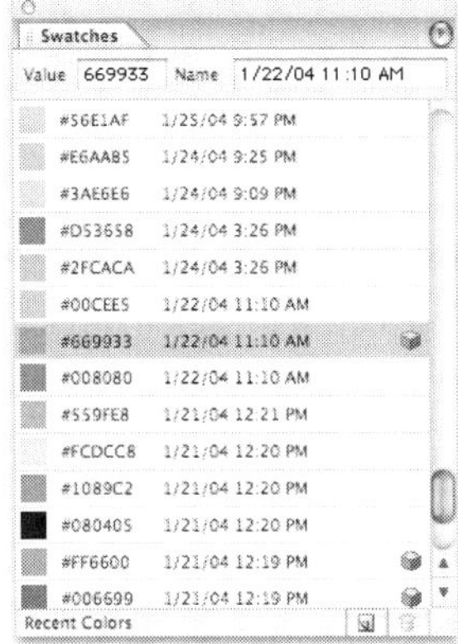

Figure 59b GoLive automatically keeps track of all the colors you've used.

Once you've decided which colors you're going to use throughout a site, you'll probably want to keep the colors consistent. Let's say you've created a specific set of colors in the Colors tab of your Site window and you want to make sure that you don't stray from those standards on the rest of the pages in the site. In the Swatches palette menu, select the Site Colors swatch set and you'll see this matches exactly with the Colors tab of the Site window (**Figure 59c**). Now you don't have to worry about accidentally using six different shades of the same green.

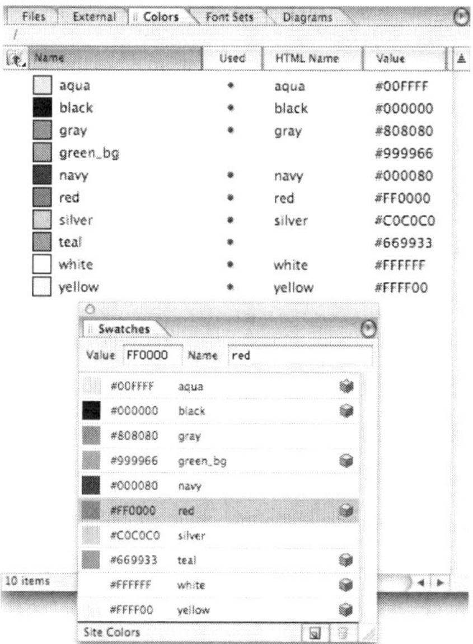

Figure 59c If you always pick from the Site Colors swatches in the Swatches palette, you can ensure consistent color usage across all the pages in the site.

TIP 60 Leveraging Common Adobe Color Management

Like the rest of the applications in Adobe Creative Suite, GoLive offers a consistent interface for color management of your images and artwork (**Figure 60**). You can open the Color Settings dialog from the application menu (Mac) or the bottom of the Edit menu (Windows).

It's beyond us to explain all the details of color management in one short tip, but the good news is that whether you use one of the presets or create your own custom settings, you can share the settings with all the Creative Suite applications. Then the color management in GoLive kicks in when you're converting native source files such as Photoshop and Illustrator to Web formats such as GIF and JPEG with the Smart Objects feature (see Tip 118). Notice that at the bottom of the Color Settings dialog you can even check the option to use color management when displaying images on Web pages in GoLive.

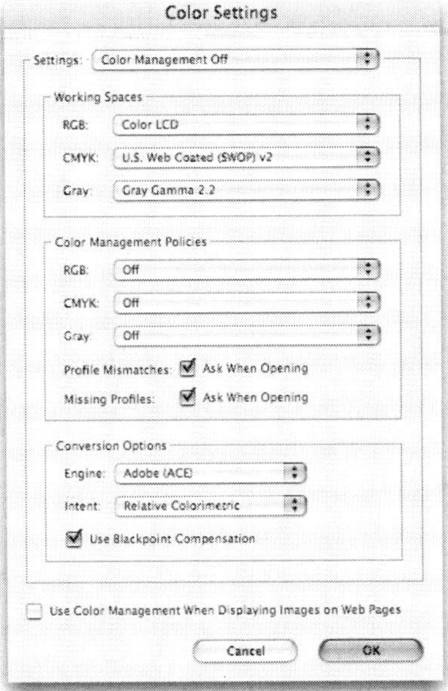

Figure 60 All the Creative Suite applications share the same color-management technology.

TIP 61 Troubleshooting Pages with the Highlight Palette

The Highlight palette is an incredibly powerful feature that can help you in so many different ways it's impossible to list them all here. Open a Web page and then open the Highlight palette from the Window menu if it's not already open (**Figure 61a**).

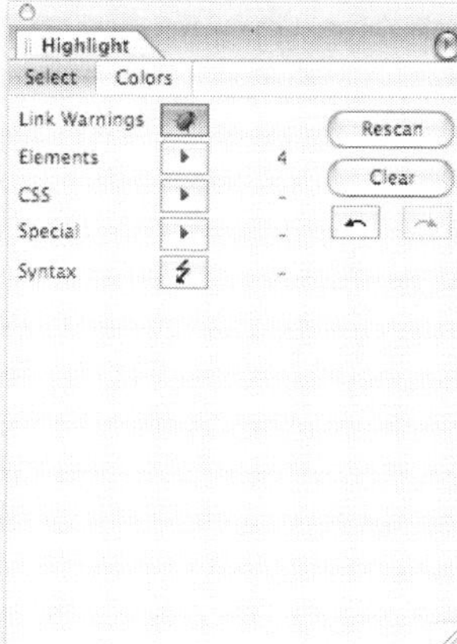

Figure 61a The Highlight palette is a great way to locate and troubleshoot different items on a page.

The Highlight palette is an easy way to toggle Link Warnings and run the Syntax Checker, but it does so much more than that. For example, the Elements pull-down menu shows you an alphabetical list of every element used in the page. Select an element, and all instances of that tag are highlighted in your page. You can even select multiple elements and get a complete count of all occurrences.

Another great way to use the Highlight palette is to quickly and easily locate CSS usage in a page. Open a page in GoLive and select a CSS class or ID from the CSS pull-down menu to instantly highlight the styled objects.

The Highlight palette also has a pull-down menu labeled Special that includes a variety of helpful items you might want to highlight in a page. One of our favorite options in this menu is JavaScript Actions, which quickly shows how many GoLive actions are in a page and where they are located.

In the Colors tab of the Highlight palette you can adjust the highlight color, opacity, and style for any from link and syntax warnings to locked and editable regions (**Figure 61b**). Check out the other options and you'll find all sorts of cool uses for the Highlight palette.

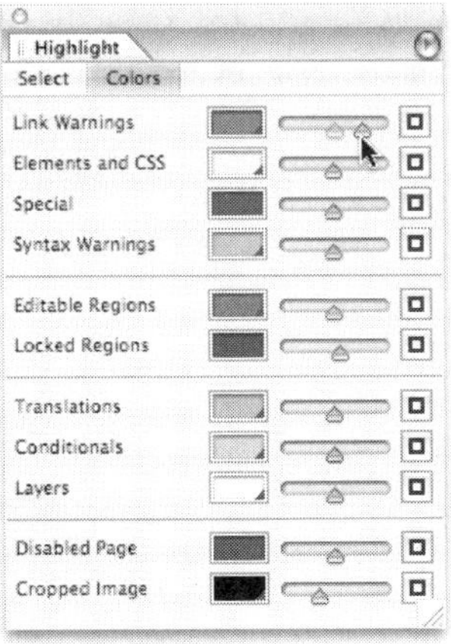

Figure 61b Use the Colors tab to customize the color and opacity of various warnings and highlights.

Using OS X Services

We want to say up front that this tip is only for Mac users, but it's so cool we just had to put it in the book. If you're not familiar with OS X Services, they are system-wide features available in the application menu of most OS X software. To use a service, select some text in the Layout Editor or a file in the Site window and choose a service from the GoLive > Services menu (**Figure 62**).

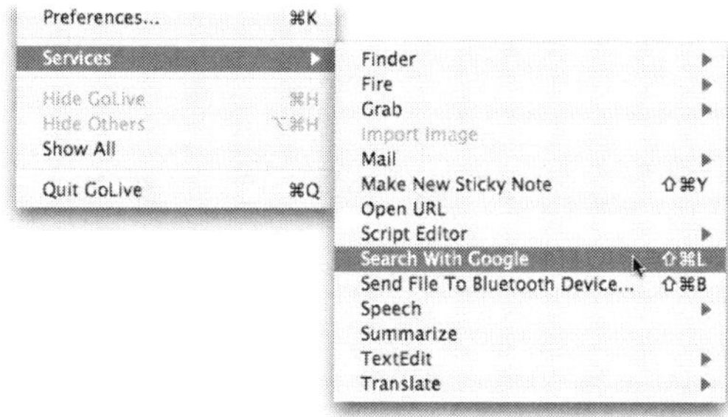

Figure 62 Manipulate your selection with a variety of OS X services.

There are a variety of services available, but some of the most practical uses include the following:

- Open URL—Select a Web site address in the Layout Editor and open the URL in your default Web browser.
- Search with Google—Use the selected text as a search at the world's most popular search engine.
- Send File to Bluetooth Device—Select a file in the Site window, such as an SMIL presentation, an MPEG movie, or a JPEG, and transfer it to a wireless device. This only works if your Mac and device are Bluetooth-compatible.
- Speech—Select text and let your Mac read it aloud to you. This is a fun way to "proofread" your writing.
- Summarize—Select all the text in a page or paragraph and let your Mac summarize the text for you. This might be an easier way to write description metatags.
- Translate—Download the Translation Service from http://www.kavasoft.com/TranslationService/ and translate text back and forth between more than a dozen languages.

TIP 63 Customizing the Document Status Bar

The status bar at the bottom of a document in the Layout Editor offers single-click access to several convenient features (**Figure 63a**). Starting on the left side and working our way across, these options include the following:

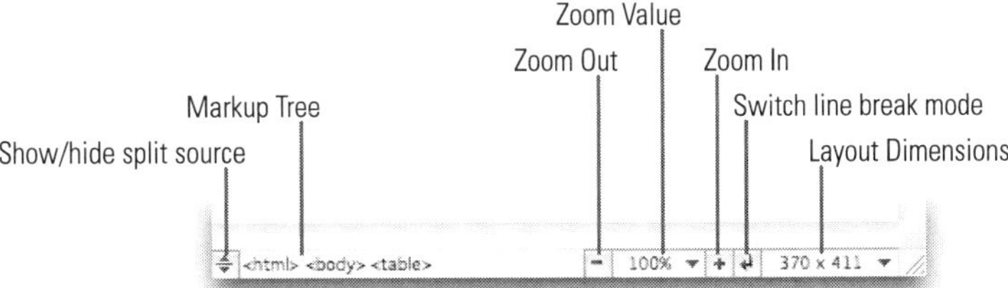

Figure 63a The status bar gives you access to several handy options.

- Show/hide split source—This toggles the Split Source View and is also available in the View menu (see Tip 28).
- Markup Tree—The markup tree allows you to logically navigate the structure of your source code while in the Layout Editor (see Tip 52).
- Zoom Out—Zooms out on the current page to the next zoom preset (see Tip 45).
- Zoom Value—Selects a preset zoom value from the pull-down menu (see Tip 45).
- Zoom In—Zooms in on the current page to the next zoom preset (see Tip 45).
- Switch line break mode—Changes the line breaks of the current page between Mac, UNIX, and Windows formats. This setting is also available under File > Line Breaks.
- Layout Dimensions—You can store and retrieve multiple presets for the document window dimensions (see Tip 46).

You might use some of these features more than others, so GoLive lets you customize the status bar to your preference. You can toggle all of these features, as well as some status bar options related to PDF preview, in the document flyout menu (**Figure 63b**).

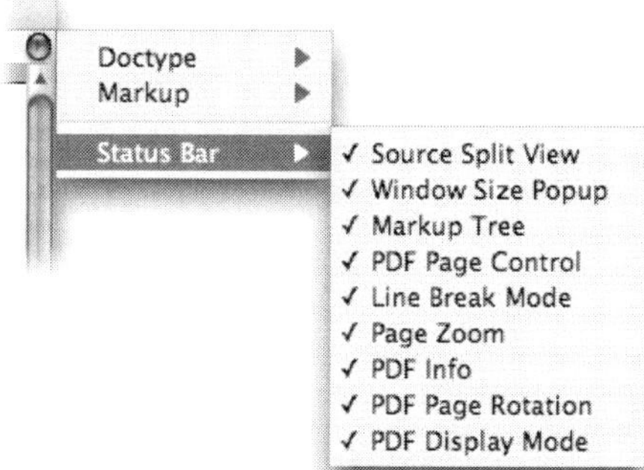

Figure 63b Turn off the status bar options you don't need.

CHAPTER FOUR

Advanced Page Editing

In Chapters 2 and 3 we give you the basics you need to get started building a site in GoLive CS. In this chapter, we go beyond the basics to introduce features in the intermediate to advanced categories. It doesn't take long to become familiar with GoLive's page-building tools, and before you know it you'll probably feel compelled to dive in deeper and become familiar with the other editing modes available to you: the Frames Editor, the Source Editor, and the Outline Editor.

In this chapter we not only demonstrate additional editing possibilities, we also go beyond that to show how to fix errors on your pages, validate your code, add DOCTYPEs, and do much more.

Once you've been totally immersed in syntax handling, we illustrate how to use GoLive's previewing tools so that you can check the work you've completed. The options for previewing in GoLive CS include Page Preview, Live Rendering, Preview in Browser, and the exceptional PDF Preview—each of which has unique features. We also journey into exciting new territory: GoLive CS's amazing ability to create and edit PDFs, including managing the links contained in them.

TIP 64 Designing with Frames

Frames are a method by which you can split up a browser window into sections, each of which can display a separate HTML page. Once a very common method of designing a Web site, frames have lost popularity somewhat due to issues that search engine spiders sometimes encounter when attempting to index framed pages. At times, though, frames can be useful, and GoLive handles framed pages quite nicely.

To build a framed page, first determine how you'd like to split up the page. Many of the common configurations can be found in the Frames set of the Objects palette (**Figure 64a**).

Figure 64a The Frame set of objects includes many popular configurations.

To use one of the frame objects, click the Frame Editor button at the top of a document window to enter the frames editing mode and then drag and drop a frame object into the page. With the frame object in place, the Inspector palette shows two tabs: Frame and FrameSet. The attributes in the Frame tab are applied to the individual sections within the frameset, whereas the attributes in the FrameSet tab are applied to the border and separators between the frames. You can also edit the frameset attributes if you click directly on one of the borders of the frameset (**Figure 64b**).

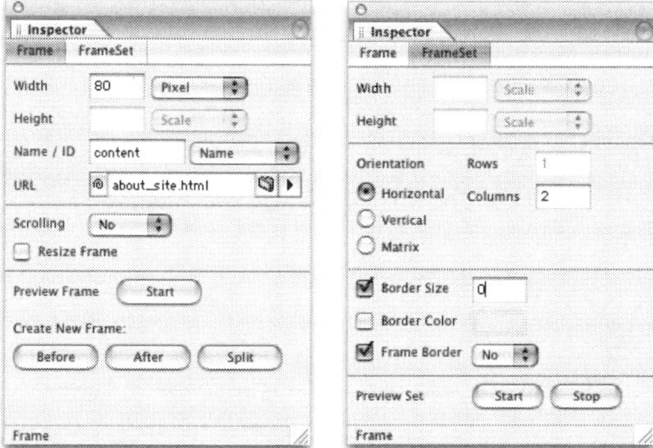

Figure 64b The Frame Inspector and the FrameSet Inspector offer easy ways to set the attributes for both the individual frames and the frameset itself.

To change the size of a frame, enter pixel dimensions into the Height and Width fields of the Inspector or drag the frame separators larger or smaller. To add additional frames to your configuration, simply drag another frame object into the page or use the Create New Frame buttons in the Inspector. Select whether or not you'd like a scroll bar to appear by choosing an option from the Scroll pop-up menu and give the user the ability to resize the frame by enabling the Resize check box.

If you don't want a border to show between the sections, enable the Border Size check box in the FrameSet Inspector and then type 0; you'll also need to click the Frame Border check box and select No from the pull-down menu. You can set border color in the FrameSet Inspector, but expect wide-ranging results in different Web browsers.

Auto DOCTYPE Correction

If you drop a frame object into a page that does not contain the appropriate DOCTYPE (see Tip 54) for frames, GoLive intelligently puts up a dialog showing the current DOCTYPE and the suggested one. To accept the change, click OK, and to leave the DOCTYPE untouched, click Cancel.

The last step is to designate which pages will appear in the sections of the frameset. To assign the pages to the frames, click in a frame and then use the URL field in the Inspector palette to link to a page in your Site window. Or drag a page from the Site window and drop it onto a frame to make the link.

It's important to give each frame in a frameset a unique name in the NameID field of the Frame Inspector. Later, when you create links on pages within a frameset, use the Target pull-down menu to select a frame name or type the frame name into the Target field in the Inspector to indicate to the browser which of the frames the link should load into (**Figure 64c**).

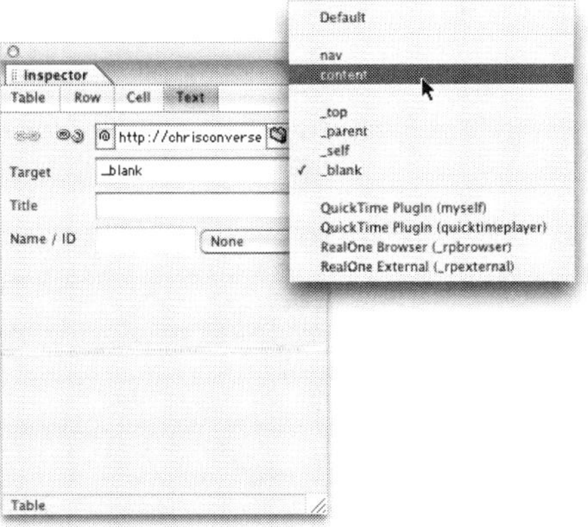

Figure 64c Be sure to select a target frame when creating links within framesets.

When you've got everything set up as you want it, you can get a temporary preview by clicking the Start button next to Preview Frame in the Frame Inspector or Preview Frameset in the Frameset Inspector. Once enabled, the button will read Stop. Click it to stop the temporary preview.

TIP 65 Creating iFrames

What is the first object in the Frames set of objects, and why can't you drag it into your frameset? That, friends, is no ordinary frame. It's an *inline* frame, better known as an iFrame, and it's not used in a frameset, but to create a frame right inside a regular HTML page. iFrames are neat because they can be placed anywhere on your page, giving the effect of a virtual window.

To create an iFrame, open a page and drag the iFrame object in. An iFrame can be placed into a layer, a table cell, or onto a layout grid to position it more precisely (**Figure 65**).

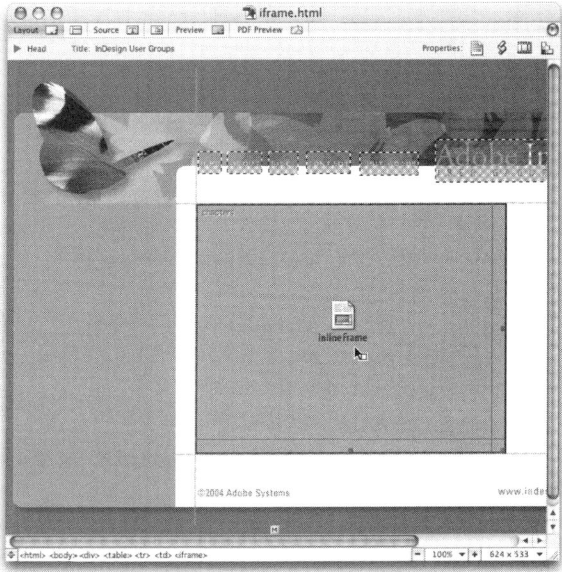

Figure 65 Position an iFrame on a page by placing it into a layer, in a table cell, or on a layout grid.

Designate the page that will load into the iFrame using the Source field of the Inspector or by dragging a page from the Site window and dropping it onto the iFrame. In the Inspector, set options such as the height, width, or alignment of the iFrame. Add a margin if desired by entering pixel dimensions into the margin fields or enable the Border check box if you'd like a border to show around the iFrame.

Note

Some older browsers do not support iFrames, so be sure to know your audience and test pages using iFrames in target browsers.

TIP 66 Customizing Source Code Formatting (Themes)

New in GoLive CS is the ability to customize the formatting of your source code by creating code themes. Themes are available in the Source Editor, the Split Source View, the JavaScript Editor, and the Source tab of the CSS Editor and are accessible by choosing an option from the Theme pull-down menu (**Figure 66a**).

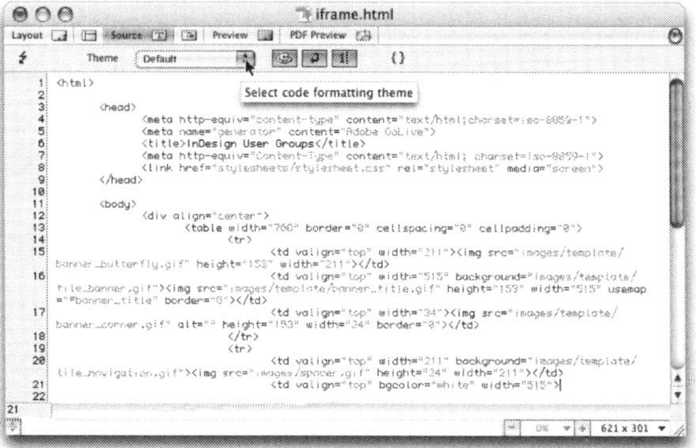

Figure 66a Choose a theme from the Theme pull-down menu in the Source Editor.

Although GoLive CS has a number of useful themes already configured, you can create your own or edit any of the default themes in the GoLive preferences. On a Mac, choose GoLive > Preferences; on Windows, choose Edit > Preferences. Next, open the Source pane of the preferences and click Themes.

> ***Note***
>
> *Themes only affect how the code looks when you edit in GoLive. It has no effect on how your pages look or work in a Web browser.*

Pick the type of syntax for which you want to create or edit a theme from the Syntax pull-down menu and then select a theme name from the Theme pull-down menu. Select the font face and size as well as the text and background colors for the theme in the upper portion of the Preferences dialog. To set specific colors and font styles for text, tags, attributes, and so on, choose an option in the text list on the left and set the styling for that option using the Color field, font face buttons, and Size pull-down menu (**Figure 66b**).

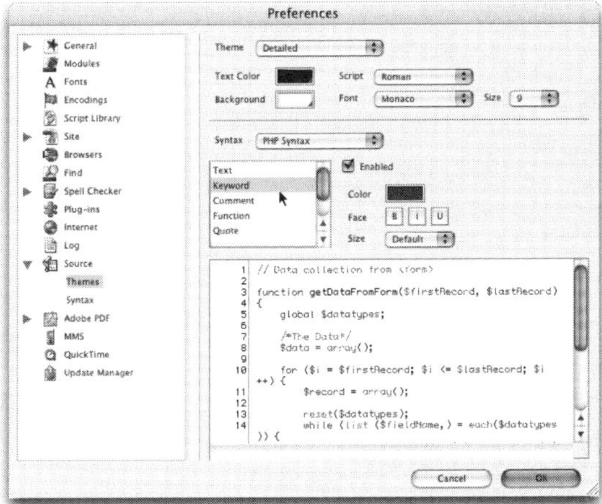

Figure 66b Edit themes in the Themes portion of the GoLive preferences.

To set the default theme as a preference, use the pull-down menu in the Source portion of the preferences. You can specify both a default theme (for viewing on screen) and a print theme, which will be used when a page of code is printed from GoLive.

ThemeManager Extension

The GoLive team has created a free extension called ThemeManager that allows you to duplicate, delete, rename, reorder, import, or export themes. See Tip 183 to learn more about extensions, and visit http://share.studio.adobe.com/axAssetDetailSubmit.asp?aID=8822 to download a copy of ThemeManager.

TIP 67 Automating Code Completion and Adjusting Settings

We have, on occasion, made a typo or two when editing source code and then spent ages trying to find what we'd done wrong. Not to worry—code completion in GoLive CS allows even the most abysmal typists to turn out perfect pages.

In GoLive's Source Editor, type an opening bracket. Notice that as you do so a list pops up, displaying a full set of tags appropriate for the type of syntax you're working with (**Figure 67a**).

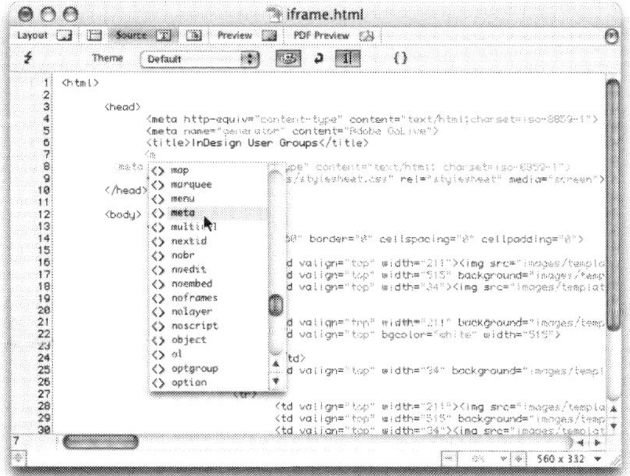

Figure 67a With the code-completion feature enabled, a list of tags you can pick from appears as you type source code.

If you type the first letter of the tag you want to use, the list will jump to the tags beginning with that letter. You can scroll through the list using the up and down arrows on your keyboard, and you can select a tag by pressing Return/Enter or by double-clicking the tag. Doing so writes the tag into the code. As soon as you type a space to continue, the list of attributes for that tag will appear. Again, simply navigate the list and make your selection.

The code-completion feature is context sensitive, so if you're working in PHP it will display the appropriate list of elements for PHP, and likewise for JavaScript. The feature is turned on by default, but you can disable it if you'd like or set options for how it responds. To set the code-completion options, choose GoLive > Preferences (Mac) or Edit > Preferences (Windows) and then select Syntax under the Source Preferences (**Figure 67b**).

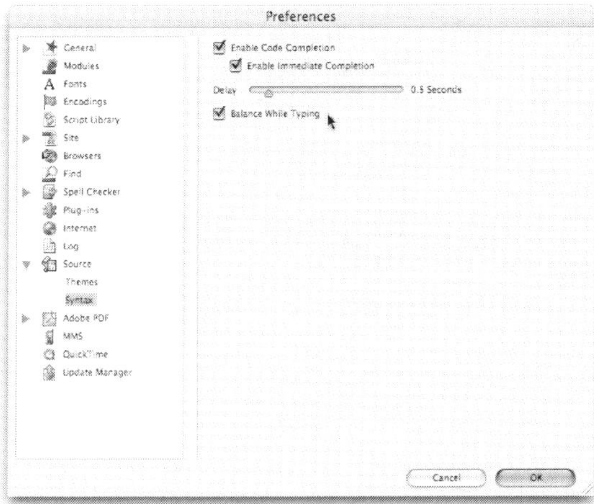

Figure 67b Disable or customize the code-completion feature in the Source preferences.

Choosing Enable Immediate Completion will insert the necessary end tags into the code. Selecting Balance While Typing automatically jumps you to the next open bracket as soon as you type a closing bracket. You can also decrease the delay of the pop-up list by dragging the Delay slider toward zero.

Disabling Code Colorization

To turn off code colorization, click the Colorize Code button in the Source Editor. This is a sticky setting, meaning that if you turn it off on one page, it will be turned off on all pages, including the source view in the CSS Editor, the Split Source View, and the JavaScript Editor.

Rewriting Your Source Code

Call us picky, but we prefer our source code written in a particular way, thank you very much. Sometimes, though, if we've been mucking around a lot in the code or cutting and pasting code from here to there, we end up with source code that is formatted inconsistently. When that happens, we invoke a command called Rewrite Source Code. Don't mistake this command for one that fixes poorly written code. Instead, it restores the formatting of your code to your specifications, including line breaks, indents, upper or lower case, and CSS formatting.

You issue the command by choosing Edit > Document Content > Rewrite Source Code. To rewrite the source code on a single page, open the page and have it in front of the Site window. If you have a Site window in front, with no files selected, the command will run on all the pages in the site. To run the command on a group of files, select them in the Site window and then choose Rewrite Source Code.

Once you invoke the command, a dialog appears offering choices on how the source code should be rewritten (**Figure 68**).

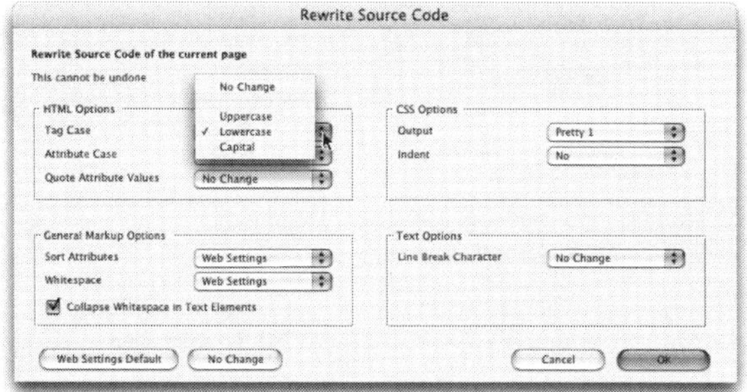

Figure 68 The Rewrite Source Code dialog offers several choices on how to format the code.

There are four sections in the dialog: HTML Options, CSS Options, General Markup Options, and Text Options. To set preferences for any of these areas, choose from the options in the pull-down menus.

What Are Web Settings?

In the pull-down menu for General Markup Options in the Rewrite Source Code dialog, you'll find a selection called Web Settings. By accessing these settings, advanced users can get very granular about how they want their code to be written by GoLive. Choose GoLive > Web Settings (Mac) or Edit > Web Settings (Windows). A word of caution, though: if you don't know what you are doing, stay away! You could end up wreaking havoc with your source code.

TIP 69 Selecting Tags Easily in the Source Editor

Here is a small but handy-dandy tip: While in the source code, double-click on the opening bracket of any tag to select the entire block of code between the opening and closing tags. For instance, to select a block of code between the opening and closing <td> tags, including the opening and closing tags themselves, double-click on the bracket in front of the <td>. If you double-click on the bracket following the <td>, you'll select the contents of the tag but not the tag itself (**Figure 69**).

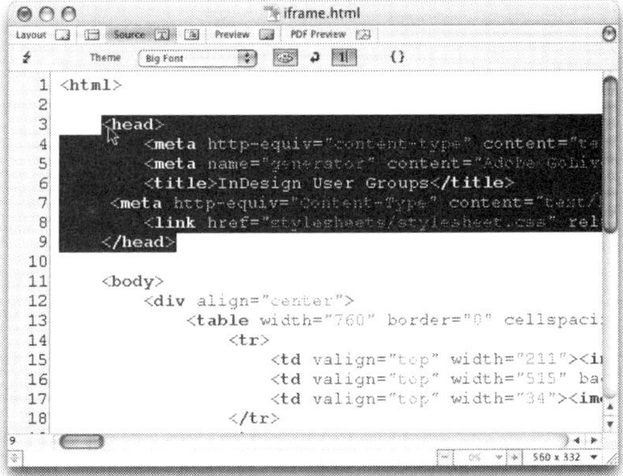

Figure 69 Double-click the opening bracket to select the whole tag. Double-click the bracket after the tag to select the contents of the opening and closing tags.

In the same manner, you can select an attribute and its value by double-clicking the equal sign that comes after the attribute. If you want to select the value of an attribute only and not the attribute itself, double-click on either of the quotation marks surrounding the value. Last but not least, to select both a CSS property and its value, double-click on the colon in front of the value.

Once you've memorized these selection techniques, you'll find working in source code a lot less time consuming.

TIP 70 Navigating Your Source Code

There's one spot in your source code that you always seem to edit. But to find that particular spot, you've got to remember the line number, right? Well, no. GoLive CS does have line numbers and even has a sweet feature that makes using them a snap, but it also has something that makes finding a certain spot in source code easy as pie.

First things first. To jump to a precise line number on a page, simply type the number into the small input field in the lower-left corner of the page and then press Return/Enter (**Figure 70**). GoLive instantly jumps down the page and places the cursor right at the beginning of the desired line.

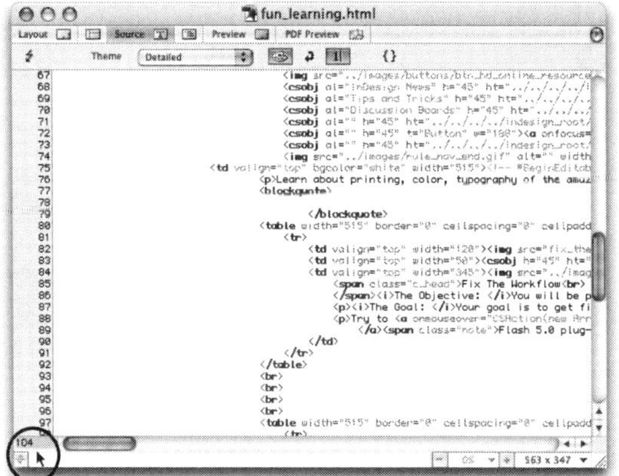

Figure 70
Type in a line number and press Return/Enter to jump directly to that line of code.

To simplify matters even more, though, use the handy new Navigate Through Code button {} in the Source, CSS, and JavaScript Editors, and in the Split Source View. This button is automatically populated with any tags in your HTML page that have the name attribute assigned (see Tip 80). In the JavaScript Editor, it's autopopulated with the functions on the page, whether you are working in JavaScript, VBScript, ASP, Perl, or Java. In the CSS Editor, it's populated with the definitions themselves. All you need to do is select an item in the list to jump directly to that spot in the code.

But what to do if the spot you want to jump to happens to be a tag that does not have the name attribute? In that case, set your own marker. Simply put your cursor in the spot you want to mark and then click the Navigate Through Code button and choose New Marker. Give the marker a name and click OK. Next time you click the button, your new marker name will be in the list.

Alphabetically, Please

The list in the Navigate Through Code button is populated according to the order in which the tags, functions, or definitions appear on the page. If you prefer to sort the list alphabetically, Command-click (Mac) or Ctrl-click (Windows) when you click the Navigate Through Code button.

TIP 71 Creating New Objects in the Source Editor

Back in Chapter 3, we explained how to take objects from the Objects palette and drag them into the Layout Editor (see Tip 25). But did you know that you could use those very same objects in the Source Editor, too? To test it out, open a new blank HTML page in GoLive and switch to the Source Editor. Next, drag a table object from the Objects palette and drop it into the page between the opening and closing <body> tags (**Figure 71**). Ta-da! Instant table. Go to the Head objects and drag a Meta object into the head portion of the page. Ta-da! Instant metatag. Double-click the word *generic* to select it and type the value you want to use. Combine use of the Objects palette with code completion and you'll be zipping through source code at high speed.

Outline Editor

So you can use objects from the Objects palette in both the Layout and Source Editors. Wouldn't it be nice if you could use those objects in the Outline Editor, too? You can! Just drag and drop. See Tips 74 and 75 to learn more about the Outline Editor.

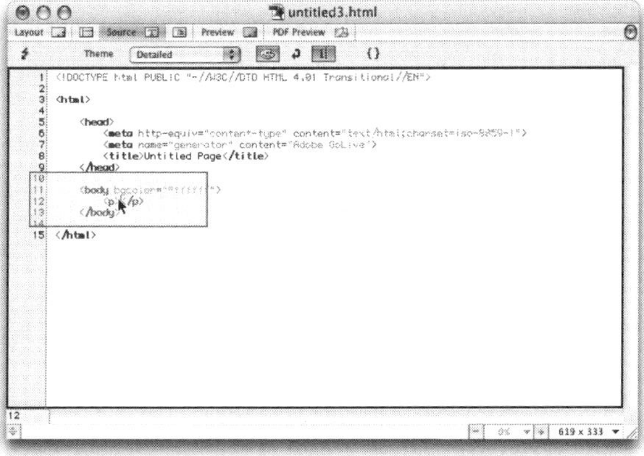

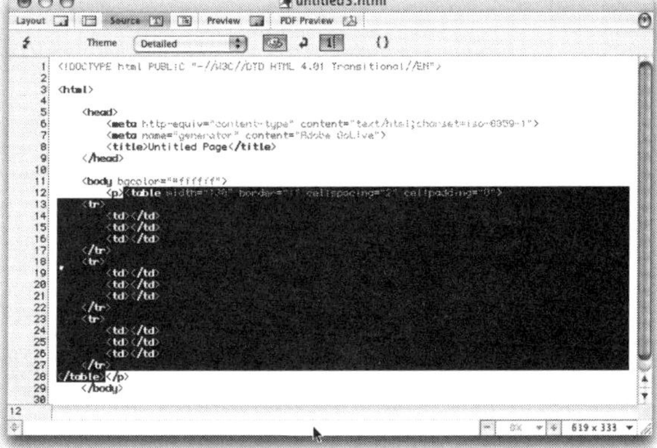

Figure 71 You can use the Objects palette to write markup in the Source Editor. Just drag and drop an object into the page. The first image shows the table object being dragged; the second shows the code that is written when the object is dropped.

TIP 72 Keeping Selections in Different Editors

The different editing environments in GoLive add up to a really potent combination, and we expect you'll want to use different modes for different tasks. Fortunately, the various editors work together smoothly as you switch from one to the other. For example, if you select an object such as an image, table, or text in the Layout Editor and then switch to the Source Code Editor, the code for that object is still selected and cued up (**Figure 72a**).

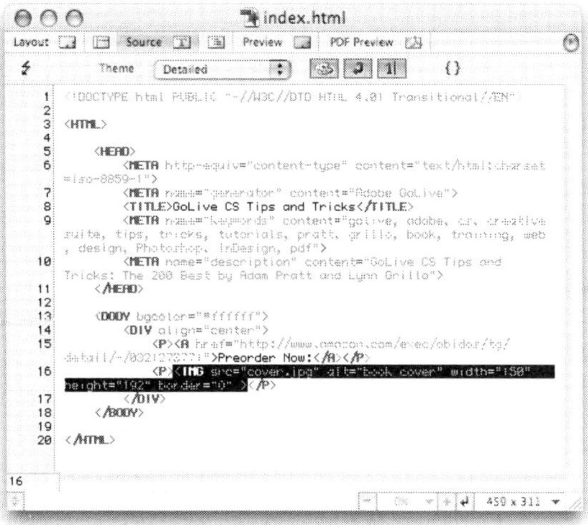

Figure 72a Selecting Cueing works between the Layout and Source Code Editors.

Now if you switch modes one more time to the Outline Editor, the same object is still selected and cued up in the Outline Editor (**Figure 72b**). And now if you select a specific attribute in the Outline Editor and switch back to the Source Code Editor, just the code for that attribute will be selected. The integration of all the editors (Layout, Frame, Source, and Outline) is just amazing.

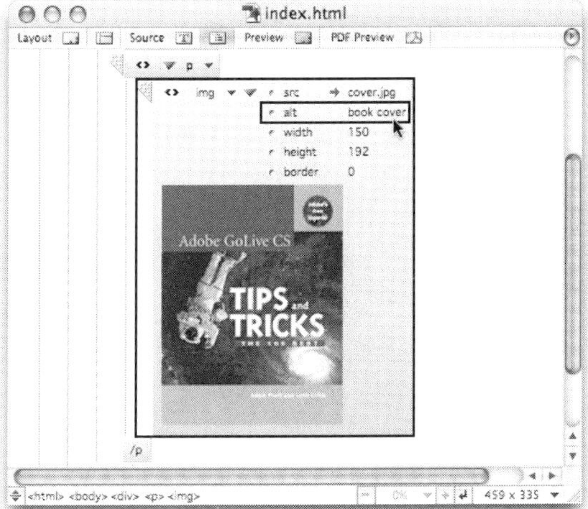

Figure 72b Selecting Cueing also works in the Outline Editor.

Selecting Cueing makes it easy to switch among the various editing modes for a quick edit, because you don't have to find your place in the page over and over again. It's also a great way to learn more about HTML; you can immediately see the source code that corresponds to your selection in a different editing mode.

TIP 73 Validating Your Source Code Syntax

You spend precious time creating pages that look good and navigate properly. To that end, it behooves you to make certain that your pages are free from errors and that they use valid syntax to ensure that they behave as expected in a Web browser.

Using GoLive's built-in Syntax Checker, you can see whether your pages are compliant with a particular DTD (see Tip 54) or whether your code is well formed (meaning all tag pairs are complete and so on). To use the Syntax Checker, choose Edit > Check Syntax, click the Check Syntax button in the Highlight palette, or Control-click (Mac) or right-click (Windows) on a page in the Files tab of the Site window and choose Check Syntax (**Figure 73a**).

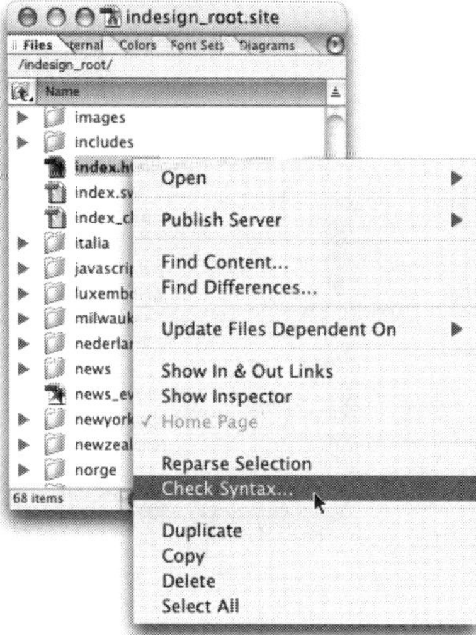

Figure 73a There's a Check Syntax button in the Highlight palette, a Check Syntax menu item in the Edit menu, and a Check Syntax command in the contextual menu, as shown here.

Once invoked, a modal dialog will open. In the Comply With portion in the upper left, choose one or more DTDs to check against by enabling the check box next to them. Alternatively, you could check for well-formedness only.

The Additionally Allowed portion in the lower left lets GoLive-specific tags and attributes go through the checker without being flagged (**Figure 73b**). If you intend to strip out the GoLive specific code while uploading (see Tip 179), enable these check boxes.

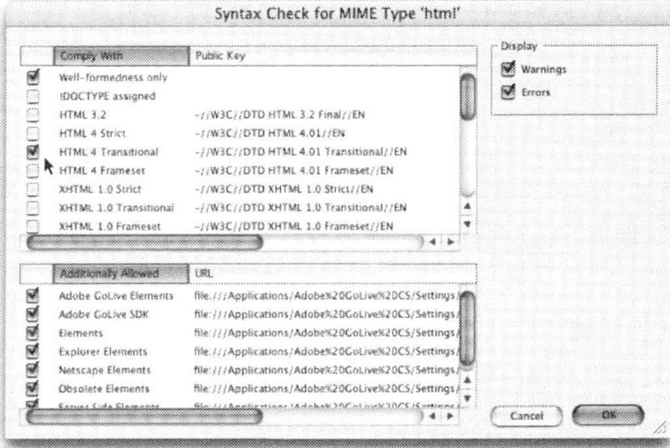

Figure 73b Choose the DTD to check against and whether to allow additional elements.

By default, the Warnings and Errors check boxes in the upper right are enabled. For the best results, leave them on. When you're done making your selections, click OK. The Syntax Checker proceeds, and GoLive then presents a list of results (**Figure 73c**). If errors or warnings are found, the problems are highlighted on the page, and the Highlight palette (see Tip 61) automatically opens.

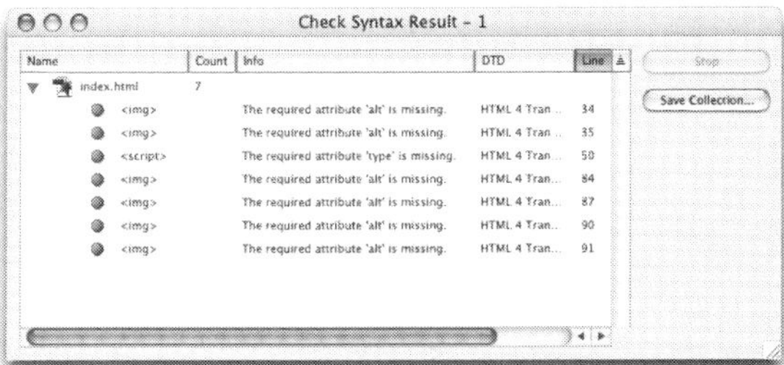

Figure 73c After running the Syntax Checker, you'll see a results list.

Dispatch the Dialog

Want to use the same settings you used last time you checked syntax? Hold down the Shift key when you click the Check Syntax icon in the Highlight palette to bypass the modal dialog and use your previous settings.

Double-clicking on a warning or error in the results list causes the page to pop forward with the problem area in view, ready for you to fix. Using the Outline Editor is the easiest way to fix errors because it not only highlights the errors on the page but also gives a brief description of the problem. If a required attribute of a tag is missing, the Outline Editor even puts a bullet next to it in the tag's attributes list, making it a snap to fix (**Figure 73d**).

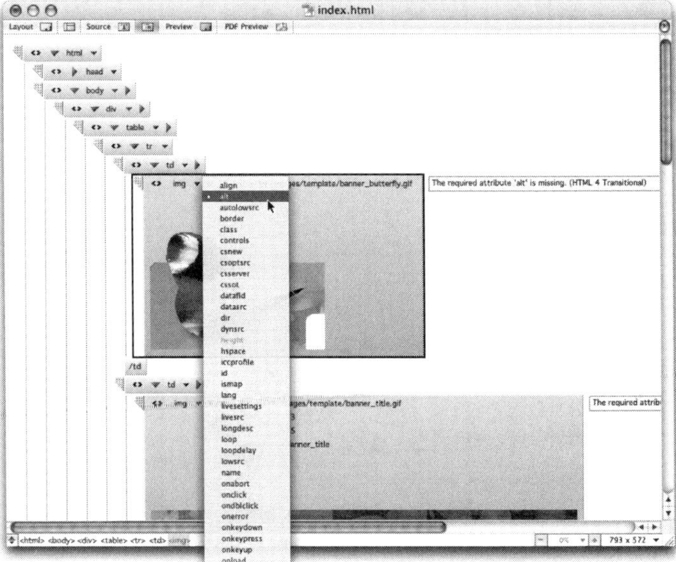

Figure 73d The Outline Editor is the best choice for fixing syntax errors.

You can run the Syntax Checker on a single open page, on selected pages in the Site window, or on the entire site if the Site window is in focus with no pages selected.

TIP 74 Working with the Outline Editor

The Outline Editor in GoLive is a unique and powerful feature that makes tedious Web-authoring tasks a breeze and helps ensure better quality code. There are lots of cool things you can do in the Outline Editor, but the essence of this mode is that it displays a fast and easy-to-use structural view of the markup of a document (**Figure 74**).

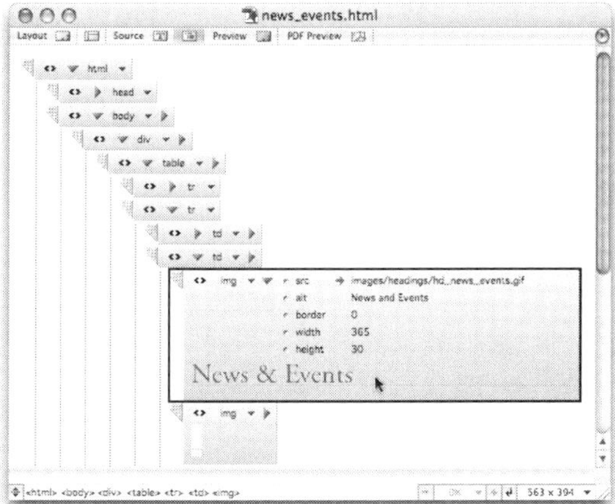

Figure 74 The Outline Editor makes newbies more comfortable and experts more efficient.

However, the Outline Editor isn't just a pretty way to look at your code. It's also a great way to edit and add to your pages. If you ever need to troubleshoot a complex page or streamline some deeply nested tables, you'll love the Outline Editor. To add to pages in the Outline Editor, just drag and drop items from the Objects palette to the appropriate location in the outline.

The Outline Editor is also a great way to learn about source code within a structured editing environment, which minimizes the tedium and mistakes of hand coding. You can study anything from the structure of tables to the attributes of images. This is a powerful tool for trainers teaching HTML basics and Web-design fundamentals.

TIP 75 Working with Elements and Attributes in the Outline Editor

It's easy to add attributes to elements correctly even if you don't remember the attribute names or proper syntax. Just select the new attribute for the selected element from the pull-down menu in the Outline Editor (**Figure 75a**).

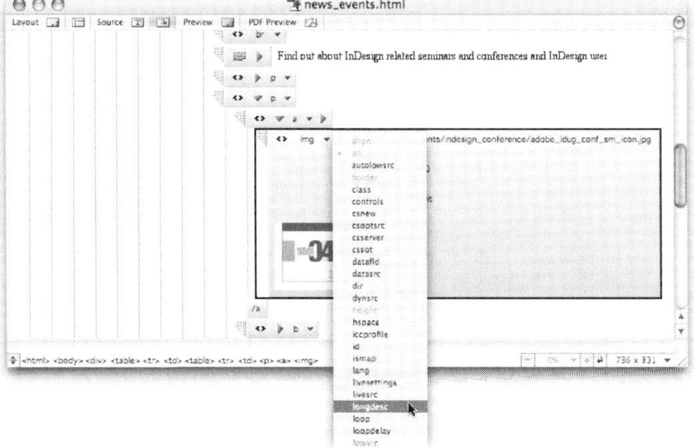

Figure 75a Adding attributes is easy in the Outline Editor.

It's just as quick to edit attributes in the Outline Editor as it is to add them. For example, the LONGDESC attribute can be used to add extended accessibility features to images, but there is no corresponding field in the Image Inspector when you use the Layout Editor. The Outline Editor makes it easy to add and edit attributes that are used less frequently and that are not available in the Inspector (**Figure 75b**).

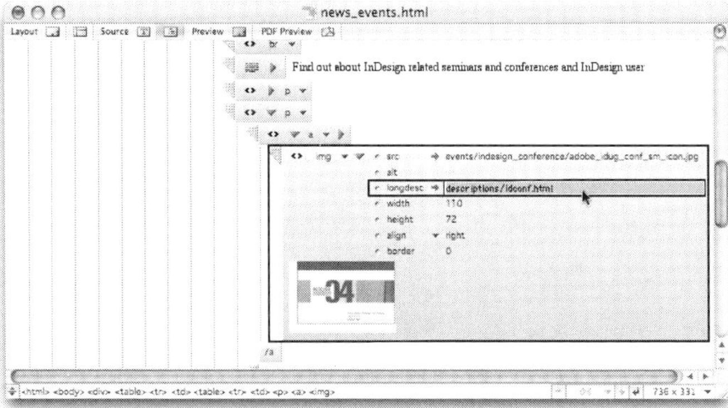

Figure 75b You can edit obscure attributes as easily as you can add them.

Controlled by DOCTYPE

The list of attributes available for a selected element is intelligently controlled by the current DOCTYPE (see Tip 54) of the page. This means that the list of available attributes for an element might be longer or shorter, depending on the current DOCTYPE. This is a great learning tool, and it also helps ensure better quality code.

TIP 76 Finding Elusive Page Errors with the Outline Editor

If there's a red bug icon in the Status column for a page in your Site window, you probably have a broken link or missing image that needs to be fixed. Open the page with the error and make sure Link Warnings is enabled in the toolbar (see Tip 31), and the obvious errors should appear with a red highlight.

However, there are times when the errors aren't as easy to locate. You might have a broken link to a deleted style sheet, an old component, or a missing single-pixel GIF that's very hard to see in the Layout Editor.

Switch to the Outline Editor and toggle the Link Warnings icon in the toolbar, and obscure errors such as missing single-pixel GIFs are instantly revealed and highlighted in the outline (**Figure 76**).

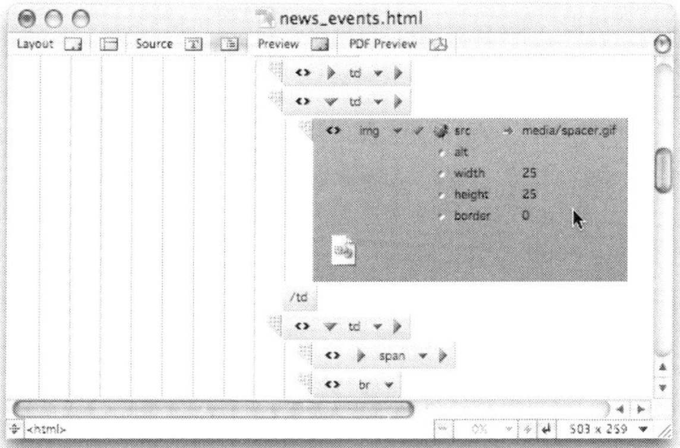

Figure 76 Toggle Link Warnings in the Outline Editor to instantly reveal and highlight obscure errors.

After you've found the error, you can fix it in the Outline Editor or select it and switch to the Layout or Source Code Editors and make the correction there.

TIP 77 Adding Missing End Tags with the Outline Editor

When you run the Syntax Checker (see Tip 73) to validate your source code, you might get an occasional warning that the closing end tag for an element is missing (**Figure 77a**). This means the opening tag of a pair such as a table, multimedia object, or layer is missing the required end tag. There are some elements such as `img` and `meta` that don't need a closing tag, but these are exceptions to the rule.

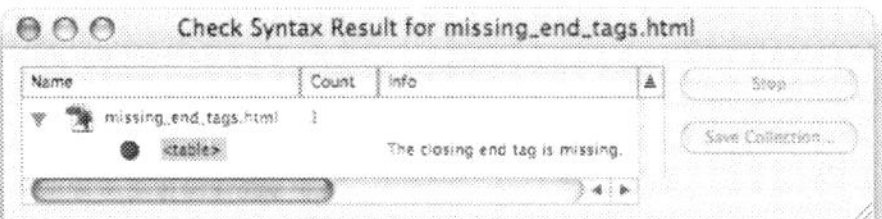

Figure 77a The Syntax Checker warns you of missing end tags.

If you need to fix a missing end tag error, switch to the Outline Editor instead of wading through lines of lines of source code trying to locate the problem. You can easily toggle an element in the Outline Editor from unary (no closing tag) to binary (closing tag) by Control-clicking (Mac) or right-clicking (Windows) on the element and choosing Binary from the contextual menu (**Figure 77b**).

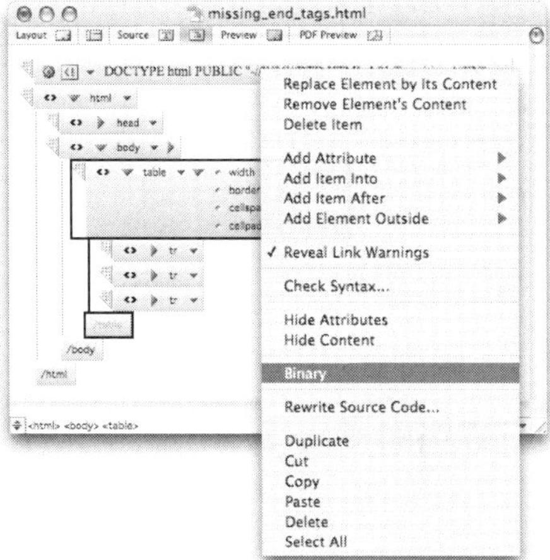

Figure 77b Add the closing tag by choosing Binary from the contextual menu.

You can also toggle between unary and binary with the Toggle Binary icon in the toolbar. GoLive is smart enough to correctly guess where the closing tag of a binary pair should be placed in the page and creates it in the correct location.

TIP 78 Viewing Images in the Outline Editor

The Outline Editor is a great way to navigate and edit your source code, but it can also be helpful to see your images in this editing mode. If you're trying to select and edit a certain image or a specific button in a navigation bar, an accurate preview of the image in the Outline Editor helps you make sure you've selected the right file.

By default, images are disabled in the Outline Editor to keep things simple, but you can turn them on with a single click. Switch to the Outline Editor and open the View palette from the Window menu if it's not open already. Then check the Images option in the View palette and you'll be able to see all images at their natural size right in the Outline Editor (**Figure 78**).

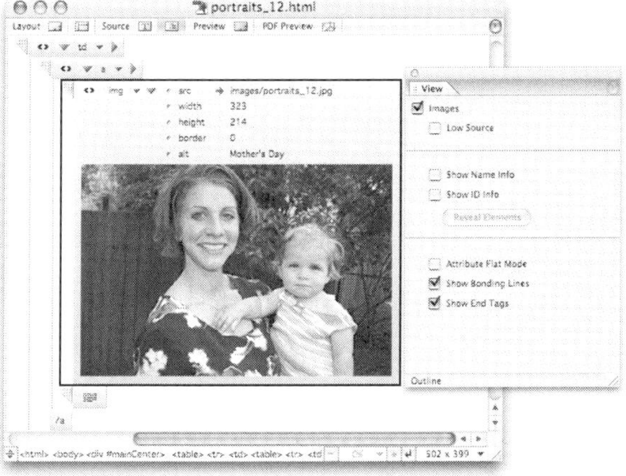

Figure 78 Use the View palette to enable images in the Outline Editor.

TIP 79 Expanding and Collapsing the Outline Editor

The Outline Editor is really one of our favorite features in GoLive, but if you use it a lot you'll find it can require a lot of mousing around the screen. You can navigate most of the features with the keyboard, and here are a few of the most helpful shortcuts:

- Unfold/collapse selected element (**Figure 79a**)—Select the element and press Return (Mac) or Enter (Windows).

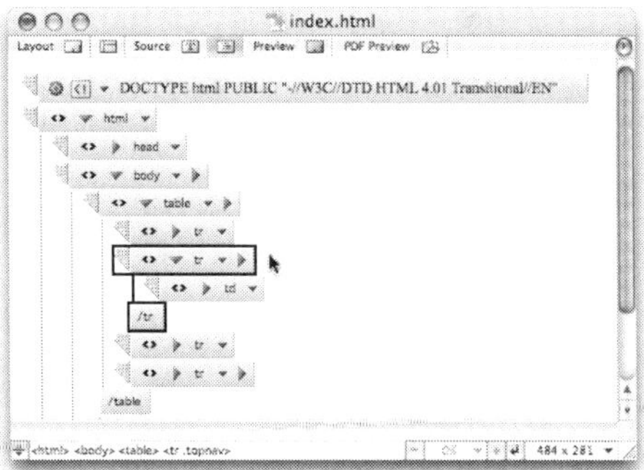

Figure 79a Unfolded element.

- Unfold/collapse selected element recursively (**Figure 79b**)—Select the element and press Option-Return (Mac) or Shift-Enter (Windows).

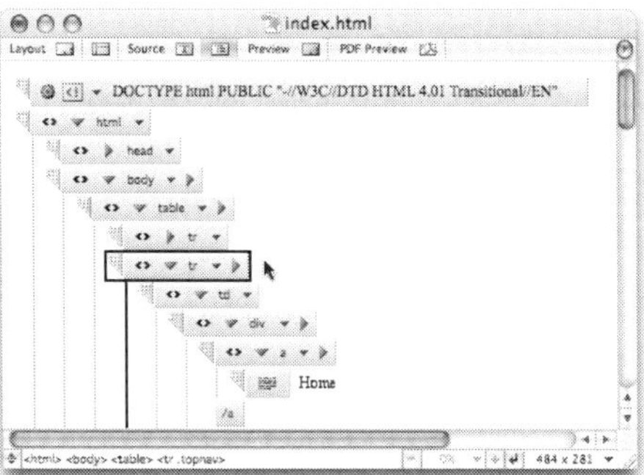

Figure 79b Element unfolded recursively.

- Unfold/collapse attributes of selected element (**Figure 79c**)—Select the element and press Return (Mac) or Enter (Windows).

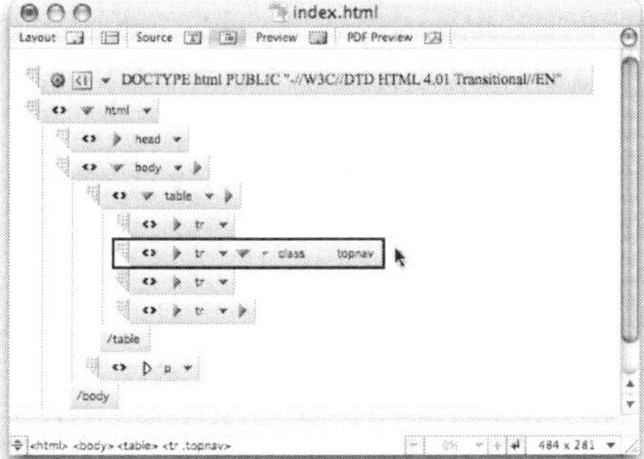

Figure 79c Unfolded element attributes.

- Unfold/collapse attributes of selected element recursively (**Figure 79d**)—Select the element and press Option-Return (Mac) or Shift-Enter (Windows).

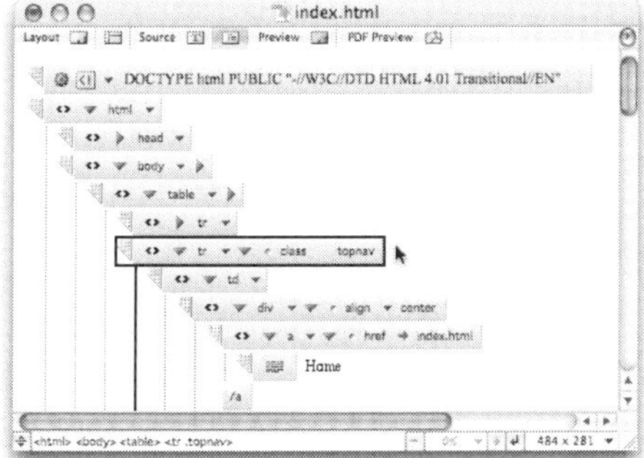

Figure 79d Element attributes unfolded recursively.

You can also navigate from one element to another using the keyboard. Use the arrow keys to navigate up and down the outline tree and press Tab to jump to the next text box.

Bonus Tip

Turn on Attribute flat mode in the View palette to avoid hiding the attributes list.

Automatically Show All Content

Hold down Option (Mac) or Alt (Windows) when you switch to the Outline Editor from any other editing mode to automatically reveal every element in the outline.

TIP 80 Showing Name and ID Information in the Outline

If you use much JavaScript or CSS on your Web pages, you'll be familiar with the name and ID attributes you can apply to objects in the page. When you assign a name or ID attribute to an object, it makes it easy to access with a JavaScript action or style with a CSS rule. You can add these attributes to objects in the Basic tab of the Inspector palette in the Layout Editor or in the Outline Editor.

To see the name and ID attribute of items in the Outline Editor, use the View palette to turn on the Show Name and Show ID options. Now you'll see a helpful column on the right side of the outline that shows all the identified objects (**Figure 80**).

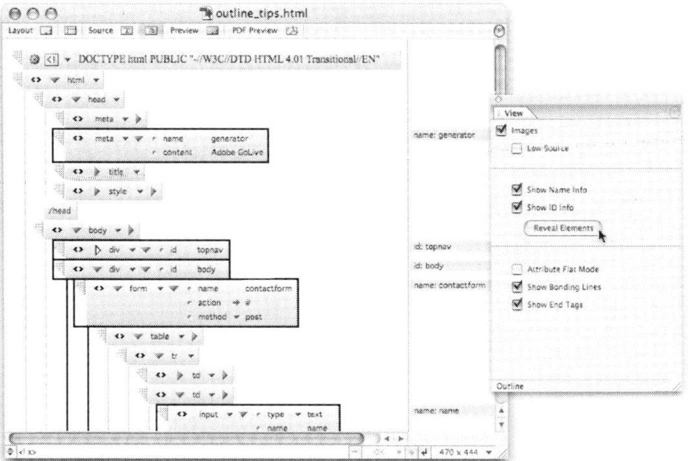

Figure 80 Names and IDs are enabled in the View palette and listed on the right side of the Outline Editor.

Most objects can have a name or ID assigned to them, but a few of the most common uses include forms, form elements, images, and DIVs for CSS layers. If you have a hard time locating all the named objects, click the Reveal Elements button in the View palette to reveal and highlight any objects with an assigned name or ID in the outline.

TIP 81 Previewing Web Pages in GoLive

When building a site in GoLive, you might like to quickly preview a page without actually leaving the application. GoLive's Preview tab allows you to do just that. On a Mac, when you enter the Preview mode what you see is an embedded version of the Opera browser. Windows versions use the system's embedded Internet Explorer browser. In both cases, since an actual Web browser powers the Preview mode, not only can you preview a page, you can also test out its links and JavaScript, too (**Figure 81**).

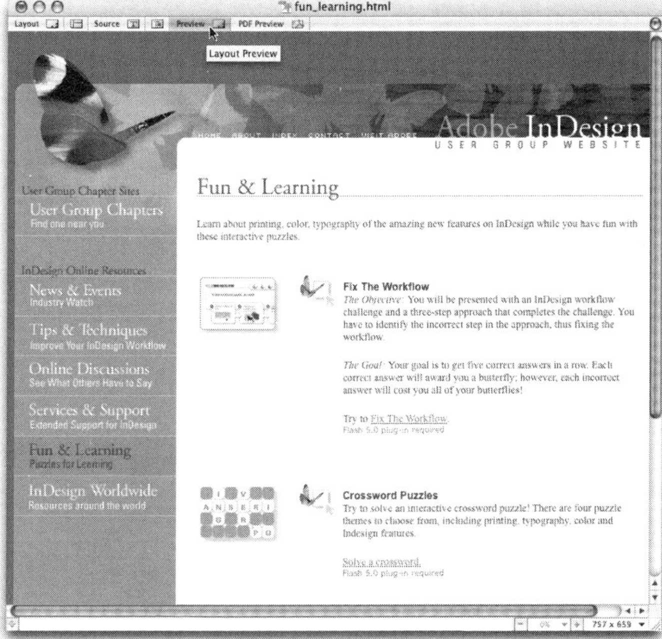

Figure 81 Use the Preview mode to test links and JavaScripts.

To preview a page, simply click the Preview button at the top of the document window. Even if you navigate away from the page as you are testing links, you are returned to the original page when you switch back to one of the editing modes. If you use the Preview mode frequently, you might like to add a keyboard shortcut to its menu command found under View > Document Mode > Preview.

Updating the Rendering Engine

Newer versions of the browsers used by GoLive's previewing modes may be released, and GoLive has a nifty way of allowing the embedded browser to be updated. Simply add the new browser to the list found in the Browser Preferences (see Tip 83), and the rendering engine is automatically updated. Sometimes new software combinations can also result in new incompatibilities. If adding a new embedded browser causes any problems, just remove it from the list of preview browsers.

TIP 82 Live Rendering with Live Update

The Preview mode is helpful for taking a quick look at how your pages are behaving, but if you've ever wished that you could edit a page in one mode and at the same time see it update in real time in another window, then the Live Rendering window is the answer.

To open the Live Rendering window, choose File > Preview in > Live Rendering. The page you have open will load into the Live Rendering window (**Figure 82**).

Figure 82 Open the Live Rendering window from the File menu to see your page update live in a separate window.

Just like the Preview mode, the Live Rendering window is an embedded Web browser, so you can use it to test page links, navigation, and JavaScript. The Live Rendering window flyout menu contains four commands—Load, Reload, AutoUpdate, and Bound—which execute the following tasks:

- Load—Choose Load to invoke the Browse dialog and select a page from your hard drive.

  Note
  Clicking the Browse button that looks like a folder in the upper right accomplishes the same task as Load.

- Reload—If you have turned off AutoUpdate, you need to invoke Reload for the page to update.
- AutoUpdate—Enable AutoUpdate to have changes made during editing of a page automatically update simply by clicking on the Live Rendering window.
- Bound—If chosen while a page is open, the Bound option will bind the Live Rendering window to that page.

You can have more than one Live Rendering window open at a time, so if you've got multiple monitors, knock yourself out. Another sweet feature is that by using the Fetch URL tool from the upper left of the Live Rendering window, you can quickly bind the window to a page in the Files tab of the Site window.

Surfing the Web and Previewing Files

If you type a URL into the address field at the top of the Live Rendering window, you can access the Web just as you would with a regular browser. Control-click (Mac) or right-click (Windows) in the window to get options for Back, Forward, Stop, Home, Copy Address, and Send Link in Email.

TIP 83 Previewing Pages in Web Browsers

A very important step toward getting the best results from your Web site is to test the pages in multiple Web browsers. In Tip 3 we outline how to set the browser preview preferences, and in this tip we explain how to invoke the Preview in Browser feature.

A button called Preview in Browser resides in the main toolbar and is easily accessible at any time. To preview a page in a browser, open a page and then click the Preview in Browser button. The browser specified as the default (in the Browser Preferences) for previewing is the one that will launch. If you have additional browsers listed in the preferences, you could launch one of them by choosing it from the pull-down list that appears when you click and hold the Preview in Browser button (**Figure 83**).

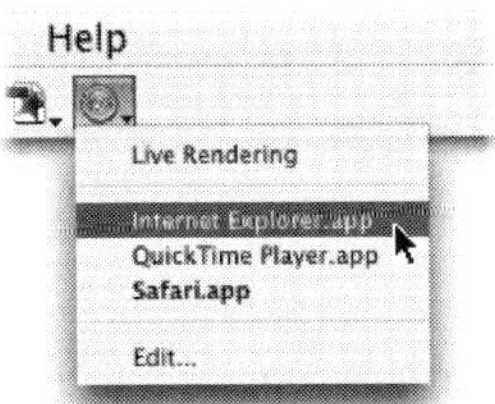

Figure 83 The Preview in Browser button has a submenu that appears when you hold the button down for a moment.

Note

The first time you click the Preview in Browser button, GoLive prompts you to select a default browser if you have not already assigned the Browser Preferences. The default browser is assigned by enabling the check box next to the preferred browser name in the Browser Preferences. If more than one browser has a checkmark next to it, clicking the Preview in Browser button will launch the page into each of them simultaneously.

An alternate method of launching the default browser is to press the keyboard shortcut Shift-Command-T on Mac (Shift-Ctrl-T on Windows) or choose File > Preview In > Default Browser.

Preview in Browser Without Opening in GoLive

To launch a page into a Web browser directly from the Site window without first opening the page in GoLive, select the page in the files list and then click the Preview in Browser button in the toolbar.

TIP 84 Exporting Web Pages to PDF

A PDF module was available separately for GoLive 6, but now an improved version is included as part of GoLive CS. The PDF Preview mode lets you convert any Web page into a PDF with one click, and we use it all the time. If you're not accustomed to converting Web pages to PDF, you might wonder why you would want to do it. Some of the most common uses include

- Preparing a page for review by a client, coworker, or art director—It's so much easer to email a single PDF than to upload to a staging server or explain how to unpack a compressed .sit or .zip archive. Anybody with a computer and a pulse can view a PDF with the free Adobe Reader (http://www.adobe.com/reader).
- Generating a print version—If you want to offer your visitors a print-ready version of a page without having to surrender yourself to the whims of browsers and printers, just use a PDF.
- Archiving a page design—We always do this before handing over a site to clients who want to do their own updates. Your great design will probably never look the same again, and PDF is a great way to preserve it.

It's easy to convert Web pages to PDF files with GoLive. Just switch to the new PDF Preview mode and click the Export as Adobe PDF icon in the toolbar (**Figure 84**).

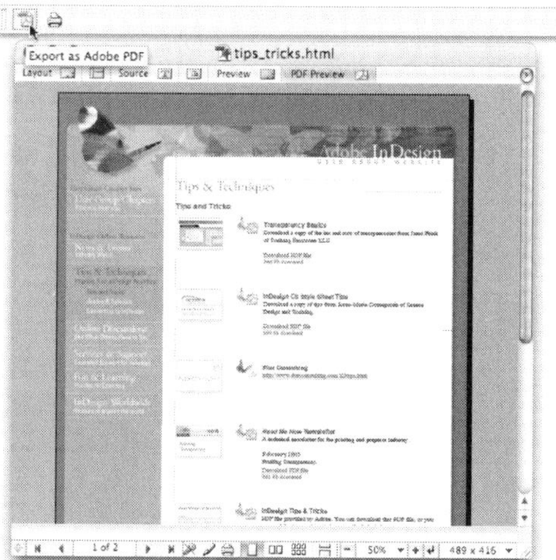

Figure 84 Export any page to PDF with a click.

Bonus Tip

Use the icons at the bottom of the PDF Preview to change the page, view, rotation, and zoom of the file.

Printing a PDF

It's easy and convenient to print PDF files right inside GoLive without launching Adobe Acrobat or Adobe Reader. Double-click a PDF file in the Site window to open it in GoLive and click the Print PDF icon in the toolbar.

TIP 85 Customizing PDF Creation Settings

When you convert a page to PDF in GoLive, you can customize several settings in the PDF Creation Inspector (**Figure 85**) that affect the exported PDF.

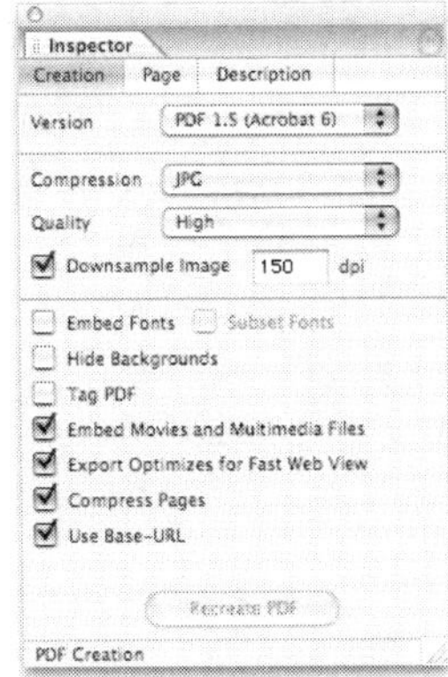

Figure 85 Use the Creation tab of the PDF Creation Inspector to adjust PDF-conversion settings.

Some of the most important settings are

- Version—Choose PDF 1.5 if you expect your visitors to have the latest version of the free Adobe Reader. Choose an older version for greater backward compatibility.
- Compression—Choose Deflate if you want lossless compression and can live with possibly larger files sizes; JPG for smaller file size and greater compatibility; or JPG 2000 for smaller file sizes but better image quality. Note that JPEG 2000 compression only works with version 6 Acrobat readers.
- Quality—If you select either of the JPEG options, you can control how much compression is applied to maximize quality and minimize file size.
- Embed Fonts—If you're using fonts your visitors won't have, be sure to enable this option.
- Export Optimizes for Fast Web View—This "streams" the PDF so the first page can be viewed even if the rest of the file has not finished downloading.

Re-creating a PDF with New Settings

GoLive doesn't automatically update the PDF as you adjust conversion settings because it could take a while on a long document. Be sure to click the Recreate PDF button in the Inspector after customizing the settings.

TIP 86 Controlling PDF Page Size and Margins

Converting Web pages to PDF documents can get tricky when the proportions of your pages don't match your intended paper size. The Page tab of the PDF Creation Inspector (**Figure 86**) lets you control several options related to page orientation, document dimensions, and margins, which will help you solve these problems:

- Paper Size—You'll probably want to select Letter, but you can choose from several defaults or create your own custom page size.
- Unit—You can change the unit of measurement to centimeters, inches, millimeters, or points.
- Orientation—Switch between Portrait and Landscape depending on the layout of the page.
- Shrink Content to Paper Width—If the content of your page doesn't fit in the paper size, trying to print can result in unexpected page tiling. We recommend you enable this option. When you do so, GoLive will shrink the page to fit your paper width and even account for custom page margins.
- Width and Height—Enter custom page dimensions here.
- Margin—Adjust the margins of the PDF here. If you want to enter a number such as half an inch, you need to type **0.5** and not just **.5**.

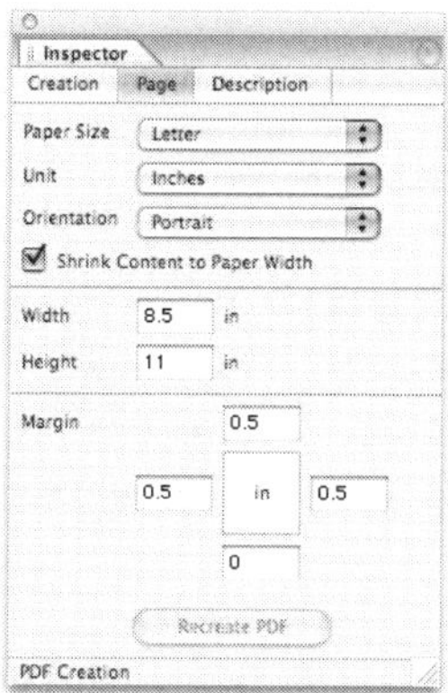

Figure 86 Adjust page size settings for PDF creation in the Page tab of the Inspector.

If you find yourself entering the same settings over and over again, see Tip 92 to learn how to set these once and for all just how you like them.

Common Printer Considerations

If you intend for your visitors to download and print a PDF from your site, you need to consider common limitations of household printers. For example, many inkjet and laser printers cannot print on the outside quarter or half inch of the paper. This is a good reason to adjust the content margins on your PDF.

TIP 87 Adding Description and Metadata to a PDF

Metadata such as author information, description, and keywords makes a better PDF because

- Search engines can more easily find the PDF.
- The PDF can be better managed by an asset-management system or database.
- The metadata is embedded in the PDF so readers know who created it and what the document is about.

Using metadata in a PDF essentially makes the file more valuable, and it's really easy to add with the PDF Preview feature in GoLive. Switch to PDF Preview, open the Description tab of the PDF Creation Inspector, and enter the document title (different from the filename), author, subject, and keywords in the four fields (**Figure 87**).

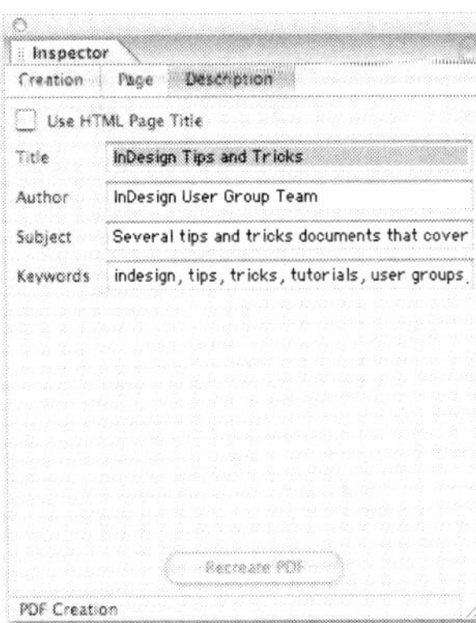

Figure 87 Add metadata in the Inspector and click Recreate PDF before you export the file.

If the Web page already has a good title, check the Use HTML Page Title option. If the page title isn't that descriptive, or if you want to customize the title, uncheck this option and type a better one in the Title field. Remember, the metadata isn't added to the file until you click the Recreate PDF button and export the PDF.

TIP 88 Hiding Page Backgrounds in PDF

Web pages with background images usually don't print very well, and the readability of text is often diminished, especially with black and white printers. To minimize ink waste and maximize readability of printed PDFs, you can check the Hide Backgrounds option in the Inspector when you create PDF files (**Figure 88**).

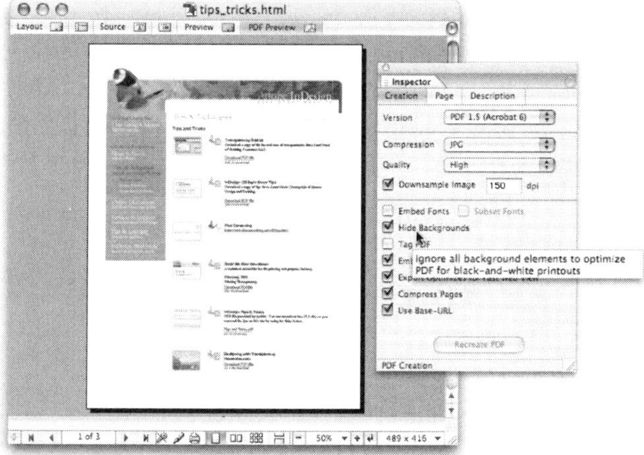

Figure 88 Hide backgrounds when you convert Web pages to PDF to improve readability and printability.

Checking the Hide Backgrounds option ignores background images and colors for tables, table cells, layers, and entire pages. It even affects background images and colors defined with CSS. The backgrounds are replaced with white to highlight the content and remove distractions. Just imagine how much ink you'll save by not making your printer print out your colored page backgrounds.

Smoothing Options

The options in the View palette to smooth text, line art, and images in a PDF only affect how the PDF looks on your computer. These settings have no effect on the final PDF because the viewer, not the PDF, controls these options.

TIP 89 Working with Links in PDF

GoLive gives you powerful control over all aspects of hyperlinks in PDF files. The links can be checked, created, and edited in GoLive whether the PDF was generated with GoLive or another application.

Checking Links

When you convert a Web page into a PDF with GoLive, all the hyperlinks are retained. Open the PDF in GoLive and you can click the hyperlinks in PDF Preview mode (**Figure 89a**). A link to a local PDF file or Web page will open the file in GoLive; a link to an external URL will open your Web browser to that address; a link to a PDF page number or bookmark will change to that PDF view; and a link to an email address will open a properly configured email client.

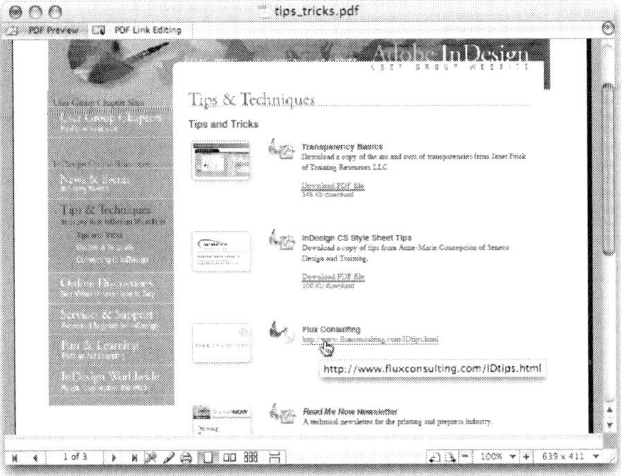

Figure 89a Open a PDF in GoLive to verify the links.

Bonus Tip

If you patiently hover your mouse pointer over a hyperlink for a moment, you'll see the link destination in the tool tip.

Creating Links

It's easy to create a new link in a PDF because the tools work just like the rest of GoLive. Open the PDF in GoLive and click the PDF Link Editing tab at the top of the document window. Select the New Link Tool in the toolbar and click and drag in the PDF to define the region of the new link. Now define the link destination in the Inspector palette as usual (**Figure 89b**).

Figure 89b Select the link region in PDF Link Editing mode and assign the hyperlink in the Inspector.

Bonus Tip

You can also Command-click (Mac) or Ctrl-click (Windows) to hyperlink a link region in a PDF with the Fetch URL tool to define link destinations.

Changing Link Highlight Color

The default highlight color for links in PDF files is purple, but you can easily change the color in the application preferences. Just look under Adobe PDF > Display in the preferences and select a new color. This can be helpful depending on the colors used in your PDF document.

Linking to a PDF Page

Did you know you can create a hyperlink to a specific page within a multipage PDF? Just select a link region in PDF Link Editing mode of an existing PDF, define the PDF you want to link to in the URL field of the PDF Link Inspector, and type the desired page number in the Page Number field (**Figure 89c**). This hyperlink will now open the linked PDF and automatically switch to the specified page number.

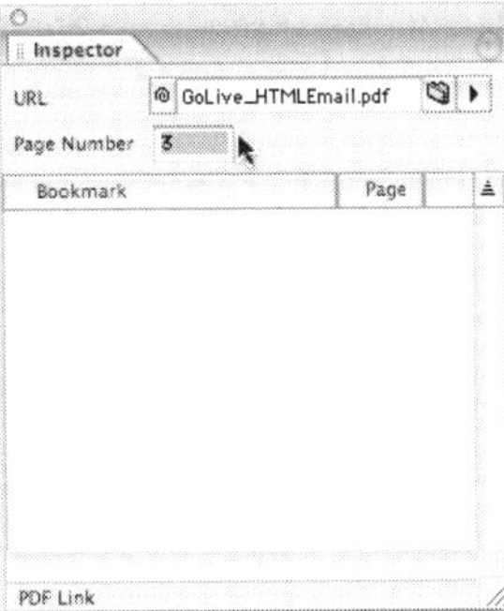

Figure 89c Link to a PDF and then enter the page number.

Linking to a PDF Bookmark

Linking to a certain page of a PDF is interesting, but linking to a specific bookmark in a PDF is even cooler. If you've taken the time and care to create well-designed PDF files, then you'll love the ability to link to the bookmarks you've already created. Create a link to a PDF and then pick any named bookmark from the list in the Inspector (**Figure 89d**).

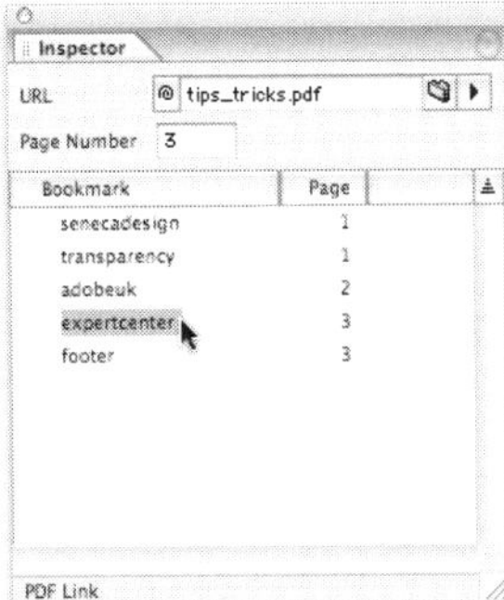

Figure 89d Link to a PDF with bookmarks and then pick from the list in the Inspector.

Bonus Tip

HTML anchors become named bookmarks when you convert Web pages to PDF with GoLive.

TIP 90 Embedding Movies and Multimedia in PDF

When Adobe shipped Acrobat 6 in May 2003, it included the amazing ability to embed interactive multimedia content such as QuickTime movies and Flash files right inside the PDF. This means Adobe PDF files can now be robust containers for compelling interactive presentations that include a variety of file formats. It can all be stored in one file that can be viewed by anybody with the free Adobe Reader (http://www.adobe.com/reader).

If your Web pages include movies, they can be embedded inside a PDF you create with the PDF Preview feature. There are two important options you must check in the Inspector (**Figure 90**) for the conversion to work correctly:

- Version—Make sure this is set to PDF 1.5, because only Acrobat 6 viewers support the new embedded multimedia content.
- Embed Movies and Multimedia Files—This embeds the interactive media in the PDF. If you don't check this option, the multimedia might still work, but you'll need to always keep the PDF and multimedia files together.

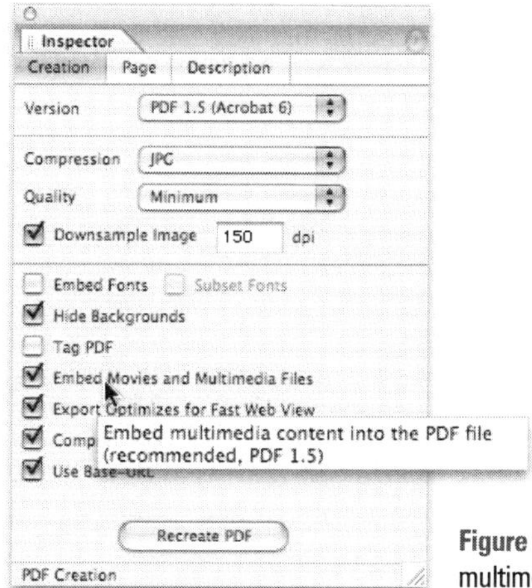

Figure 90 Adjust the settings so the multimedia is embedded in a PDF 1.5 file.

Deleting Comments

To delete a Note comment, just select it in GoLive and press the Delete key. If you make a mistake you can always use the multiple undo feature by pressing Command-Z (Mac) or Ctrl-Z (Windows).

TIP 91 Working with PDF Comments

You can add, edit, and delete PDF comments that interchange seamlessly with other GoLive, Acrobat, and Adobe Reader users. PDF comments are a great way to document a process, give feedback, and share ideas right inside the PDF.

Adding Comments

Open a PDF in GoLive and select the Comment Tool in the toolbar. Click in the PDF with the Comment Tool to create a new comment anywhere in the document. Make sure the comment is selected and write a note in the Inspector palette (**Figure 91**). Notice that GoLive automatically records the date and time of the comment so it's easy to keep track of the feedback. When you save the file, the comments are added to the PDF for others to read and review.

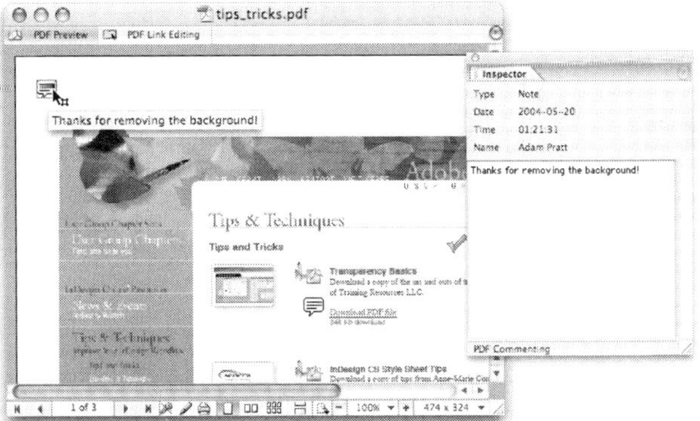

Figure 91 Click with the Comment Tool and add a note in the Inspector.

Editing Comments

You can view just about any kind of PDF comment in GoLive and you can edit Note comments using the Inspector palette. Select the comment in the PDF and edit the note in the Inspector. Notice how the time and date are updated to reflect your changes.

TIP 92 Customizing PDF Preferences

If you use the PDF Preview frequently to convert Web pages to PDF, you might find yourself entering the same settings over and over again in the Inspector. To save yourself time and ensure consistent quality, you can change the application preferences for how PDF files are created. Select GoLive > Preferences (Mac) or Edit > Preferences (Windows) and choose the Adobe PDF section on the left side. Click the triangle (Mac) or the plus mark (Windows) next to the Adobe PDF item to reveal all the categories of related preferences (**Figure 92**).

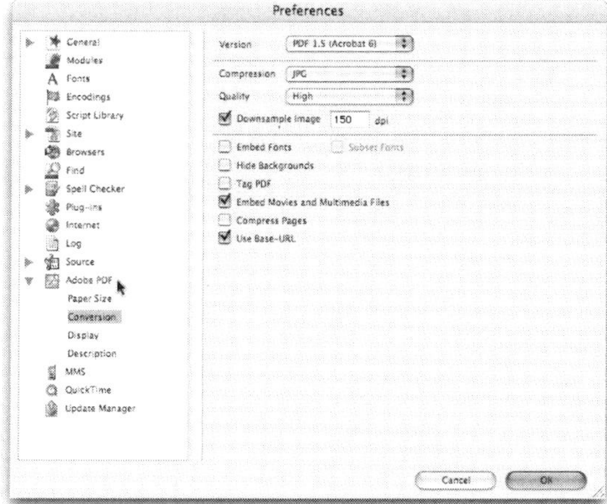

Figure 92 Adjust the preferences to customize all new PDF files you create with GoLive.

Customize the settings here, and they will affect all new PDF files you create with GoLive. The most common settings you should adjust are the PDF version (for compatibility), the paper size (for printing ease), and the description (for accurate metadata).

CHAPTER FIVE

Working with Cascading Style Sheets

If you have time to pay attention to current trends, you've certainly seen the impact that Cascading Style Sheets (CSS) are having on the Web design industry. CSS is changing how designers approach everything from text styling to layout to accessibility. It's saving people time, making site redesigns easier, and "future-proofing" the code.

GoLive has always been on the leading edge of Web technologies, and its use of CSS is no exception. Although GoLive has supported CSS for several years, GoLive CS received a complete makeover in the CSS department this time around. The engineers worked hard to consolidate the interface, streamline the workflow, and support all the latest CSS technologies. We're sure you'll be impressed.

If you're still not convinced that learning CSS is worth your time, read the internationally acclaimed CSS presentation at www.hotdesign.com/seybold/. Adam co-presented this material with CSS guru and Web standards evangelist Bill Merikallio at Seybold Seminars in fall 2003. When you've read this presentation, we're confident you'll be convinced—just be sure to come back and read this chapter.

TIP 93 Exploring the CSS Editor

The CSS Editor in GoLive CS is a complete rewrite from the previous version, and the overhaul adds a ton of impressive features. To open the CSS Editor for the internal CSS in a Web page, click the CSS Editor icon ( ) in the top-right corner of the page in Layout mode. If you'd rather work with an external CSS file, you can create a new one with the File > New Special > Cascading Style Sheet command.

When the CSS Editor opens (**Figure 93a**), you see existing rules on the left, while on the right are icons and menus that help you create new rules, including powerful, advanced features such as @import statements. To create the various types of CSS rules, click the appropriate icon on the right side or at the bottom of the window.

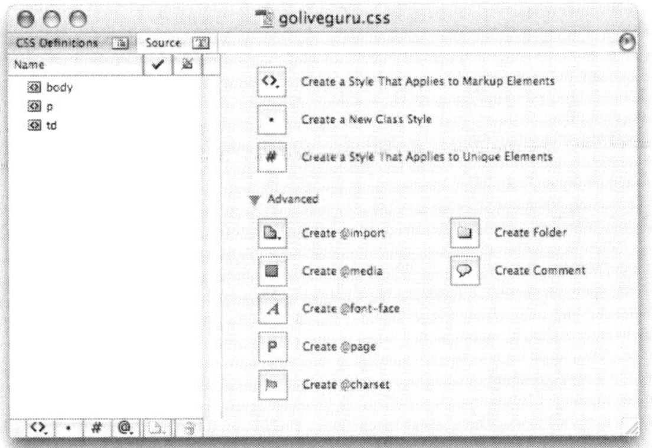

Figure 93a The default view of the new and improved CSS Editor with the advanced options revealed.

When you select one of the items on the left (called a *selector* in CSS terminology), the CSS editor changes to show eight different editing tabs on the right. Use the style properties in these eight tabs to customize the CSS rules you select on the left.

In the bottom-right corner you see a live preview so you don't have to guess what the changes will look like (**Figure 93b**). That's right—no saving, no updating, and no reloading. Just make your CSS edits and see an accurate preview immediately! The styles preview is rendered with Opera on the Mac and Internet Explorer on Windows.

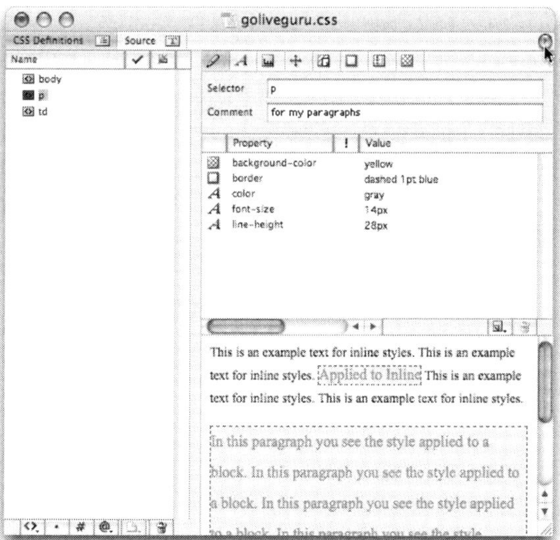

Figure 93b Edit and preview your CSS rules on the right side of the CSS Editor window.

Code-savvy users will love the new CSS Source code mode that is accessible at the top of the CSS Editor window (**Figure 93c**). All of the cool Source Code Editor features you learned about in tips 57–64 work the same here because it's the same source-editing environment throughout GoLive.

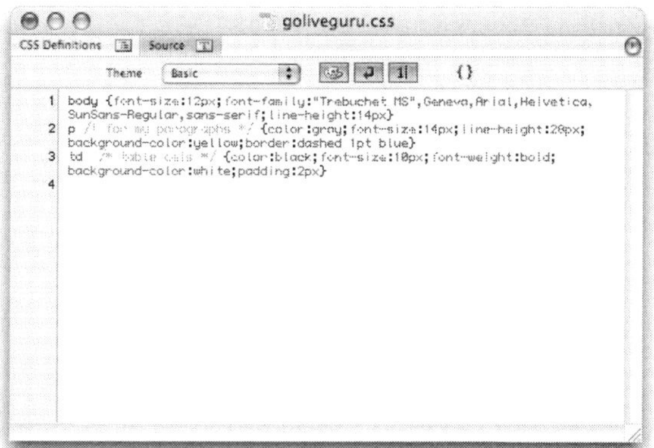

Figure 93c GoLive's powerful Source Code Editor is also helpful when you're working with CSS.

Customizing the Preview

If you want to make the preview area larger, just resize the window. To turn the preview off, uncheck View > Preview Styles from the flyout menu.

TIP 94 Saving Time with Pull-down Menus

Whether you're a CSS beginner who needs help getting started or an experienced coder hoping to save time, you'll love the pull-down menus throughout the CSS Editor. Some of the new style icons on the right side and bottom edge of the window have small black triangles on them. These triangles indicate that if you click and hold on the icons you'll see an automatically populated list of options to choose from (**Figure 94**).

For example, if you click and hold on external or @import icons, those menus are autopopulated with all the .css files from the active site. The Elements pull-down menu also features several of the most common elements for which you'll want to create CSS rules.

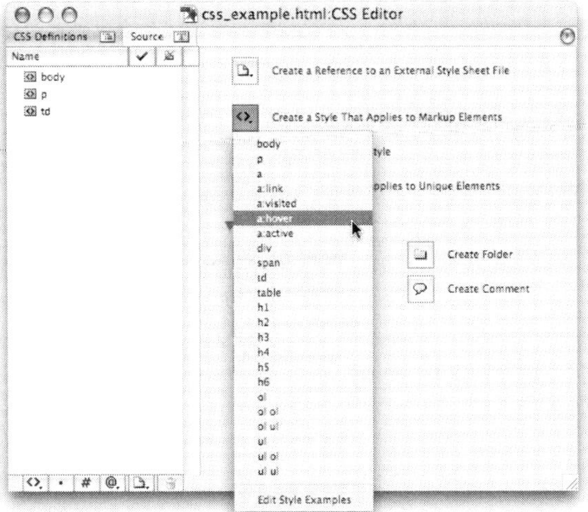

Figure 94 The pull-down menus in the CSS Editor help you learn and save time when editing CSS.

Customizing the Elements Menu

From the bottom of the Elements menu, choose Edit Styles Example to open the settings file. If there's an obscure element or style property you plan to use a lot, edit it here and it will be added to the pull-down menu.

TIP 95 Understanding the CSS Editor Tabs

You can edit dozens of different CSS style properties and attributes, and they are broken into several logical categories in the different sections of the CSS Editor (**Figure 95**). Let's start on the left side and work our way across.

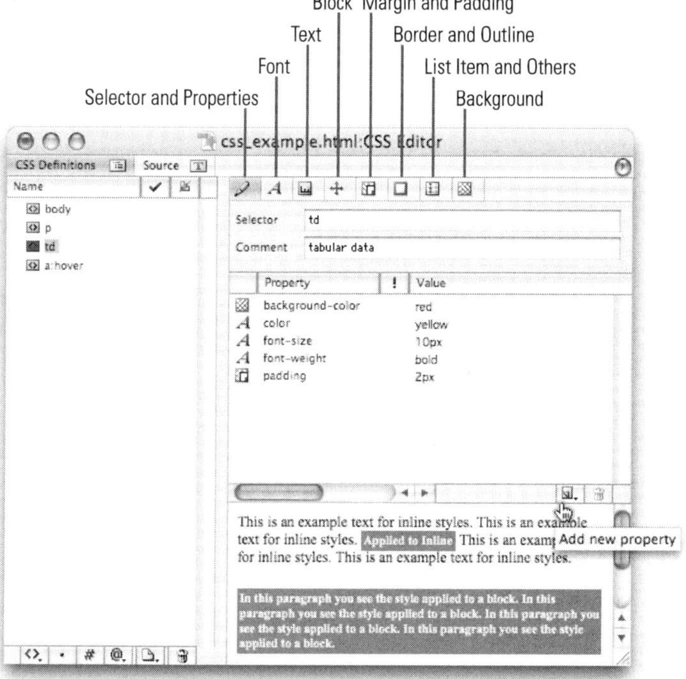

Figure 95 The CSS Editor includes eight categories of properties you can edit for a CSS rule.

Selector and Properties

Change the selector (name) of the rule and add a comment here. You can see a list of all the active style properties and even add new properties by clicking the New Property icon. This ensures compatibility with future releases of the CSS specification.

Font

Customize the font family, size, color, and line height (like leading in print design) in this section. Remember that site

Blue Cues

With a quick click through the various tabs, it can be hard to identify where you made changes. The labels of any fields you've edited for the selected rule change from black to blue. If these blue labels annoy you, you can turn them off in the CSS Editor flyout menu using the View > Mark Used Properties command.

Editing Multiple Rules

You can select multiple rules on the left and change their common properties all at the same time.

visitors will see the fonts you select only if they have the same ones installed on their computer. It's a good idea to stick to the font families included here.

Text
Adjust text spacing, alignment, and indenting in this section. You can also make text uppercase and lowercase and use small caps in this section, but not all properties will render accurately in the Layout Editor. Be sure to use Preview mode for a more accurate rendering.

Block
You can edit the size, position, and visibility of an item here. Advanced users will want to use the float and clear properties.

Margin and Padding
The margin is the space between the item and other items, and padding is the space between the item outline and any interior content. When you edit these properties, decide whether you want to have the same value on all sides or edit the top, right, bottom, and left independently.

Border and Outline
Change the thickness, color, and style of borders for items in this section.

List Item and Others
List bullets can be customized and even rendered from images using the properties in this section.

Background
Customize the background color or image of an item, such as the body element, in this section. You can also control the tiling behavior of background images.

TIP 96 Using the CSS Editor Properties List

All the style properties for the selected rule are listed in the first tab of the CSS Editor so you can quickly see an overview of the rule. If you're comfortable with CSS, you can add any existing or future property by clicking the New Property icon, naming the property, and assigning it attributes. An advanced user can add and edit all the style properties in this list instead of switching to all the different tabs. Even if you're used to hand coding, the Properties list will save you time and minimize typing errors.

If you click and hold on the New Property icon, you can choose from an extensive list of all possible CSS properties. The list is so long it can't all fit in the screenshot, as seen in **Figure 96**.

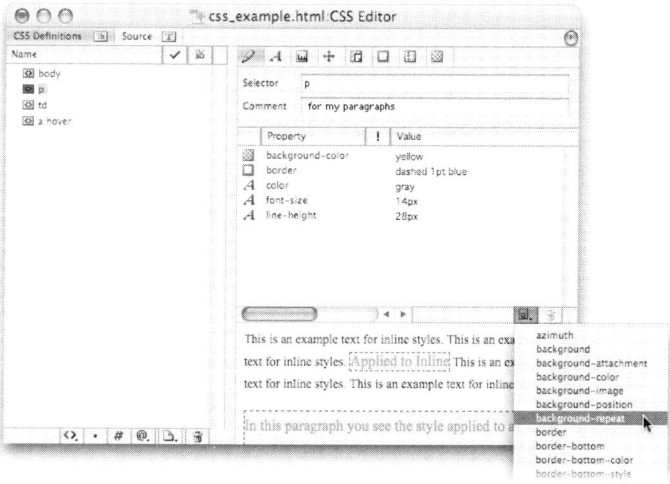

Figure 96 The New Property drop-down list is preloaded with all the possible CSS properties.

To delete a property in a CSS rule, select the property in this list and click the trashcan icon. This method is much easier than trying to find all the properties in the appropriate tabs. To delete several properties, Shift-click to select them all and then delete them at once.

TIP 97 Applying CSS Styles

Element styles such as body, td, and h1 are applied automatically at every instance of the styled element, but class and ID styles must be applied by hand.

You can apply CSS classes with the Type > CSS Span, Type > CSS Paragraph, or Type > CSS Div commands, but selecting Type > CSS Style is the easiest method. When you invoke this menu command, a small floating window appears by your selection in the Layout Editor, and with one click you can apply the class as an inline style, block, or style, or apply it to the active HTML element (**Figure 97a**). An alternative method of applying CSS classes is to open the CSS palette from the Window menu and apply the class by clicking next to the desired class in the appropriate column. If the CSS Editor window is still open, you can even drag and drop classes directly from the CSS Editor into a selection in Layout mode.

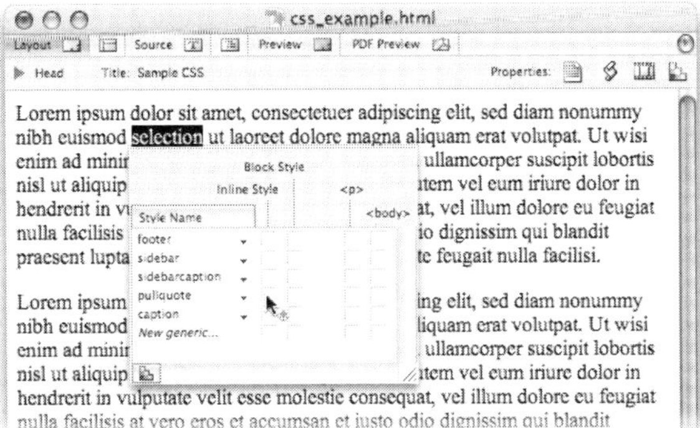

Figure 97a You can apply CSS classes with one click in this hovering window or the CSS palette.

To apply an ID style, select the element in the markup tree at the bottom of the document window (see Tip 52 to learn about the markup tree), right-click (Mac) or Ctrl-click (Windows) on the selected element, and select the ID from the Apply ID contextual menu (**Figure 97b**). Remember that you can apply an ID only once per page.

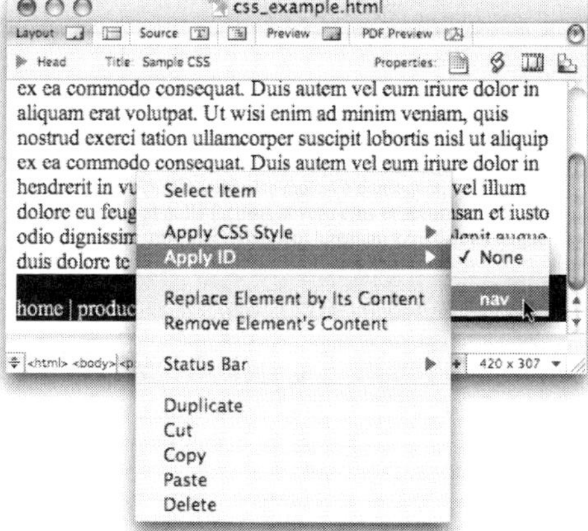

Figure 97b You can apply ID rules with the markup tree and contextual menus.

The Chicken and the Egg

What happens when you want to apply a class you haven't created yet? Well, just make your selection in the Layout Editor and click in the appropriate column next to the New Generic item in the CSS palette. This will let you create, name, and apply the new style all at the same time. Edit the properties for the new class in the CSS Editor window that will open automatically for you.

Previewing CSS Styles

Before you apply a class with the hovering CSS menu or the CSS palette, you can get a quick preview to help you make the right text styling decisions (**Figure 98**). For example, when you place your mouse pointer over the Inline Style and Block Style check boxes for a moment, a small preview window will pop up and show you an accurate preview of how the style will appear when applied in different ways.

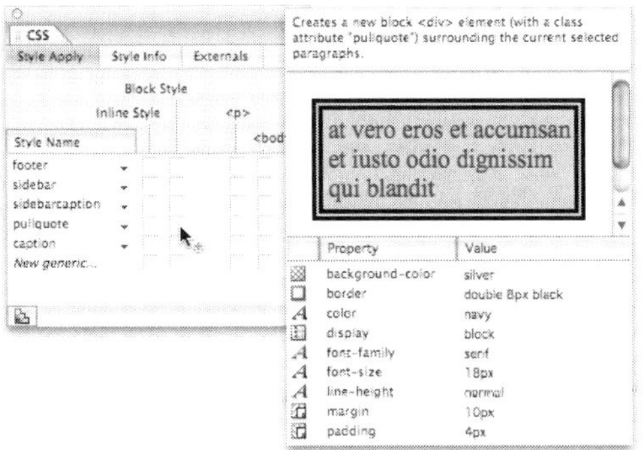

Figure 98 This preview takes the guesswork out of applying CSS styles.

At the top of the preview is a nicely written description of how the style will be applied. In the middle is a visual preview of how the style will appear when applied as an inline style, as a block style, or when applied to a specific HTML element. The comprehensive list of properties at the bottom shows an accurate cascade of all the styling information that will make the CSS gurus drool.

Opening the CSS Editor

If you decide your CSS rules need a few tweaks, just click the shortcut icon ( ) in the bottom-left corner to make some last-minute changes.

TIP 99 Viewing the Cascaded Style Info

Cascading Style Sheets are an amazing technology that can make life much easier for a Web designer. At the same time, style sheets can make you pull your hair out with frustration and confusion. When you're dealing with multiple complex style sheets, it can be hard to keep track of how all the style properties cascade and inherit to render the final results.

To help you keep everything straight, the CSS palette in GoLive CS includes an innovative new feature that shows you the complete CSS style information of your selection in the Layout Editor. Make a selection in the Layout Editor and open the Style Info tab of the CSS palette (**Figure 99**). This information on this tab will help you understand the effect of the inheritance and cascade of the styles on your selection.

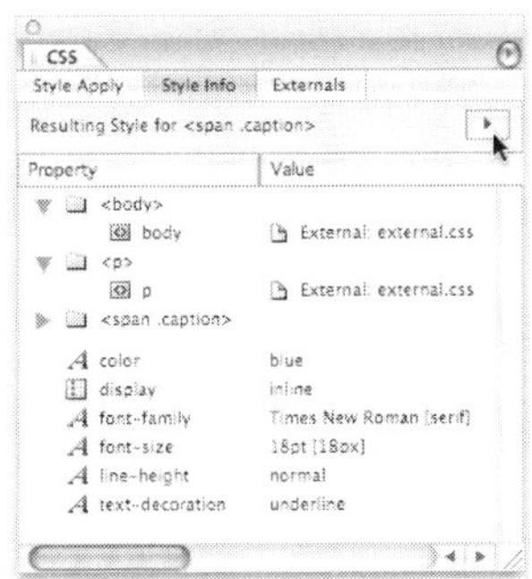

Figure 99 The Style info section of the CSS palette shows the complete final cascade and inheritance of the selection.

For example, the cascade rules of CSS determine that if an external style sheet says captions are red but an internal style says captions are blue, then the internal definition "wins" and the captions will be blue.

Changing the Active Element

To evaluate the cascaded style info of other items on the page, select the element or span from the menu in the top-right corner of the CSS palette.

TIP 100 Shortcut to CSS Editor from CSS Palette

When you have multiple pages and multiple CSS files, keeping track of which styles are defined where can be challenging. GoLive CS makes this tedious task a piece of cake with a secret shortcut in the CSS palette (**Figure 100**). Click and hold the small black triangle next to any of the class names in the CSS palette and select the Edit In command to open the file where the class is defined. If the rule is defined in multiple locations, GoLive lets you pick from all the appropriate options.

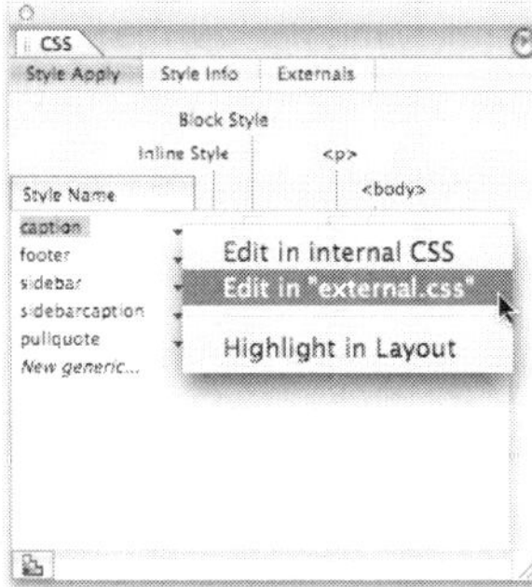

Figure 100 Double-click a class in the CSS palette to open the corresponding style sheet.

You can also double-click a class in the CSS palette to open the correct style sheet automatically. If the selected rule is defined in multiple files, the last reference in the source code is the one that is opened when you double-click the class name.

For example, if you have two external style sheets applied to one page, GoLive is smart enough to open the correct .css file and even select the rule you want to edit. Because it's automatically selected for you, all you have to do is make your edits, evaluate the results with the Live Preview, and save when you're done.

TIP 101 Applying External CSS to Multiple Pages

If you're creating a new site with CSS you'll probably assign an external CSS file to your template pages. But if you have an old site that isn't based on templates, the prospect of retrofitting it with CSS can be pretty daunting. Fortunately, GoLive makes it easy to apply an external style sheet to multiple pages at one time with the CSS palette.

Follow these three easy steps:

1. Select the Web pages in the Files tab of the Site window. You can even select files in multiple and nested folders (see Tip 18 about selecting files).
2. Open the CSS palette from the Window menu if it's not already available.
3. Use the Point and Shoot tool in the CSS palette to choose the .css file in the Files tab of the Site window, as seen in **Figure 101**.

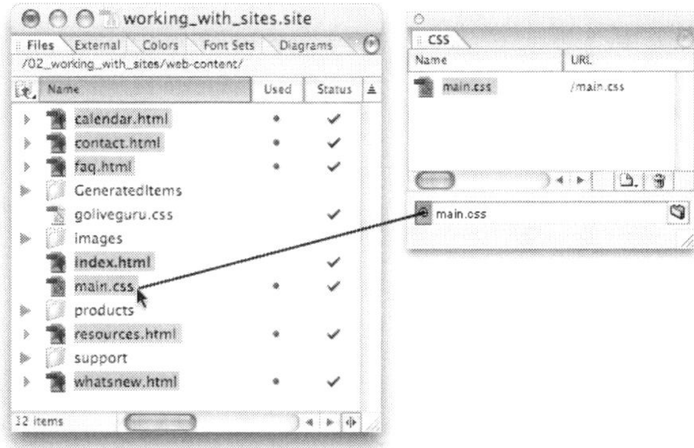

Figure 101 It's easy to assign an external .css file to multiple pages with the CSS palette.

The Secret Pull-down Option

Another shortcut to applying an external style sheet file to multiple pages in the Site window is to select the .css file from the New Link pull-down menu in the CSS palette. This pull-down menu is automatically populated with all the .css files in the active site.

TIP 102 Exporting Internal Styles

Importing External Styles

Using the same menus, you can import external styles just like you export internal styles. It's a two-way street.

Sometimes you'll create some nice internal styles that you decide would work well on other pages. You could copy and paste the source code from page to page, but there must be a simpler way, right? It's easy to export an internal style sheet with the CSS Editor.

Follow these steps to export an internal style sheet:

1. Open the page with the internal style sheet.
2. Select File > Export > Internal Style Sheet.
3. Name and save the new .css file. If you intend to use it in the site you are currently working in, select Root folder from the Site pull-down menu in the Save dialog. This will automatically choose the root folder of your site.

Another way to export an internal style sheet to a separate file is to select Export internal CSS from the flyout menu of an internal style sheet, as seen in **Figure 102**.

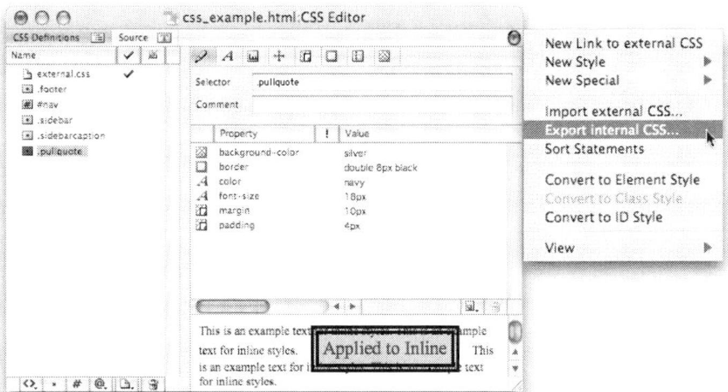

Figure 102 Exporting an internal style sheet and using the results with Tip 101 is a great way to retrofit an old site with new technology.

TIP 103 Using the CSS Samples in the Library Palette

It can be intimidating to get started with a new technology you're not familiar with. Sometimes the best way to learn a new Web design technique is to dissect somebody else's work. With this in mind, the GoLive product team included dozens of prebuilt style sheets in the GoLive CS Library palette that you can use and learn from.

1. Open the Library palette, select the Templates section (the right-most tab), and twirl down the css folder in the Application-wide folder to reveal dozens of sample .css files (**Figure 103a**).

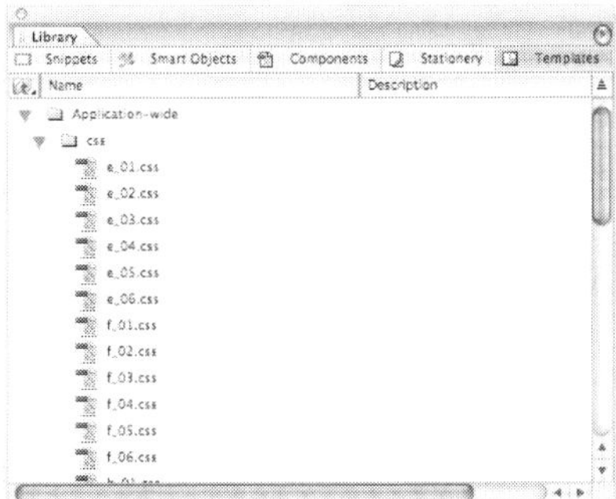

Figure 103a Dozens of CSS examples await you in the Library palette.

2. To test how a particular style sheet file will affect the appearance of your page, drag a CSS file from the Library palette into the page's head section (**Figure 103b**). Notice how the page immediately takes on a new look and feel. If you don't like the look of one CSS file, press Command-Z (Mac) or Ctrl-Z (Windows) to undo and select another CSS document to test. You can do this as many times as you like until you find a combination that suits you.

(continued on next page)

Clean Up Your Mess!

Be sure to delete any CSS markers left in the head portion of the sample page that you may have left behind while you were experimenting because they will be incorrectly linked to CSS files in the Library palette. Delete the marker by selecting it in the head section and pressing Delete on your keyboard.

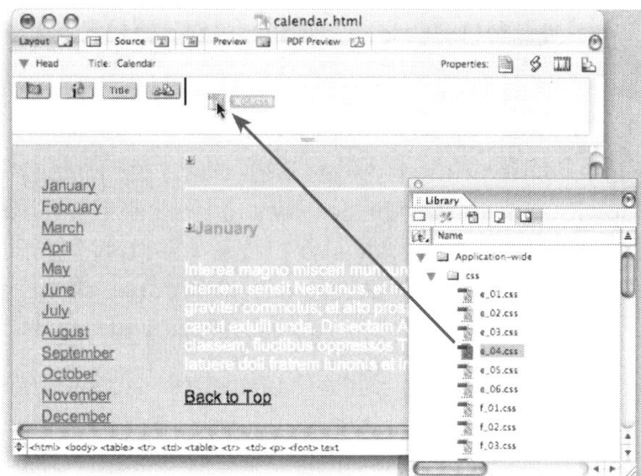

Figure 103b Drag and drop the .css file into the head section of your page to give it an instant makeover.

3. When you've decided which CSS document you'd like to use, add it to your site by dragging it from the Library palette to the Files tab of your Site window. It's a good idea to rename this external CSS file now.

4. Clean up the test page by deleting the CSS markers you placed in the head section while experimenting. (See the sidebar "Clean Up Your Mess.")

5. Now that you've found a style sheet you want to use, you might want to customize it further or learn from the example file. Open the .css file from the Site window and examine the various rules in the CSS Editor window (**Figure 103c**).

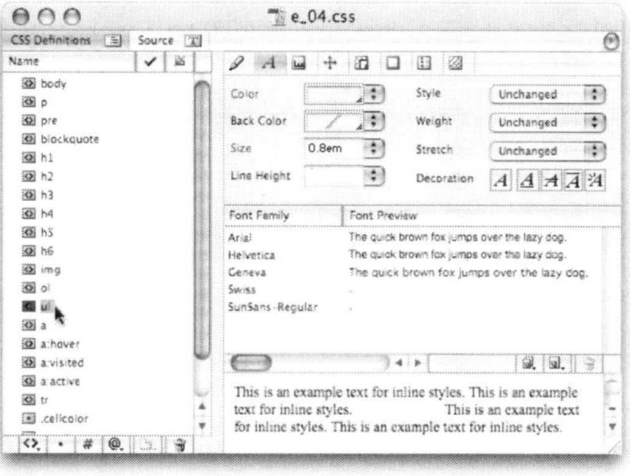

Figure 103c Use the CSS Editor to reverse-engineer the styles in the Library palette.

TIP 104 Creating CSS Comments and Folders

When you create complex CSS files, you'll want to organize the rules in a way that makes them easy to remember, easy to manage, and easy to share with others. The advanced comments and folders options in the CSS Editor make these challenges a breeze (**Figure 104**).

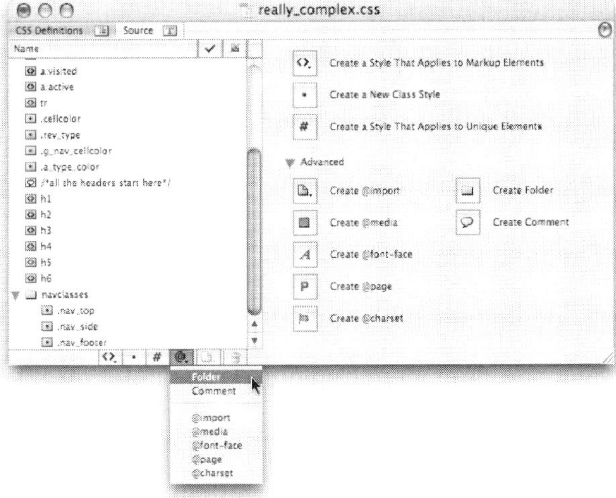

Figure 104 Comments and folders help you organize and document complex CSS files.

Create a comment in your CSS source code to leave yourself a reminder, document your work, or communicate style standards to coworkers. Just click the Create Comment button on the right side of the CSS Editor or select Comment from the Advanced pull-down menu at the bottom of the window. Type the text of your comment in the right side of the window and you're done. You can go back to edit or delete your comments at any time.

You can also create folders to organize complex style sheets. Folders in the GoLive CSS Editor are really just comments in the source code that look like folders in the list of CSS definitions, so there's nothing wrong with the code and it's a nice editing convenience. Create a new folder by clicking the New Folder icon on the right or by selecting Folder from the Advanced pull-down menu at the bottom of the window. Remember that the order of the folders does affect the cascade of the CSS.

Dragging to Re-sort Statements

To change the order of CSS rules and move rules in and out of folders, just select the rules and drag them into their new location in the list on the left side of the CSS Editor window.

TIP 105 Removing Link Underlines

One of the most common requests in any Web design forum is "How do I remove the underlines from all my text links?" You've probably figured it out by now, but you'll need to use CSS to achieve this common effect. You *can* remove link underlines with internal style sheets, but that's inefficient because it means you need to open and edit every page individually. Instead, here's an easier solution that uses an external style sheet. Just follow these steps:

1. Create a new external style sheet by selecting File > New Special > Cascading Style Sheet.
2. Select the *a* element from the New Element pull-down menu on the right to create a new style sheet rule that affects how hyperlinks are displayed in your Web pages.
3. With the CSS rule for the *a* element selected on the left, select the Font tab (*A*) in the CSS Editor and click the No Text Decoration button to remove the underlines (**Figure 105**). Notice that you can also change properties such as the color, size, and background color of your hyperlinks in the same tab of the CSS Editor.

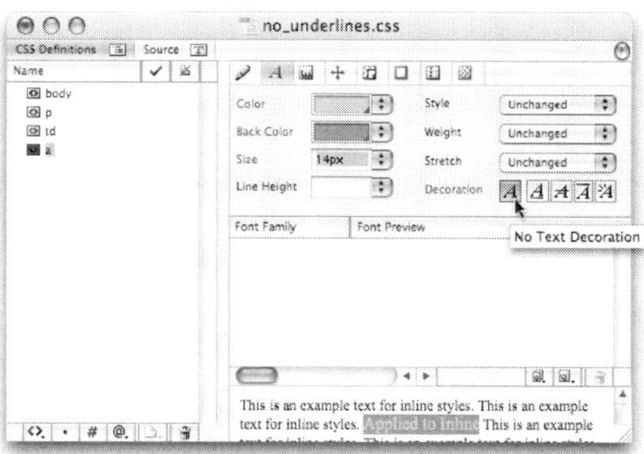

Figure 105 You're not stuck with underlined links if you follow these steps.

After you save this external .css file into your Web site follow the steps in Tip 101 to apply this effect to all the pages in your site. Isn't it amazing how much time GoLive is saving you?

TIP 106 Creating CSS Text Rollovers

You know the effect where you mouse over a text link and the text changes color, or even the background of the link changes color? If you guessed this is done with CSS, you're on the road to great Web wisdom and success. Just be aware that this CSS rollover effect may not work in older browsers, but the links themselves will work just fine.

Follow these steps to create CSS text rollovers:

1. Open your style sheet (internal or external) in the CSS Editor.
2. Add an element style for the `a:hover` element by selecting it from the New Element pull-down menu on the right side of the CSS Editor window, as seen in **Figure 106a**.

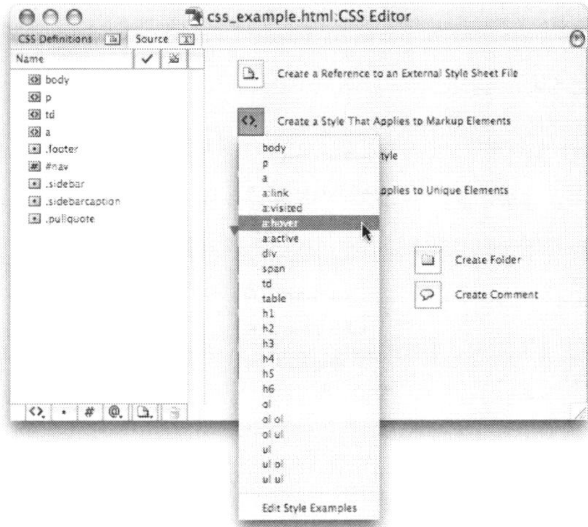

Figure 106a Select `a:hover` from the New Element pull-down menu.

(continued on next page)

3. With the a:hover rule selected on the left side of the window, change the text color in the Font Properties tab of the CSS Editor, as seen in **Figure 106b**. This will be the color of the text when you hover your cursor over the text link.

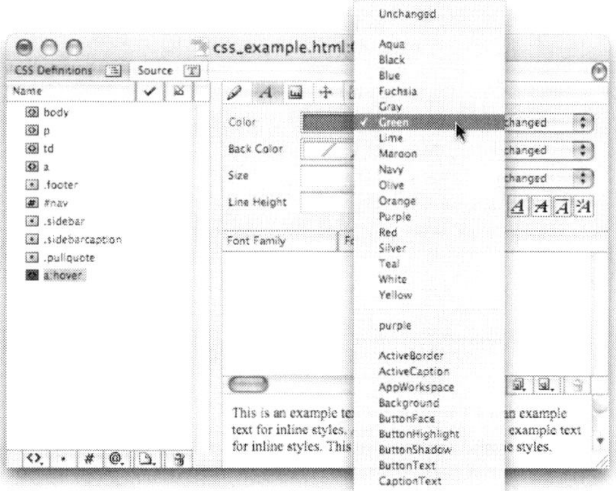

Figure 106b Change the color of the rollover text in the Font Properties tab of the CSS Editor.

4. If you also want to change the background color of the text link, edit the Back(ground) Color field in the same tab of the CSS Editor.

Now all pages that use this style sheet will have this new rollover effect on text links. To test the effect, switch to Preview mode (see Tips 72 and 73 for more about previewing) and hover your mouse pointer over the text links in your page (**Figure 106c**). Voilà!

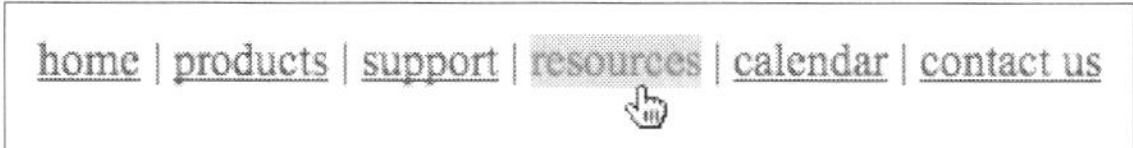

Figure 106c This simple navigation bar shows the CSS rollover effect in Preview mode.

CHAPTER SIX

Automating Repetitive Tasks

The copy and paste feature is a lovely thing, and years ago it was practically the only way to reuse elements when building a Web site. But back in 1998 a feature was introduced into GoLive (at that time called GoLive CyberStudio 3) that allowed you to save part of a page as a "component" and then reuse it on other pages. The coolest thing about it was that if you changed the original component, all the pages where it was used were automatically updated to reflect the change.

Well, that was only the beginning. Since then, every release of GoLive has added new features to help you quickly build and maintain Web sites and to automate time-consuming repetitive tasks.

In this chapter we concentrate on four features that we rely on daily to automate our design process: snippets, components, stationery, and page templates, all of which are neatly tucked into the Library palette. (Although Smart Objects are stored in the Library palette, too, we don't discuss them in this chapter because they are covered extensively in Chapter Seven.) We also cover the process for checking the spelling on your pages prior to making it live for the world to see.

TIP 107 Navigating the Library Palette

Start by opening the Library palette from the Window menu. This little palette is multitalented. It stores items that are available for use application-wide as well as items specific to any open Web site projects.

Across the top of the Library palette are five buttons, and if you hold the mouse pointer over them a tool tip will pop up showing you the button's name. From left to right the buttons are Snippets, Smart Objects, Components, Stationery, and Templates. To see what's in the Snippets area, click the Snippets button; to see what's in Templates, click the Templates button; and so on.

In the area below the buttons is a folder called Application-wide, along with folders representing any sites that you have open. These folders work like the folders in the Files tab of the Site window. They can be toggled open or closed by clicking the gray arrow to the left of the folder name (click the plus sign in Windows), or you can drill down into a folder by double-clicking it. Use the up arrow in the upper-left corner to move back up a level (**Figure 107a**).

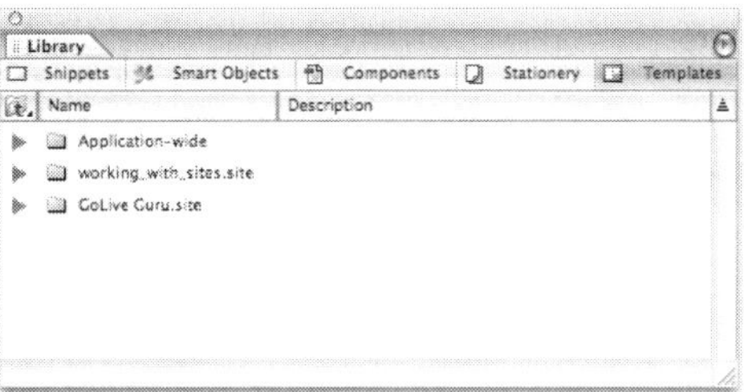

Figure 107a The Library palette.

You can drag items into the folders in the Library palette to store them, and drag them from the folders onto pages or into the Site window to use them.

In the Library palette's flyout menu are options to turn the Preview feature on and off and to have the preview appear at the right instead of the bottom. This choice comes in handy when you're previewing a template or component, but the feature can be a little tricky to use. We suggest you resize the Library palette larger before enabling Preview because sometimes the resize corner is hard to grab when Preview is turned on (**Figure 107b**).

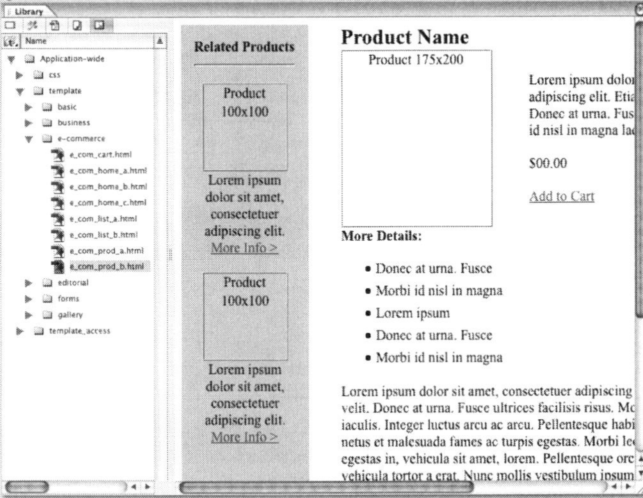

Figure 107b Viewing one of the included page templates in the Library palette with Preview enabled and on the right.

Stored in Site Extras

Notice that the sections of the Library palette correspond with folders in the Extras tab of the Site window. All you need to remember is this: Reusable items are *stored* in the Extras tab, but to *make use* of them we strongly suggest you drag from the Library palette.

TIP 108 Using Snippets

Try the Samples

Some very handy samples are included in the Snippets area of the Library palette. Go through and drag some of them onto a page to see what's there. Note that some of the included snippets are for use in the body of a page, whereas others, like the meta snippets, are for the head portion of the page. Likewise, some snippets are easily used in Source mode, while others are perfect for Layout mode. Play around and you'll see how flexible snippets can be.

Snippets are, very simply, pieces of a page that you can use over and over again. Examples include an address, a table of data, or a piece of JavaScript. If you find that you are using one element on lots of pages, turn it into a snippet for drag-and-drop ease of use.

Let's create a snippet so that you can get the hang of it. Follow these steps:

1. Choose File > New Page to start with a new blank page.
2. Type your name and address onto the page.
3. Select everything you typed and drag it into the Application-wide folder in the Snippets area of the Library palette.

The folder will automatically pop open, and you'll see a new file there called snippet.agls. The filename will be highlighted so you can easily rename it. Call it address.agls (**Figure 108**).

Now follow these steps to complete the process:

1. Choose File > New Page to get another new blank page.
2. Drag the snippet you named address.agls onto the new page.

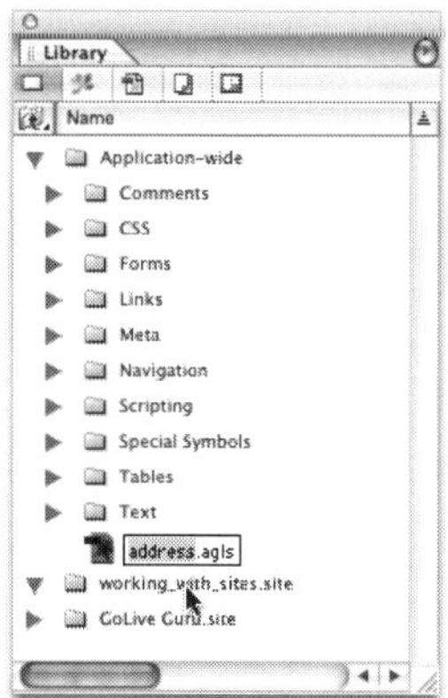

Figure 108 When you create a new snippet, give it a descriptive name.

Tada! You have successfully created and used a snippet. Remember, you can create a snippet out of anything on a page—grids, tables, text, images, and more. If you have a styled table that includes an image and text, and it's surrounded by additional text, you can grab the whole kaboodle and save it as one snippet.

To modify a snippet, double-click the file in the Library palette, make the changes, and then save the document. The changes will affect only the snippet you've edited, not the pages on which the snippet was already used.

TIP 109 Using Components

There is one major difference between snippets and components: If you create a snippet and use it on 10 pages, and then change the snippet file, no change is made to the pages that already use that snippet. Not so with components. If you create a component, use it on 10 pages, and then change the component file, every page that uses the component will automatically be updated to reflect the change.

"Ah-ha," you're thinking, "this is going to save me some time." Right you are. Here are specific examples of when components are perfect: navigation bars, copyright notices, or any item that is used on multiple pages but needs occasional updating.

The process for creating a component is a little different than for creating a snippet. Instead of dragging items off a page and into the Components section of the Library palette, you'll need to save the whole page as a component. To do so, either choose File > Save as and then choose Components from the Site Folder pop-up menu in the Save dialog box or choose Save as > Save as Component from the document's flyout menu (**Figure 109a**). Use a descriptive name when you save the file so that you know which component is which when you later go to use one on a page.

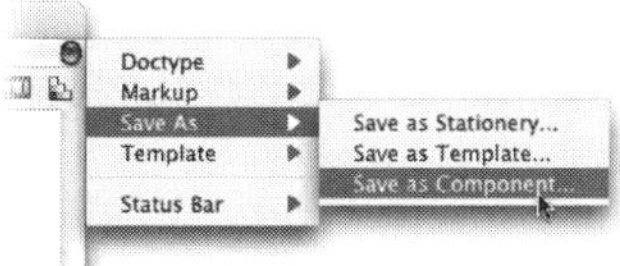

Figure 109a Use the handy Site Folder pop-up menu to save directly into the site's component folder or save the file as a component via its flyout menu.

Warning! Application-wide Library Items

The Application-wide folder in the Library palette is great for storing text-based items, but be wary of storing items there that reference an object that does not physically exist in your site, such as an image. Unless you are 100 percent sure that no object used in your snippet, component, stationery, or template is referenced outside your site, stick with the site-specific folder.

When the component is saved, it will appear both in the Components folder of the Site Extras and in the Components section of the Library palette. To use it, drag it from the Library palette onto a page (**Figure 109b**).

Figure 109b To use a component, drag it from the Library palette and drop it onto a page.

To edit a component, double-click it in the Library palette, make your changes, and then save the file. When you save the component, any pages using that component will be automatically updated (**Figure 109c**). A dialog box will inform you when the update has been completed. Click OK.

Figure 109c GoLive shows you which pages reference the component and will therefore be updated.

Note

After you change a component that is used on other pages, remember to upload the changed pages to the Web server.

TIP 110 Using Stationery

Anyone who has seen a stack of company letterhead will be familiar with the term *stationery*. If you take a piece of letterhead, type a letter on it, send it to your mom, and then subsequently redesign the letterhead, your mom's letter would remain unchanged. GoLive's stationery pages work precisely the same way.

Design a stationery page as you would any other page, but instead of saving it into the Files tab of the Site window, save it into the Stationery folder. There are two easy ways to do so: Choose File > Save as and then choose Stationery from the Site Folder pop-up menu in the Save dialog box or choose Save as > Save as Stationery from the document's flyout menu.

Your new stationery file will appear in both the Stationery folder of the Extras tab in the site window and in the Stationery section of the Library palette. You can use it from either location, but we suggest the Library palette because it's so easy to use. To create a new page from the stationery, do one of the following:

- Drag the stationery file from the Library palette and drop it into the Files tab of the Site window. The page is copied into your site, and the filename is automatically highlighted so that you can type in an appropriate name (**Figure 110a**).

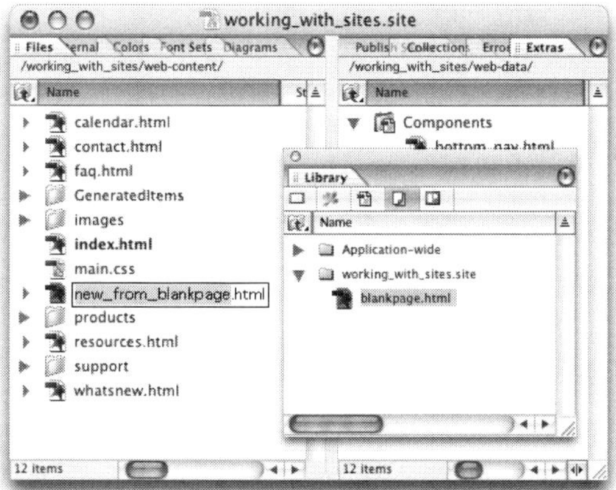

Figure 110a GoLive helpfully highlights the portion of the filename that needs to be changed.

(continued on next page)

Stationery vs. Templates

Stationery pages are great for those times when you're modifying the original and don't want to affect pages created from it—for example, a newsletter or archive. However, when you want to update multiple pages with ease, template pages are the best choice because any page created from a template will be updated to reflect changes made to the original file.

- Double-click the stationery file in the Library palette. A dialog box will ask if you want to modify the file or create a new one. Choose Create, and a new page will be created and opened, ready for you to work on (**Figure 110b**).

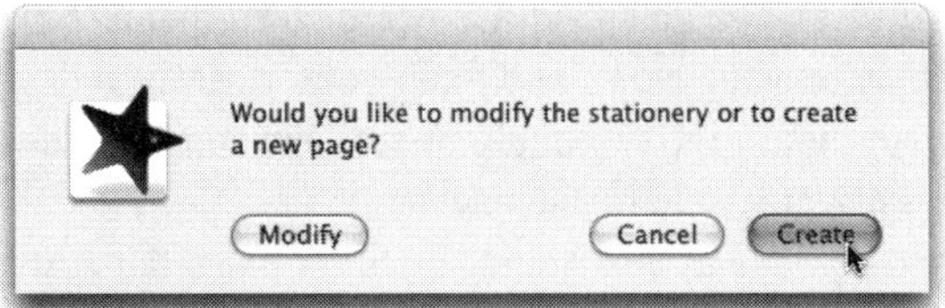

Figure 110b Choose Create to make a new page based on the stationery, or choose Modify to change the stationery file itself.

If you would like to change the stationery file, double-click it in the Library palette and choose Modify. Make your changes and then save the file. None of the pages that were created from the stationery page will be affected by the modification of the original.

TIP 111 Creating a Template

Of the four brethren, snippets, components, stationery, and templates, templates are by far the most powerful. By building a template-based site, you can update the entire look of your Web site quickly and easily. Templates require a little more setup than stationery pages, so we devote the next five tips exclusively to the topic of templates.

> ***Note***
> *Another powerful way of making site-wide visual changes is to employ Cascading Style Sheets (see Chapter 4).*

The idea behind a template is that certain areas of the page are locked and unchangeable while other areas are editable. Locked areas typically include the parts of the page that repeat throughout the site, such as navigation bars, whereas editable regions contain elements that will vary on each page, such as the text.

As you create your template page, you specify which areas of the page are editable via the Template Regions palette, found in the Window menu. To create an editable region, make a selection on the page and then click the Create New Editable Region button in the Template Regions palette. GoLive will automatically name text regions according to the first few words in the selection. Images, tables, grids, and other objects are simply named Region. You can rename any region by clicking on its name in the Template Regions palette and pressing Enter, or by clicking a second time (**Figure 111a**).

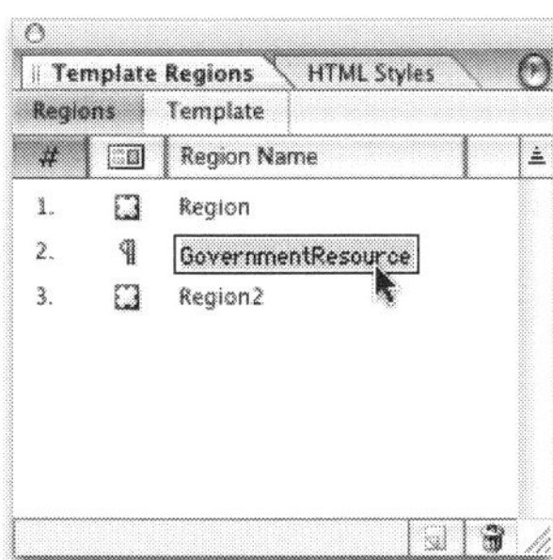

Figure 111a GoLive automatically gives newly created regions a name, but they are easily edited.

Editable CSS in the Template Head

Here's a nifty trick: If you have CSS written into a template page, when you make new pages from the template the CSS will be locked. You can't use the Template Regions palette to assign editable regions in the head, but you can go into the source code and add the necessary syntax yourself. Just add `<!-- #BeginEditable "CSS" -->` right before the `<style>` tag and `<!-- #EndEditable -->` right after the closing `</style>` tag. Although these regions won't show up in the Template Regions palette, when you create a page from the template you will be able to edit the CSS by double-clicking the CSS head tag in the page.

You can turn off the automatic naming of regions by disabling Selection Defines Region Name in the Template Regions flyout menu. Turning it off means that GoLive will name all new regions Region2, Region3, and so on. Editable regions are highlighted on the page in green, making them easy to identify (**Figure 111b**).

Figure 111b Editable regions that appear light gray here are highlighted in green on your template page.

Create as many editable regions on the page as you need and then save the page as a template by choosing File > Save as and then clicking Templates from the Site Folder pop-up menu in the Save dialog box (or choose Save as > Save as Template from the document's flyout menu). The new template page will appear in both the Templates folder of the Extras tab in the Site window and in the Templates section of the Library palette.

Note

You must specify at least one editable region on a page before the template will perform like a template. When no editable regions are indicated, GoLive treats the page as a normal page, and you won't be able to create new pages from it.

TIP 112 Creating Pages from a Template

When your template page is complete, the next step is to build additional pages from it. Choose one of the following methods to create a new page based on your template:

1. Drag the template file from the Templates section of the Library palette and drop it into the Files tab of the Site window. The page will be copied into your site with the filename automatically highlighted so that you can type in an appropriate name.
2. Double-click the template file in the Library palette. A dialog box will ask if you want to modify the file or create a new file. Click Create, and a new page based on the template opens. All the editable regions show in their normal color while the locked regions (any area *not* designated as editable) are highlighted in purple. You can try to select or edit a highlighted area, but you won't be able to because those areas are protected, hence, not editable. You can, however, modify any editable region. When you're done, save the page into your site (**Figure 112a**).

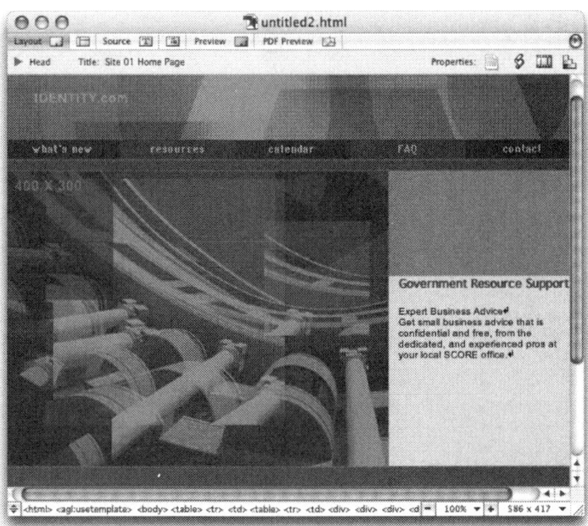

Figure 112a Pages created from a template highlight locked areas while editable regions appear normally.

Highlight Color

You can change both the color and the type of highlighting used to indicate editable regions in the Highlight palette. Choose Window > Highlight and then click the Color button at the top of the Highlight palette. Move the sliders to make the editable region's highlight color more or less opaque, or click the Show Border Only button on the right of the opacity slider to highlight only the region's border. To change the color entirely, click the color well and choose a new color from the Color or Swatches palette.

Applying Templates

What if you have an existing page that already has content on it and you want to drop that content into a template? Here's how.

One method is to open the page and then, from the document flyout menu, choose Template > Apply Template > *yourtemplate.html*, where *yourtemplate.html* is the name of the template you are applying. A dialog will ask you to specify the editable region where the page's content will go. Make your choice, and voilà! The page assumes the look of the template page.

An optional method is to open the page to which you want to apply the template and then, from the Special menu, choose Template > Apply Template. The Open dialog box appears with the templates folder already loaded. Choose the template you want to use and click Open. Again, you're asked to choose the editable region where the page's content should be placed. Select the region name and click OK (**Figure 112b**).

Figure 112b When applying a template to an existing page, select the region where the page's content will be placed.

TIP 113 Redefining Templates

Let's say you've entirely based your site on templates. Well done. Now let's say you get in a creative mood one day and come up with a completely new design. How do you take all those pages built upon one template and port them over to a new template? It's simple, really.

First save the new design as a template, making sure that you define its editable regions. To make porting pages to a new template a snap, it is important that you *use the same editable region names* in the new template that you used in the original. Using the same region names allows the content to flow seamlessly from the old template to the new one.

Let's first explore how to redefine a single page and then we'll see how to redefine multiple pages at once.

To redefine which template a page uses, employ one of the following methods:

- Open the page and then from the document flyout menu choose Template > Apply Other Template > *newtemplate.html*, where *newtemplate.html* is the filename of your new template (**Figure 113a**).

Figure 113a Choose a different template to base the page on from the document flyout menu.

- Open the page and then click the Template button in the Template Regions palette. Use the Fetch URL tool to point and shoot at a new template file in the templates folder of the Extras tab of the Site window (**Figure 113b**). (See Tip 29, for more on *point and shoot*.)

(continued on next page)

Redefining Components

You can use the In & Out Links palette to redefine components as well as templates. Follow the steps outlined for redefining page templates site-wide, but select the original component inside the Components folder found in the Extras tab of the Site window and then point and shoot to the replacement component.

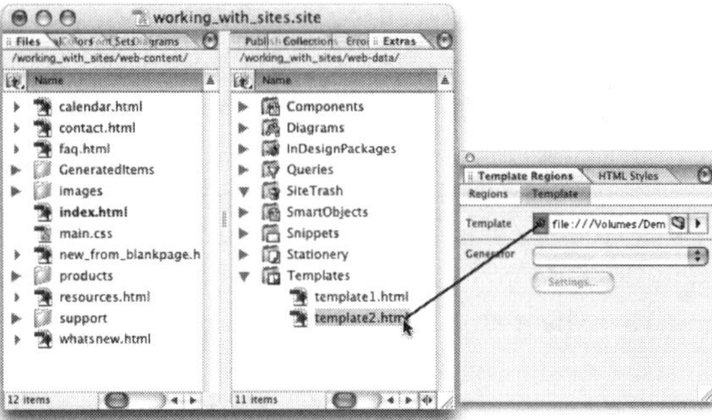

Figure 113b Use the Fetch URL tool from the Template Regions palette to redefine a page's template.

In both cases, if the editable region names match, the new template is automatically applied. If you don't use the same region names in both templates, you get a dialog asking you to choose an editable region from the list. This can be tricky because you can select only one region from the list.

To redefine the template used on multiple pages, use the In & Out Links palette as follows:

1. Open the In & Out Links palette from the Window menu.
2. Select the original template file by clicking it once. You should find it in the Templates folder in the Extras tab of the Site window. The In & Out Links palette will show all the pages connected to the old template.
3. Use the Fetch URL tool next to the template name to point and shoot to the new template in the Templates folder (**Figure 113c**).

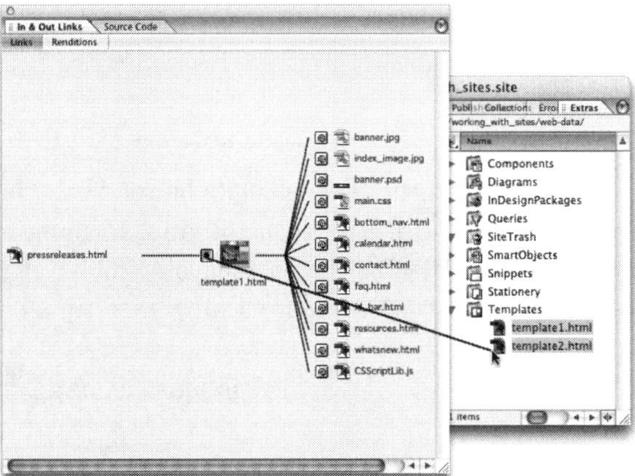

Figure 113c Easily redefine the template used on multiple pages by using the In & Out Links palette.

TIP 114 Detaching Templates

There may come a time when you no longer want a page to be attached to a template. If that's the case, you can easily detach it. When you do so, the page's design remains the same, but the connection with the template is broken. Any subsequent updates to the template page will no longer affect the detached page.

To detach a page from its template, begin by opening the page. From the document's flyout menu, choose Templates > Detach From Template or choose Template > Detach from Template from the Special menu. The highlighting of locked areas is removed, and the entire page becomes editable (**Figure 114**).

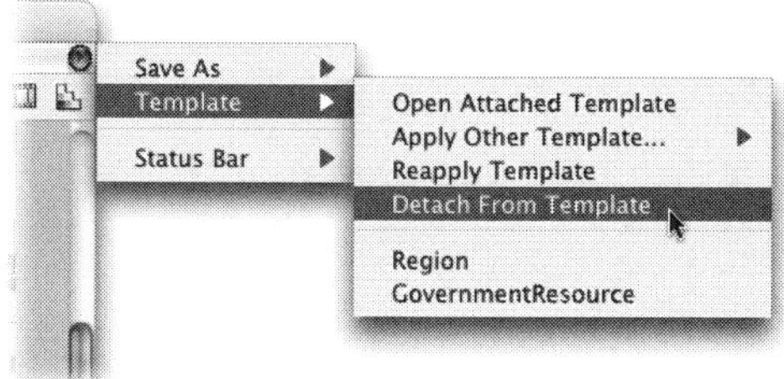

Figure 114 A page detached from its template becomes fully editable again.

Detaching Components

Not only can you detach a page template from its source document, you can detach a component as well, thereby breaking the link back to its original version. Simply Control-click/right-click on a component in a page and choose Component > Detach Selected Component. You can also choose Detach All Components or Detach Single Component and then select the component's name from the list. From then on, changes made to the original component are updated in the detached version.

TIP 115 Using Sample Templates

You might have noticed that in the Templates section of the Library palette a number of page templates and Cascading Style Sheet (CSS) templates are tucked into the folder labeled Application-wide. Let's take a look at what's there and how you can make use of them.

First open the Library palette and select the Templates section. Enlarge the palette by dragging its lower-right corner and then turn on Use Preview and Preview on Right in the palette menu. As you browse through the templates, a preview of the page appears in the preview area, making it easy for you to find a page to choose (**Figure 115**).

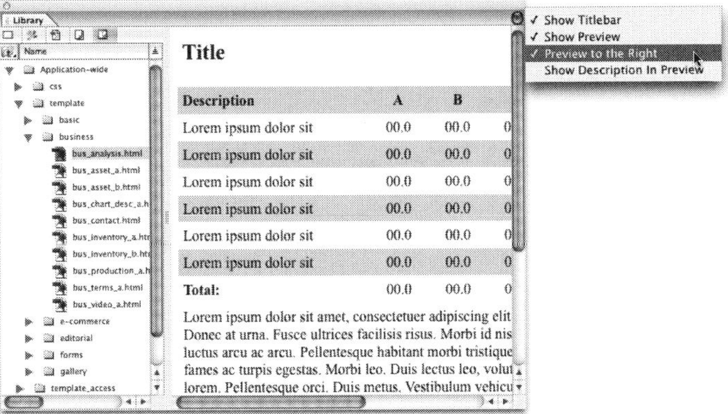

Figure 115 Dozens of page templates are included in the Library palette.

Drag the page you've chosen into the Templates folder in the Extras tab of the Site window and give it an appropriate name. You can now create new pages from the template, as explained earlier in the chapter, or modify the template to better suit your needs.

You may need to unlock the page to make modifications, but you can lock it again when you are done. To unlock the page, choose Special > Template > Unlock Page. Replace the image placeholders with images of your own, substitute the placeholder text with your own text, and then save the template. You can now use it as you would any other template in your site.

The fun part comes when you combine the page templates with one of the included CSS templates. You can change the entire look of a page (or site) by attaching an external style sheet to a template. For instructions on how to use the included CSS templates, see Tip 103.

TIP 116 Spell-checking

An interesting thing about the two authors of this book is that Adam is a better speller than Lynn, but Lynn is a better typist than Adam. Either way, we both make plenty of errors, so having the ability to run a spell-check on one page, a series of pages, or an entire site is immensely helpful and a huge time-saver.

Start by opening the Check Spelling window from the Edit menu. A spell-check begins at the position of the cursor on an open page. To run the spell-check from the top of the page, enable the From Top check box. To check a selection only, select text on the page and then initiate the spell-check.

If you need to perform the check on multiple files or on a complete site, enable the Check in Files check box in the Check Spelling window and then click the gray arrow to reveal the lower portion of the dialog. You can then choose your site's name from the pop-up list or drag files from the Files tab of your Site window directly into the Check Spelling window (**Figure 116**).

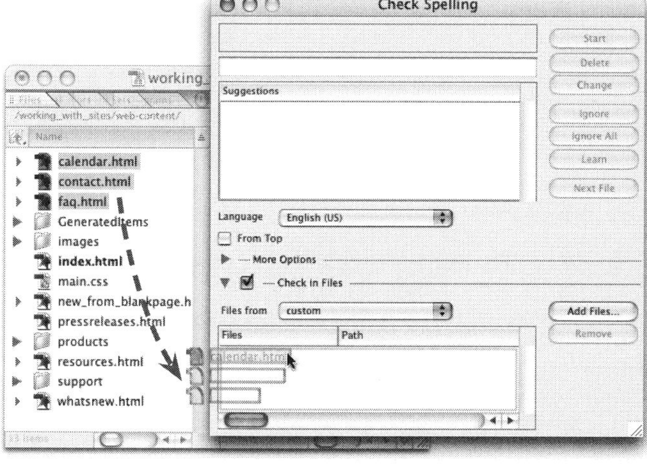

Figure 116 You can drag multiple files directly into the Check Spelling window.

Creating a Personal Dictionary

When checking the spelling of a document you can add a word to your personal dictionary by clicking the Learn button when the word is flagged as incorrect. This adds the word to your personal dictionary, and from then on it is no longer considered an error. You can also add words to your personal dictionary in the Spell Checker section of the application preferences.

Choose your preferred language from the pop-up menu and select the appropriate options for your spelling check. Then click Start to begin the spell-check. As the check proceeds, you'll choose from several options:

- Delete removes the word.
- Replace replaces the questionable word with the top one in the list.
- Ignore skips over the word with no modification.
- Ignore All skips all instances of the word.
- Learn adds the word to your personal dictionary.
- Next File moves to the next document in the site.

TIP 117 Changing Documents Site-wide

There may be times when you need to make site-wide changes, such as updating the DOCTYPE of every page. GoLive CS offers an easy method for making this kind of change quickly and accurately.

The five site-wide document content changes that you can make are: Change Encoding, Rewrite Source Code, Convert to HTML, Convert to XHTML, and Change Doctype. Choose Edit > Document Content and then select one of the five options from the submenu (**Figure 117**).

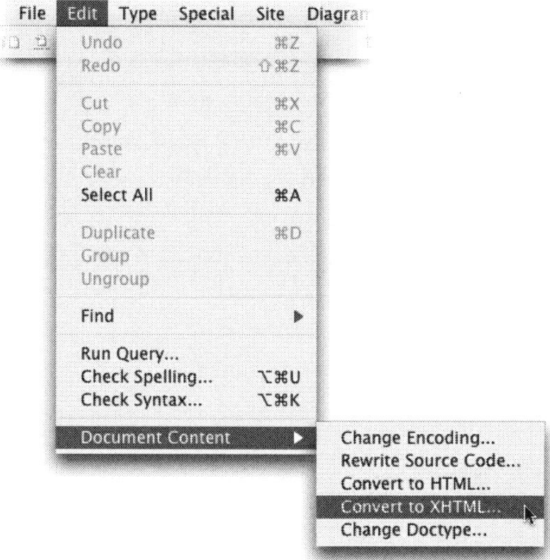

Figure 117 You can select a document content change from the submenu.

Here's a brief description of what each option does:

- Change Encoding changes the selected charset (character set) in the page's syntax.
- Rewrite Source Code cleans up the way the source code is formatted.
- Convert to HTML converts XHTML syntax to HTML.
- Convert to XHTML converts HTML syntax to XHTML.
- Change Doctype allows you to assign a different DOCTYPE to the page or pages.

You can choose to run one of these options on a single page, on multiple pages, or on an entire site. Here are the choices:

- To run a Document Content command on one page, open the page (in front of the Site window) and then invoke the command.
- To run a Document Content command on multiple files, open the Site window (in front of any pages) and select the files in the Files list on which you want to run the command. Then invoke the command from the menu.
- To run a Document Content command on an entire site, open the Site window but *do not select any files*. Then invoke the command from the menu.

Regardless of which of the five Document Content options you choose, you'll be greeted with a dialog that acts as both a safety net (what if you really didn't want to convert your whole site from XHMTL to HTML?) and as an opportunity to fine-tune the changes that will be made.

For more information on document encodings and DOCTYPEs, see Tips 32 and 54.

CHAPTER SEVEN

Creative Suite Integration

Can we see a show of hands from anybody here who uses Photoshop? That's what we thought. Virtually everybody uses Photoshop. Most designers also use Illustrator. Everybody deals with Adobe PDF files. More and more designers are switching from QuarkXPress to InDesign every day. All this is important for GoLive users because using files and designs from other Creative Suite applications in GoLive is easier than ever before.

Whether you're using Web layouts from ImageReady, digital photos from Photoshop, logos from Illustrator, print layouts from InDesign, or Adobe PDF files from Acrobat, GoLive CS makes it easy to incorporate all that content in your Web site. Smart Objects let you use native Adobe source files in your site, and the new Package For GoLive feature in InDesign CS allows you to easily repurpose print layouts for the Web. We explore these two features and much more in this chapter. We're confident that by the end of this chapter you'll agree that the Creative Suite is greater than the sum of its parts.

TIP 118 Introducing Smart Objects

You use GIF and JPEG images on your Web pages, right? Well, Adobe makes it as easy as drag and drop to convert a variety of source files, such as layered Photoshop documents or high-resolution TIFF images, into Web-friendly GIFs and JPEGs right inside GoLive.

You can store your Smart Objects source files in the SmartObjects directory in the Extras tab of the Site window. This method of storage makes it easy to use the files, and GoLive can keep track of them if you move them. To place a Smart Object, select a source file in the SmartObjects directory and drag and drop it into your Web page layout, as shown in **Figure 118**.

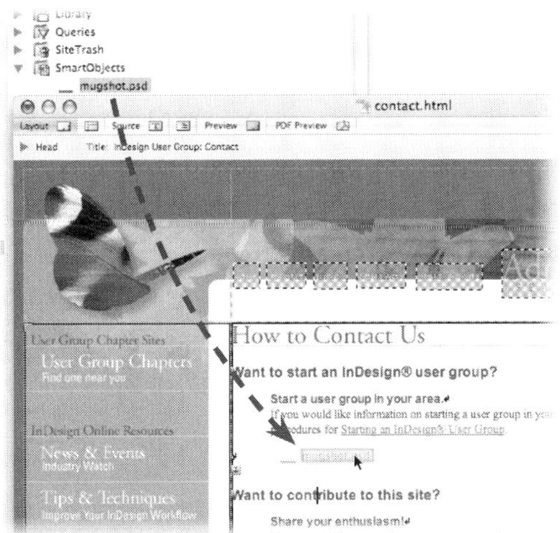

Figure 118 Drag and drop native source files into the Layout Editor to place a Smart Object.

After you place a Smart Object, choose the image optimization settings in the Save For Web dialog (see Tip 119 for more details about Save For Web) and save the target file in your Site Root folder.

Here's a complete list of the file formats supported by Smart Objects:

RGB File Formats	CMYK File Formats
Adobe Illustrator (.ai and .aisvg)	Adobe Illustrator (.ai and .aisvg)
Adobe Photoshop (.psd)	Adobe Photoshop
BMP	EPS
Clipboard	JPEG
EPS	JPEG2000
GIF	PDF
JPEG	PDF with security
JPEG2000	SVG
PICT	SVGZ (compressed)
PCX	TIFF, flat
PDF	TIFF, layered
PDF with security	TIFF, JPEG compression
Pixar	
PNG	
SVG	
SVGZ (compressed)	
Targa	
TIFF, flat	
TIFF, layered	
TIFF, JPEG compression	

CMYK TIFF for Print-to-Web Workflows

Smart Object source files that are high resolution are automatically converted to 72 dpi, and CMYK images are instantly and seamlessly converted to RGB. This makes print-to-Web publishing a reality!

TIP 119 Optimizing Images with Save For Web

The Save For Web interface (**Figure 119**) in GoLive lets you quickly optimize your source files to image formats such as GIF, JPEG, and PNG. The powerful optimization algorithms allow you to maximize quality and minimize download times all in one dialog. Let's take a quick tour through the major features.

GIF vs. JPEG

You should select GIF when compressing images such as buttons, banners, logos, and other images with lots of flat color or repeating patterns. Choose JPEG when you're compressing photographic images and files with smooth gradients.

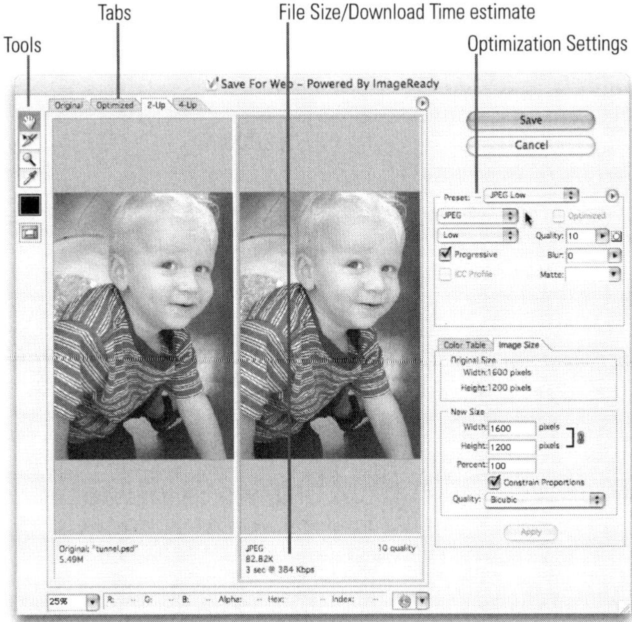

Figure 119 The Save For Web dialog optimizes all your Smart Object source files into Web-friendly target files.

Across the top of the Save For Web window are four tabs that show you (in order from left to right) the Original uncompressed image, an Optimized view with real-time compression preview, a 2-Up view, and a 4-Up view to compare multiple settings side by side.

On the right side you can select an optimization preset from the pull-down menu or create your own settings with the available options. You can choose from JPEG, GIF, PNG-8, PNG-24, and WBMP—but JPEG and GIF will be your most likely choices.

As you adjust your optimization settings, you can see a real-time compression preview in the image previews on the left as well as estimated file size and download time at the bottom of the dialog. Use the preview and the download estimates to decide which optimization settings work best for each image.

On the left side there's a small toolbar with four tools. Use the Hand tool to pan around the image; double-click this tool to fit the entire image in the window. Also notice that as you pan in 2-Up and 4-Up modes, all the images pan together so you can compare areas of detail with different optimization settings. Click with the Zoom tool to zoom in and Option/Alt-click to zoom out.

Adjusting Image Size in Save For Web

To change the dimensions of the target file without affecting the source image, enter the new image dimensions in the Image Size tab in the bottom-right corner of the Save For Web window. Make sure you click the Apply button instead of pressing Return or Enter because Return/Enter confirms *all* the changes and not just the image size changes.

TIP 120 Working with Source and Target Files

Being able to compress native source files into Web graphics right inside GoLive is cool, but it's just the beginning when it comes to Smart Objects. The real powers of Smart Objects are the amazing ways the Source and Target images work together (**Figure 120**).

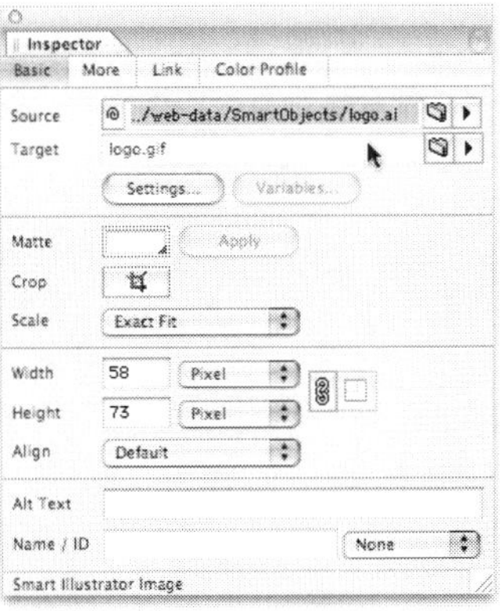

Figure 120 The smart connection between the Source and Target files makes the magic of Smart Objects happen.

For example, if you resize a Smart Object in the Layout Editor (hold Shift to constrain proportions), GoLive automatically generates a fresh Target file using the same optimization settings. The new Target file is saved over the previous version with the same name in the same place so you don't end up with cluttered files. This makes it easy to make last-minute tweaks without any hassles.

To change the optimization settings for a Smart Object, click the Settings button in the Inspector palette and adjust the compression options. Click Save, and a new Target file is saved into your site for you. The most important thing to note about all these changes is that they're completely nondestructive to the original Source file. This means you can change the size and compression of a Smart Object a hundred times, yet the Source file is never altered, and the Target file is always regenerated based on the original so you'll never see any generational quality loss or recompression.

To really blow your mind, try double-clicking on the Smart Object in the Layout Editor. Instead of opening the JPEG or GIF Target file, the Source file is opened in its creator application, such as Photoshop or Illustrator. Make any changes you want to the Source file, such as adding layers, deleting layers, editing text, and adding adjustment layers, and save it when you're done. When you switch back to GoLive, the program instantly recognizes the changes you've made in the other Creative Suite applications and automatically updates all your Target images.

TIP 121 Integrating with Photoshop CS

You can easily place native Photoshop documents by dragging the PSD from the SmartObjects folder (or from anywhere on your drive or network) and dropping it directly onto the GoLive page. When the Save For Web window opens, compress the image in the format of your choice and then save it into your site.

If you prefer, you can put a Photoshop Smart Object placeholder on the page first and size it to fit your layout. Drag the placeholder from the Smart section of the Objects palette onto the page and then use the Inspector palette to locate the Source file by clicking the Browse button, which has the icon of a little folder on it and appears to the right of the Source field (**Figure 121**).

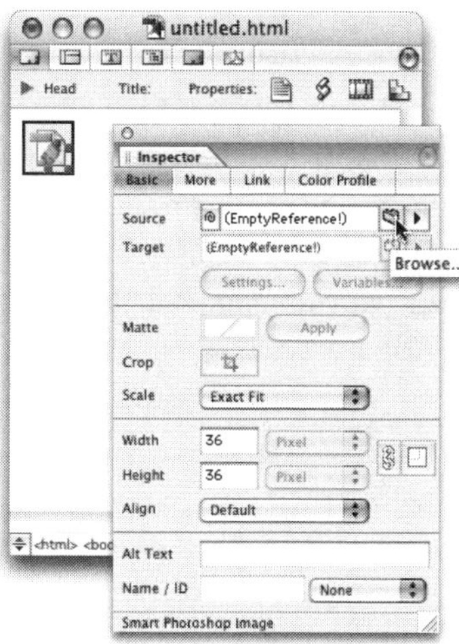

Figure 121 You can use a Smart Object placeholder and browse to the Photoshop document from the Inspector.

When you select the Source file, the Save For Web window opens and displays a version of the image that fits the dimensions of your placeholder exactly. Choose your compression settings and save the Web-ready version of the file into your site. Using this method, you can also choose file types other than PSD to use as the source, such as EPS or TIF. See Tip 118 for a list of usable file formats.

Editing Original Source Files

Double-click to open the PSD in Photoshop and make such changes as adding or deleting layers, editing text layers, using the Healing Brush, changing colors, running filters, adding adjustments, and extracting the background.

TIP 122 Optimizing Photoshop Layouts

Most users place normal Photoshop files, but you can also place entire page comps complete with slices. Create your layout in Photoshop or ImageReady, slice it as desired, and then use either of the two methods outlined in Tip 121 to place the sliced PSD file onto your GoLive page. As expected, the Save For Web window opens and displays the entire document, including the slices. To set the compression for a slice, select it with the Slice Select tool on the left side of the Save For Web window and then adjust the settings using the options on the right (see Tip 119 for more on Save For Web).

Note

If you've used ImageReady to create the sliced layout and have already set your compression settings there, those settings will be honored when you use the PSD in GoLive.

When you're done fine-tuning your settings, click Save and save the resulting files into your site. You'll notice in the Save dialog box that the file extension is .data. Upon saving the .data file you'll see that GoLive has created a folder whose contents include an automatically generated HTML file, a settings.opt file, and an images folder containing the slices from the PSD (**Figure 122**).

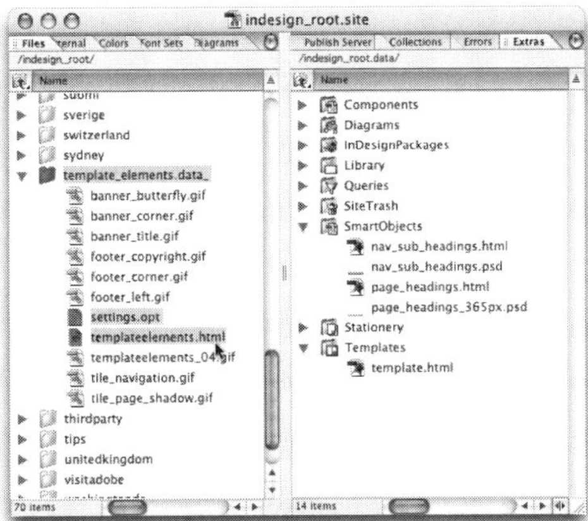

Figure 122 GoLive automatically generates a folder with a .data extension that holds an HTML file, a settings file, and a folder of images.

You might wonder why there is an HTML page in that folder, and which you should use—the page you placed the Smart Object on, or the page in the folder that was subsequently created? The choice is yours, but there are benefits to each:

- If you choose to use the page where you originally placed the Smart Object and later you want to adjust the design, you can simply double-click on the edge of the Smart Object, and the original PSD file will open in Photoshop or ImageReady for you to edit. When you save the PSD file, GoLive will update the Smart Object, including its slices. In GoLive, you can adjust the size of the entire image, crop it, or change the matte color as you can with any other Smart Object. However, you cannot adjust the table, add text to any of its cells, or add functionality such as Actions to the slices. This method works best if you don't need to edit the design itself in GoLive.
- If you choose to use the automatically generated HTML page, you can edit the table that holds the slices, add text inside cells, add actions, and so on. However, altering the original PSD will not update the page, nor can you crop, resize, or matte the individual slices in GoLive. This method works best if you intend to use the page as a template or component.

ImageReady and Illustrator Layouts

You can use the very same methods outlined in Tip 122 to place sliced Illustrator or ImageReady documents into GoLive as well. The bonus to using ImageReady is that it supports slices, rollovers, remote rollovers, hyperlinks, and more. For yet another method for using ImageReady layouts in GoLive, take a gander at Tip 125.

TIP 123 Customizing Text Variables

If you have ever used a layered PSD file as a Smart Object and had a text layer as the topmost layer in the Photoshop file, then you've probably seen a dialog like the one here (**Figure 123**). The Variable Settings dialog lets you customize some parts of a Smart Object without the original authoring application.

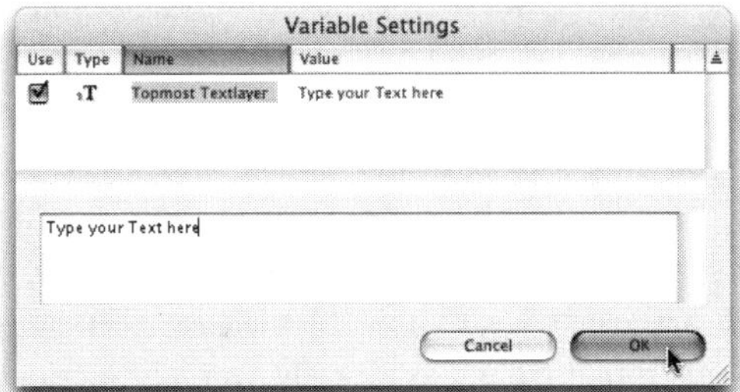

Figure 123 The Variable Settings dialog box.

You use this box to easily change the text string in the PSD file. Simply enable the check box next to the words *Topmost TextLayer* and then, in the input field that appears, type in the new text. When you click OK, the Save For Web window opens, and you can save a Web-ready version of the image that uses the new text string instead of the original. This is handy for creating multiple headings, buttons, or other items that need the same styling with different wording. It's also a good solution for those times when the font you want to use is not a typical Web font.

Using Photoshop Type on a Path

Photoshop CS now includes the ability to create type on a path—a long-standing feature request from many users. As long as the type on a path is the topmost text layer or assigned as a variable in ImageReady, then even type on a path can be customized as a variable.

TIP 124 Converting Text to Images

GoLive includes the ability to convert HTML text to a Web graphic by combining Adobe's incredible Smart Object and Variables technologies. This is an easy way to create consistent and visually compelling navigation buttons, graphical subheads, and banner ads.

Here are the steps:

1. Create a Photoshop file that has a text layer as its topmost layer or use the Image > Variables > Define command in ImageReady if you want to use a layer other than the topmost text layer. You can also use Adobe Illustrator SVG files with text variables.

2. Save the Smart Object Source file in the SmartObjects folder of your Site window.

3. Select some HTML text in the Layout Editor and choose the Special > Convert Text to Banner command (**Figure 124a**).

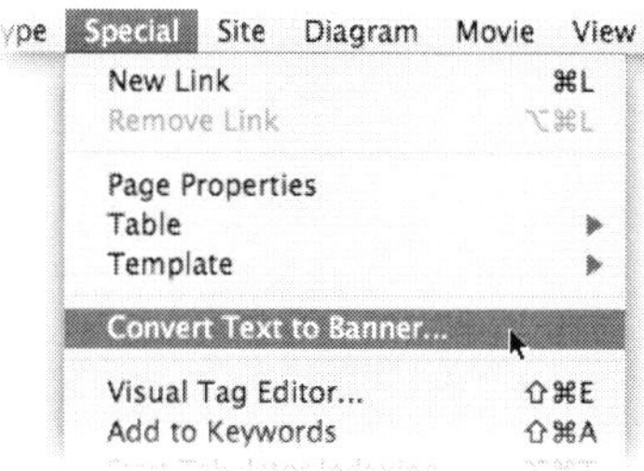

Figure 124a Select text in the Layout Editor and choose Special > Convert Text to Banner.

4. In the Open dialog, select the Smart Object Source file you want to use and click OK.

5. Notice that the Variables Settings dialog automatically copies your selected HTML text and applies it to your Topmost Textlayer variable. Change the text variable if you need to and click OK.

Bonus Tip

See the little red 1 character next to the T icon? That helps you differentiate the topmost text layer from other variable text objects.

(continued on next page)

ALT Tags from Variables

Look at the ALT Text field in the Inspector and notice how the variable text data is automagically written into the ALT attribute.

Stripping GoLive Data from Media Files

Optimization and variables settings data is stored inside the target files (GIF, JPEG, PNG, SWF, and SVG) that you view in a Web browser. That makes the target files a little larger (typically 100 to 300 bytes per image) but doesn't affect their display at all. To get rid of the unwanted size overhead, you can strip out that data on site export/upload/publish by checking the "Strip GoLive data from media files" option. This setting is found under Site > Settings in the Upload/Export category.

6. Compress the new Target file using Save For Web and save the graphic in your Site Root folder.

   Bonus Tip

   GoLive intelligently names the Target file using your variable text data.

7. Your Text-to-Banner conversion is complete (**Figure 124b**). If you need to alter the variable values, just select the image in the Layout Editor and click the Variables button in the Inspector. Now whenever you need to change the graphic headers or navigation buttons on your Web site, all you have to do is change one Photoshop file (change a color, choose a different font, add a drop shadow, and so on), and all the Smart Objects in your site are updated automatically.

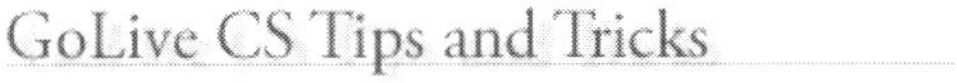

GoLive CS Tips and Tricks

Figure 124b Your HTML text is now a beautiful graphic using all the type and layer effects that couldn't be created with HTML and CSS.

TIP 125 Using ImageReady CS Output

Tip 122 explains how to drop a complete sliced layout into a GoLive page, but there is another method that we use even more. With a design open in ImageReady, choose File > Save Optimized As. A save dialog will open. Near the bottom a pop-up list labeled Format offers the options of saving HTML and Images, Images Only, or HTML Only (**Figure 125**).

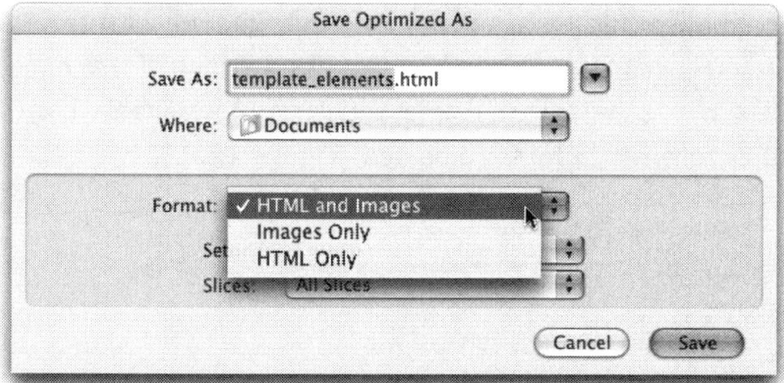

Figure 125 Select Save Optimized As from the File menu to save the HTML, the images, or both.

You can fine-tune your settings by using the Settings pop-up list and select which slices you want to save by choosing from the Slices pop-up list. When you've made your selections, click Save and save directly into the root folder of GoLive.

> ***Note***
>
> *If you have slices selected when you invoke the Save Optimized As command, you will see the Selected Slices option in the Slices pop-up list.*

Next, switch to GoLive and refresh the Site window by clicking the Refresh icon on the main toolbar. The assets you saved will now appear in the Files tab of the Site window. If you've saved HTML and images, simply double-click the HTML page to open it in GoLive. If you've saved images only, you can now drag and drop the images as you would any other images in your site.

This can be an effective way to work if you don't expect to make frequent changes to the design. Combine this with the ability to export just slice selection sets from ImageReady for a great way to build navigation bars that you'll save as reusable components in GoLive.

TIP 126 Customizing ImageReady SWF Variables

Using ImageReady CS, you can include a text variable in an SWF animation (Flash animation) and edit that text after you place it in your GoLive page. This comes in very handy when, for example, you have an ad banner whose design remains constant but whose text must change. Using a text variable, you can change "This week's special, 4 days in Florida, only $399!" to "This week's special, 5 days in New York, only $699!" and use the same SWF both times.

To accomplish this, create the animation complete with text variables in ImageReady and then choose File > Export > Macromedia Flash SWF. When the export dialog appears, select Enable Dynamic Text and choose which fonts to embed (**Figure 126a**).

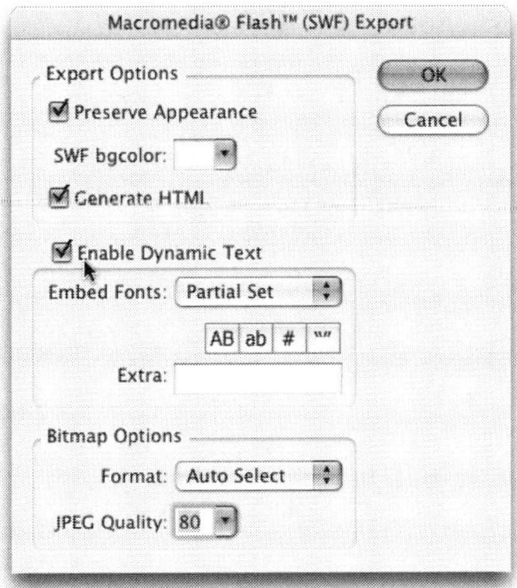

Figure 126a Choose Enable Dynamic Text when importing to SWF to make the text variables accessible in GoLive CS.

When you've placed the text in a GoLive page, you can edit it by following these simple steps:

1. Select the SWF on the page.
2. Click the right-facing arrow at the far right of the File field in the Inspector.
3. Choose Edit from the list.
4. In the Edit URL dialog, select a Query Parameter from the list.

5. Edit the text value (**Figure 126b**).
6. Click the Update button.
7. Click OK.

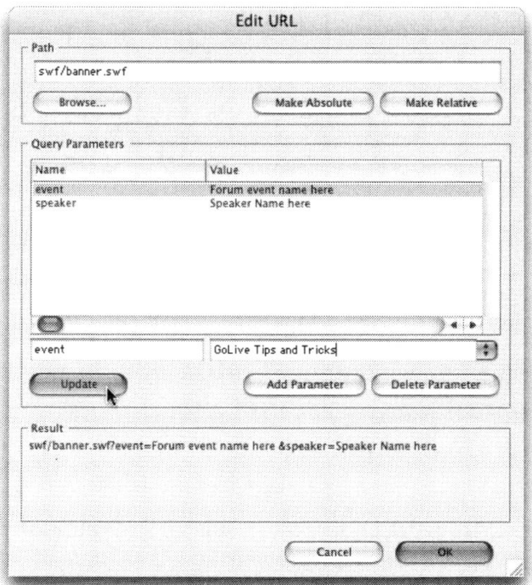

Figure 126b Change the dynamic SWF text variable from within GoLive CS using the Edit URL dialog.

Now, go back to your page and preview the animation. The original text will be replaced by the new text you just entered.

TIP 127 Integrating with Illustrator CS

You can drag and drop Adobe Illustrator files (.ai) just as you can any other Smart Object, but when you do you get a dialog offering a few extra file formats: SWF, SVG, and SVG Compressed. If you choose the Bitmap Formats option, you see the standard GIF, JPEG, PNG, and WBMP options in the Save For Web window (see Tip 119). However, if you choose SWF, SVG, or SVG Compressed, Illustrator launches instead. You need to choose the appropriate options in the Save For Web window inside Illustrator because there are a few more options available here that control SWF and SVG Output.

Note

If you don't have Illustrator installed, you can only choose the Bitmap options.

Illustrator also offers the ability to use text variable and layer visibility variables. To create variables in Illustrator, open the Variables palette from the Window menu. Designate which pieces of text you want to make dynamic and which layers' visibility you want to turn on and off in GoLive. Then—and this is the important part—save the file as SVG, *not* AI.

When you drag the SVG file onto a GoLive page, a Variable Options window opens, allowing you to turn layers on and off and to change text strings (**Figure 127**).

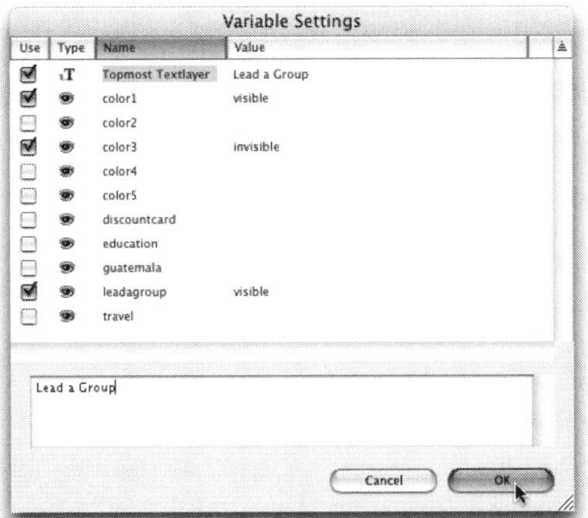

Figure 127 The Variable Options window gives both text string and layer visibility choices.

Don't Forget ImageReady!

Remember, you can also assign variables in an ImageReady file. However, ImageReady does not have a Variables palette like Illustrator. Instead, choose Variables either from the Image menu or from the Layer palette flyout menu.

TIP 128 Creating PDF Thumbnail Galleries

Lots of folks make PDF files available on their Web sites. If you have multiple PDFs, you've probably thought about the best way to present the links.

One of our favorite tricks is to create a little thumbnail version of the PDF in GoLive and then add a link to the original PDF so that users can quickly see what they're getting. The process for creating thumbnails of your PDFs is easy. Drag and drop a PDF file into the Layout Editor. If the PDF has more than one page, you get a dialog called PDF Options (**Figure 128**) asking you to choose which page you want to use to create the image.

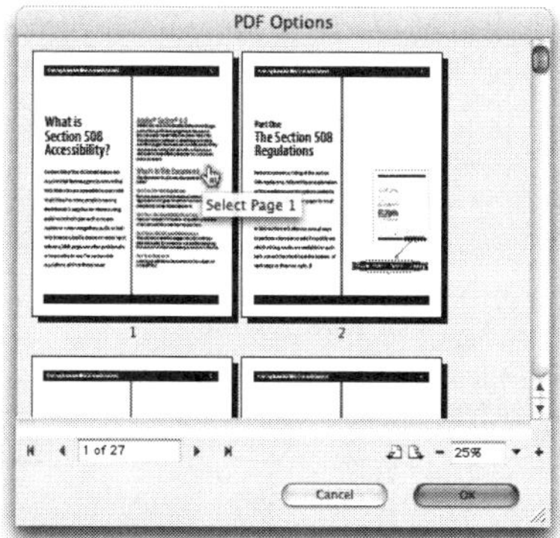

Figure 128 Select which page of the PDF you want to use to create a thumbnail preview image.

Make your selection and click OK. When the Save For Web window appears, compress the images as a GIF or JPEG and resize it so that it's tiny.

Note

Be sure to click the Apply button in the Image Size area before pressing Return/Enter on your keyboard, or the resize will be dismissed before it has been applied.

When you are all done with the settings, click Save and save the image into your site. Now visitors don't have to guess what's inside the PDF file they're about to download because they'll see a nice thumbnail preview. Using this method on a page with multiple PDFs, you can quickly and easily create an attractive PDF gallery.

Linking to the Original PDF

Once your PDF thumbnail is on the page, simply select it, click the Link tab in the image Inspector, and then point and shoot to the original PDF to create the link (see Tip 29).

TIP 129 Cropping Smart Objects

After a Smart Object is placed on a page, you may decide you don't want to use the entire image on the Web. A perfect example of this would be when you use a Photoshop image for a print piece in Adobe InDesign, but then want to use just a portion of that image on your Web site. Instead of creating and managing two versions of the same Photoshop file, just use GoLive's crop feature to customize the Target file for appropriate Web use.

Select the Smart Object in the Layout Editor and choose the Crop tool in the Inspector palette. When you select the Crop tool, a new set of options appears in the toolbar (**Figure 129**).

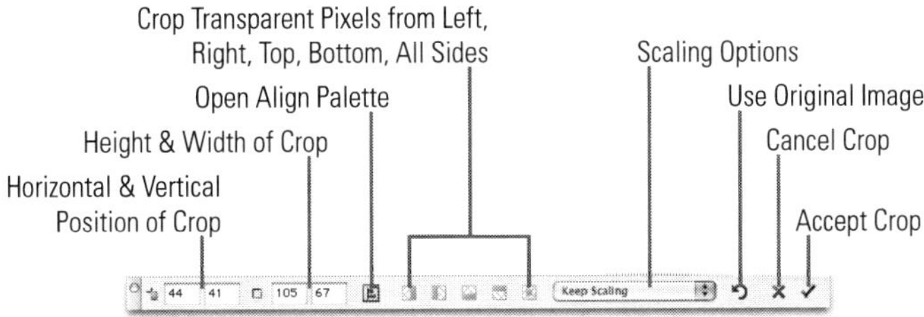

Figure 129 When cropping a Smart Object, you can use the tools in the toolbar to achieve various results, such as trimming transparent pixels from one or more sides.

Click and drag over the Smart Object you want to crop just as you would in Photoshop. As you drag, the parts of the image that will be cropped out are dimmed. Click one of the icons in the toolbar to crop transparent pixels from any or all edges of the image. If you want to align the crop to the image itself, click the Open Align Palette icon in the toolbar and use the Align palette to line up the edges perfectly. The Scaling Options pop-up list offers some neat options. For example, choose Keep Scaling if you simply want to crop off parts of the image. Select Keep Object Size, and you can then use the Crop tool to select an area that fills the image at its current size. Choose Scale to Source Size to select an area with the Crop tool and have only that area render at the image's original size.

Confirm a crop with the checkmark icon in the toolbar, cancel a crop with the X icon in the toolbar, and revert a crop with the circle arrow icon in the toolbar. Remember that any crop you make here only affects the Target file and never the Source file.

TIP 130 Scaling Smart Objects

When you scale Smart Objects, hold the Shift key to constrain the proportions of the image (**Figure 130a**). Holding Shift to constrain proportions is pretty typical in most graphics and layout applications and will probably give you the results you expect.

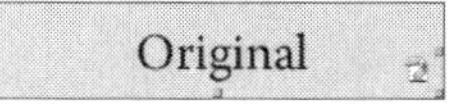

Figure 130a Hold Shift to constrain proportions when you scale a Smart Object.

However, when you scale the bounding box of a Smart Object nonproportionally, GoLive gives you three unique ways to scale the results. The option you choose will depend on the composition of the image and how it fits with the other objects on the page. The three scaling options in the Basic section of the Image Inspector are as follows:

- Exact Fit (default option)—This option forces the image to fill the entire bounding box of the image. If the Smart Object is resized nonproportionally, the image will be distorted (**Figure 130b**).

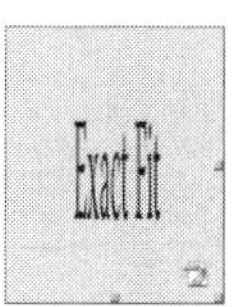

Figure 130b Resize a Smart Object nonproportionally with Exact Fit, and the image will be distorted.

- No Border—If you scale a Smart Object proportionally with this option, nothing peculiar happens, and the image just scales. It gets interesting when you scale the Smart Object nonproportionally (from an edge or the corner without the Shift key). The No Border option maintains the proportions of the image and fills the entire image's bounding box with image data. If the proportions are uneven, then any extra pixels are cropped off (**Figure 130c**). This setting is great if you want to use text variables in Smart Objects for navigation buttons but want the images to be different sizes.

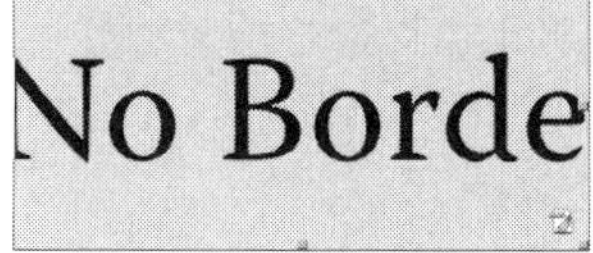

Figure 130c The No Border option crops image data but preserves the proportions of the image.

(continued on next page)

- Show All—This option scales the image proportionally as large as possible within the image's bounding box and adds transparent or matte-colored borders to whichever sides need the padding (**Figure 130d**). This setting is particularly helpful if you have a Smart Object that needs to be resized to fill a table cell or a template region but you don't want to crop off any of the image data.

Figure 130d The Show All option maintains image proportions, crops nothing, and adds padding as needed.

TIP 131 Matting Smart Objects

Have you ever tried to eliminate the amateur-looking white fringe around transparent images? It's normally a pain in the you-know-what, but with GoLive Smart Objects it's a piece of cake.

First, place a Source file that has a transparent background. Then select the Matte field in the Inspector palette and select the appropriate color with the Eyedropper tool from the Color palette or a swatch from the Swatches palette. When you have the right matte color selected, click the Apply button in the Inspector palette.

Here's a good before-and-after comparison of the benefits of using a custom matte color to eliminate the anti-aliased fringe. See the yucky white halo in the top example and the perfect anti-aliasing on the bottom (**Figure 131**)?

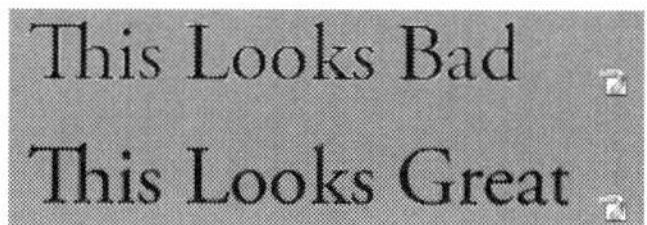

Figure 131 Use the matte feature for Smart Objects to remove the amateur-looking white fringe on transparent images.

Adjusting matte works with Adobe Photoshop, Illustrator, and PDF files and even works with target file formats that don't support transparency, such as JPEG.

Note
Smart Illustrator objects that use the SVG or SWF format do not support a matte color.

One-Click Trick

Another way to set the matte color is with contextual menus. Just Control-click (Mac) or right-click (Windows) on the Smart Object in the Layout Editor and select the appropriate option. Select Background to quickly matte the transparency to the background color of the Web page as defined in the HTML code.

TIP 132 Tracing Images

Cropped Images Are Smart Objects

All the images that are cut out of a tracing image behave like Smart Objects. This means that if you make changes in the tracing image file, all the cutouts update automatically. This is an effective way to prototype new page designs quickly.

You can use a design comp from an application such as Photoshop or Illustrator as a quick way to start a new page design. Just as you can place a sheet of tracing paper over a printed design and trace over parts of it, you can place an image in the background of a GoLive page and trace parts as well. Such an image is called a *tracing image*. Open the Tracing Image palette from the Window menu, click the Source check box, and then point and shoot to the tracing image you want to use as the basis for your design. You can change the position of the tracing image as required by using the Hand tool in the palette, and you can change the opacity depending on how much you visibility you need (**Figure 132**).

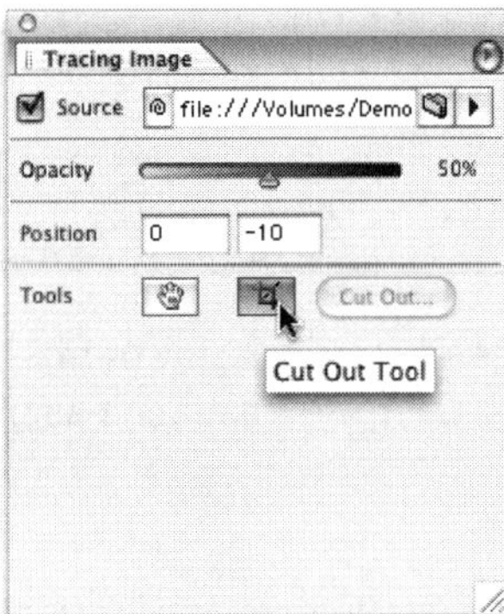

Figure 132 Use the Tracing Image palette to place an image in the background of a page and then cut out the parts you want to use.

Next, start cropping. Drag the Crop tool over the part you want to use, and click Cut Out to use that piece. When you cut out a part of the tracing image, the Save For Web window opens—this is where you set the compression options and save the resulting image into your site. The cutout pieces are automatically placed into CSS layers, and you can easily rearrange the layers to experiment with the layout. When you're done, you can turn off the tracing image by disabling the Source check box in the Tracing Image palette.

If you want to convert the design to a layout grid, select the Convert to Layout Grid command in the Layers palette menu. If you want to then convert the layout grid to a table, click Special > Layout Grid to Table and click OK.

TIP 133 Organizing Smart Objects

We're convinced Smart Objects will save you so much time that that you'll want to use them as often as possible. Managing lots of files in the SmartObjects folder could get unwieldy, so to manage them more effectively, create subfolders in the SmartObjects folder in the Extras tab of the Site window.

To begin, select the SmartObjects folder in the Extras tab of the Site window and click the new folder icon in the toolbar to create a subfolder (**Figure 133**). Notice you can even create subfolders inside subfolders. Give the new subfolders logical names and organize them however you want.

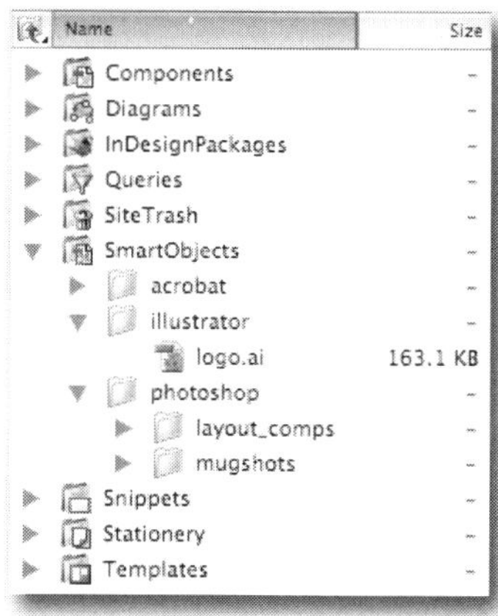

Figure 133 Use subfolders to organize your Smart Object Source files.

By storing your Source files in the GoLive Site window, you leverage the powerful site-management capabilities of GoLive and gain an extra level of control over how your files are organized. For example, you can create subfolders for different file types such as Photoshop, Illustrator, and PDF. Another option would be to organize the files according to the different phases of the design cycle, such as originals, retouched, and final.

TIP 134 Updating Pages Based on the Library

GoLive generally does a great job of automatically updating pages that use library items such as templates and components, but sometimes it needs a little nudge. For example, if you repackage an InDesign layout or make changes to a Smart Object on a closed page, you can force GoLive to update all the dependent pages with a quick menu command.

Open the Site window and select Site > Update Files Dependent On > Library. GoLive checks all the library items (templates, components, snippets, Smart Objects, and InDesign Packages) and updates all the pages in your site as necessary (**Figure 134**).

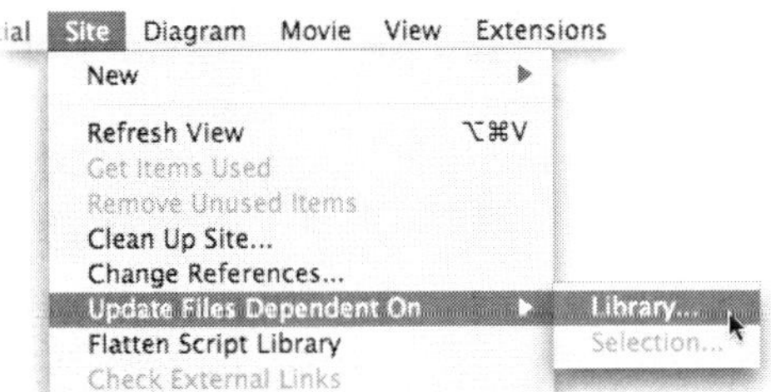

Figure 134 You can force pages with library items to update in the Site window.

To force pages to update based on a specific library item, select the files in the Extras tab of the Site window and choose Site > Update Files Dependent On > Selection.

TIP 135 Integrating with Version Cue

Version Cue is a new workflow-management tool that comes with the Creative Suite and adds versioning and checkout features to all the CS applications. Users of the Web Workgroup Server will recognize Version Cue as the latest version of this powerful collaboration technology. In this tip, we cover a few of the basics that you'll need to know to get started with Version Cue. Version Cue is installed by default with the Creative Suite, but you have to turn it on before you can use it. You do this in the System Preferences on a Mac and in the Adobe Version Cue Control Panel in Windows (**Figure 135**).

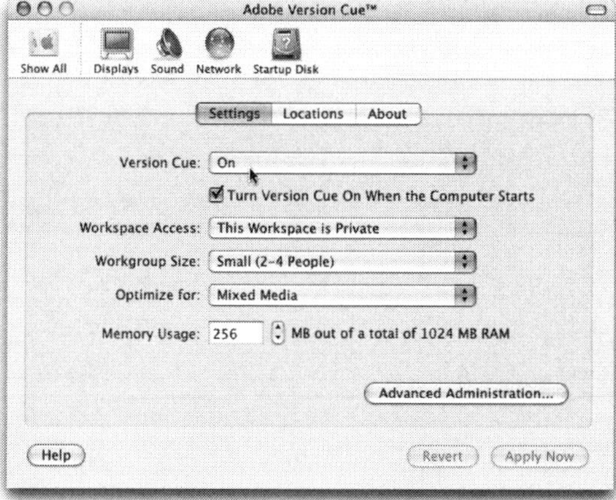

Figure 135 Turn on Version Cue in the Mac OS System Preferences or in the Adobe Version Cue Control Panel in Windows.

Note

Once Version Cue has started up, you can use it in GoLive CS. However, the other Creative Suite applications—Photoshop CS, Illustrator CS, and InDesign CS—require that you enable Version Cue in their individual preferences under File Handling.

Version Cue and the Internet

Yes, it's possible to share Version Cue files over the Internet. Just remember that to connect to a Version Cue project over the Internet from GoLive CS, you must use the Site Wizard rather than the Connect to Version Cue command in the File menu.

To create a new Version Cue project, you can use the Site Wizard (as explained in Tip 11) or you can use the administrative interface. To open the administrative interface, click the Advanced Administration button in the Version Cue preferences or Control Panel, and your default Web browser is launched. The first time you launch the admin controls, you are asked to change the System Account. Be sure to write down what you input here because you'll need it the next time you go to access the admin area. Once you're in the admin area, take note of the Help link at the upper right. It provides all the info you need to create projects, users, and more.

To mount an existing Version Cue project in GoLive CS, simply choose File > Connect to Version Cue from the menu. With a Version Cue site mounted, you can check out pages, create new versions, compare versions, roll back to previous versions, and more.

TIP 136 Understanding the Print to Web Workflow

InDesign CS and GoLive CS offer a radically new approach to repurposing print content for the Web called Package For GoLive and Import from InDesign. Design the print piece in InDesign CS however you want to, for example, and the Package For GoLive feature takes care of converting it for use in GoLive. This means you don't have to do anything special, such as tagging or structuring the content in special ways.

When the print piece is done and ready to be repurposed for the Web, click File > Package For GoLive in InDesign CS (**Figure 136a**). The package exports all the text stories to XML files, saves all the images and multimedia files into subfolders, and includes a visually accurate PDF of the original print layout.

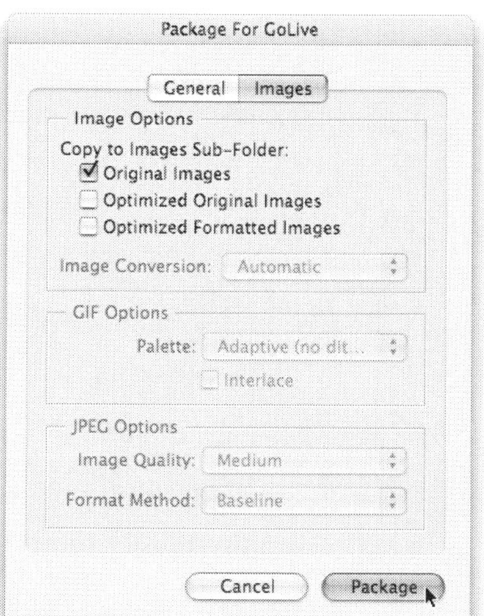

Figure 136a Package the layout for GoLive and include the original images so you can leverage Smart Objects when you place the images in your Web pages.

If you haven't already done so, design a Web page in GoLive with the look and feel and navigation you need for your site and leave room for any text, image, or video content you want to use from the InDesign package. You can even use GoLive templates to make long-term site updates easier.

Customizing the Package with Layers

If a layer is hidden in InDesign when a GoLive package is created, then the items on the hidden layer are not exported to GoLive. This is an easy way to differentiate print-specific and Web-specific design elements.

When creating the package, you can choose an option to have it automatically open when complete. If you didn't tell InDesign to open the Package automatically, choose File > Import > From InDesign in GoLive and select the InDesign Package folder you generated. When you're asked if you want the package copied into the site, click Yes. GoLive copies the package to the InDesignPackages folder in the Extras tab of the Site window. Double-click the package, and the default view of the Package window shows a PDF of the print layout, where you can change the zoom value and page number with the buttons at the bottom (**Figure 136b**).

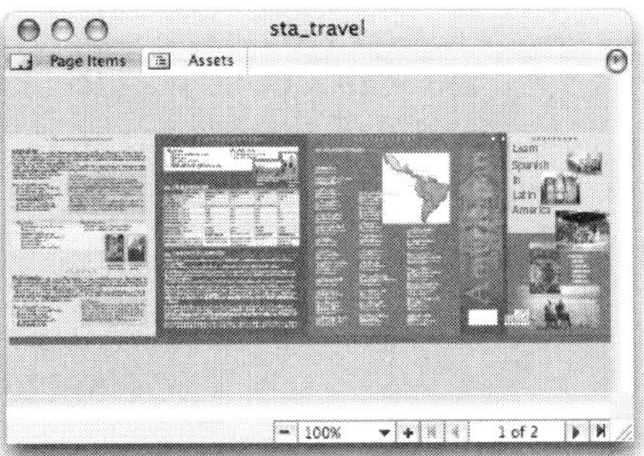

Figure 136b The Package window shows a PDF preview of the original InDesign layout.

Stories and images in the Package window are highlighted when you place your mouse pointer over them, so you can easily drag and drop chunks of content into your Web pages.

TIP 137 Finding and Selecting Package Objects

Open an InDesign Package in GoLive, and you can select objects by hovering your mouse pointer over them in the Package window. The colored highlight lets you know which item you can grab, but sometimes you'll have arranged or layered objects in InDesign in a way that makes them difficult to select in the Package window. An easy way to select overlapping objects is to Control-click (Mac) or right-click (Windows) in the Page Items view of the Package window and select the object you want from the Select submenu (**Figure 137a**).

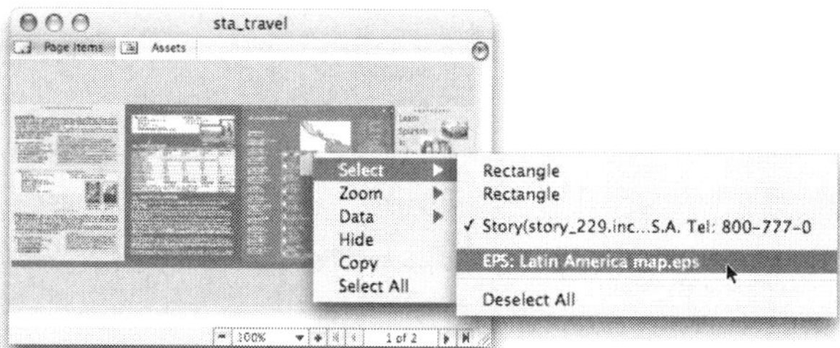

Figure 137a Use contextual menus to select stacked objects in the Package window.

Another way to select hard-to-grab objects in the Package window is to switch to the Assets section, where you can see a simple list view of all your stories, images, and multimedia content. You can search for items by filename in this list view. Control-click (Mac) or right-click (Windows) on a file in the Assets list and choose Reveal in Document to focus the selected object in the Inspector palette and confirm that it's the correct item. When you have the right item, you can drag and drop directly from the Package window into your GoLive layout (**Figure 137b**).

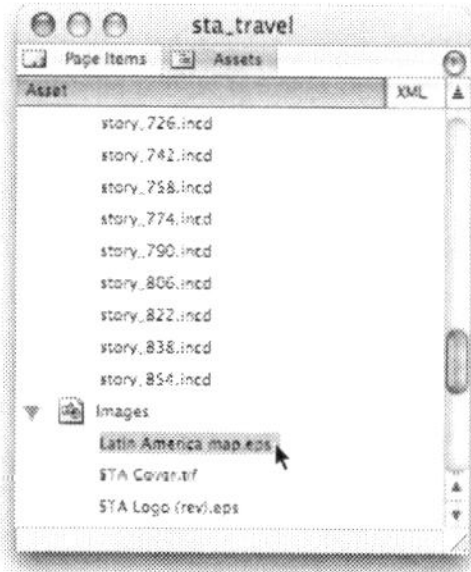

Figure 137b The Assets list makes it easy to find an object when you already know its filename.

Dragging and Dropping from the Inspector

Just as you can with a normal file in the Site window, you can drag and drop from the Inspector to the Layout Editor.

TIP 138 Placing Text, Tables, Images, and Movies from InDesign

Placing assets from an InDesign Package into your GoLive layouts is as easy and drag and drop. This tip gives some details and explains the process.

Text and Tables

When you drag text stories from the Package window into GoLive's Layout Editor, they are placed as XML components (**Figure 138**). These XML components behave just like normal components (see Tip 109), so updating your Web pages based on updates in your InDesign print layouts is a piece of cake (see Tip 142). If the InDesign story was threaded across multiple frames or multiple pages, the entire story is placed in GoLive when you drag and drop. This is a huge time-saver compared with the typical copy and paste method of content repurposing. InDesign tables work the same as text stories and are placed as an HTML table in a component.

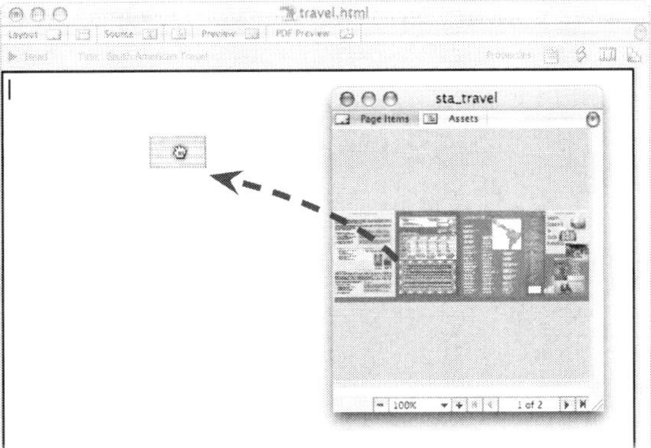

Figure 138 If you can drag and drop, you can convert InDesign layouts into Web pages with GoLive.

Images

Drag images into your Web page from the Package window, and the Save For Web dialog opens so you can resize and compress the graphics into Web-friendly formats such as GIF and JPEG. Select the appropriate image format, adjust the compression options, and click Save. Part of the magic of the package integration between InDesign and GoLive is that CMYK images are automatically converted to RGB, and high-resolution images are instantly downsampled to 72 dpi. This feature makes repurposing print content for the Web easier than ever before.

Movies and Sounds

InDesign CS now lets you place multimedia files such as QuickTime movies. To use a movie or sound from the Package window, drag and drop it into the Layout Editor just like an image. Smart Objects don't work for movies because the files tend to be larger and have very different compression factors. If you need to resize or recompress the video, you should always go back to the source footage instead of resizing the movie in the Layout Editor.

TIP 139 Customizing Package Options

When you drag a text story from the Package window into GoLive's Layout Editor, the default behavior is to place the story as an XML-based InCopy component (see Tip 131). This is what most users will want because your GoLive Web pages can be updated automatically based on changes to your InDesign layout. However, if you want to break the connection between the print and Web layouts, or if you want to edit or stylize the text in GoLive, you can place the story directly as plain text instead of as an XML component.

To change the settings for a text object in the Package window, click once to select it and then click the Options icon in the toolbar at the top of the screen. In the Content Usage pull-down menu, the default setting is Component, but if you choose Direct, then the text will place as normal HTML text instead of as a component (**Figure 139**).

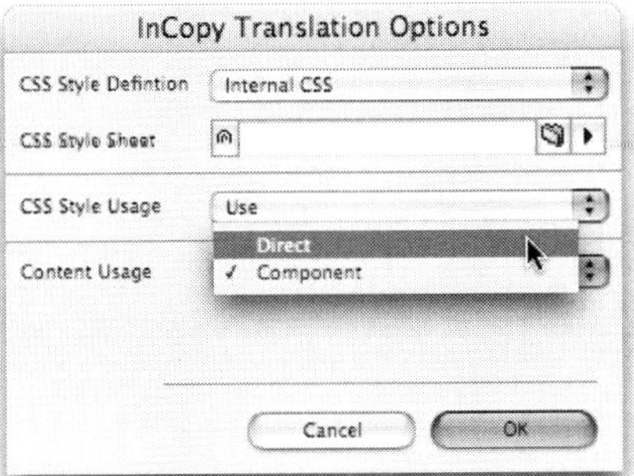

Figure 139 The InCopy Translation Options dialog lets you control how stories are translated for Web use.

GoLive also defaults to converting InDesign type styles to equivalent CSS styles (see Tip 140). If you want to place the story as plain, unstyled text, choose Do not Use from the CSS Style Usage pull-down menu. After you've adjusted the translation options, click OK and place the story with the new settings.

Applying Settings to All Package Objects

If you hold down the Option (Mac) or Alt (Windows) key when you click OK in the InCopy Translation Options dialog, your settings apply to everything in the Package.

TIP 140 Converting InDesign Print Styles to CSS

When you drag text stories from the Package window into a GoLive Web page, the character, paragraph, and nested styles can be converted to a close approximation using CSS. This is a significant time-saver that helps ensure visual consistency between print and Web publications without requiring any extra effort. Be aware that certain InDesign typography features—such as baseline shift, ligatures, tracking, kerning, hyphenation, and optical margin alignment—cannot be retained in a Web page because equivalent features don't exist in CSS.

First, select the story in the Package window and click the Settings icon in the toolbar to open the InCopy Translation Options dialog (**Figure 140**). To make sure print styles are translated to CSS styles, check that the CSS Style Usage option is set to Use. Then in the CSS Style Definition pull-down, choose from None, Internal CSS, and External CSS. You probably don't want to use None because that means none of the styles will be translated. You can use Internal CSS, but that writes the CSS definitions into every page, which is usually redundant and makes the pages harder to update. We recommend choosing External CSS and selecting a .css file from your site to use as the CSS definitions. Now when you place InDesign stories in your GoLive Web pages, the external .css file can be the default style sheet for all the package content, and GoLive will automatically link to the .css file.

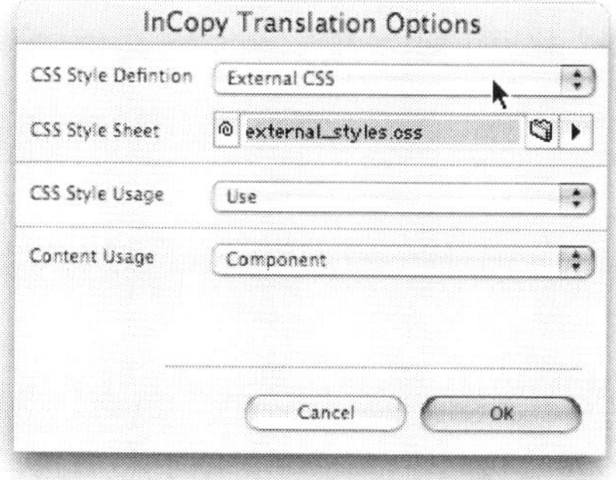

Figure 140 Adjust the InCopy Translation Options so that text from InDesign packages uses an external style sheet.

Exporting CSS from a Package

From the flyout menu in the Package window, choose CSS Styles > Save to Site. When you refresh the Site window, you'll see a new .css file based on the styles from your InDesign document. Now you can edit the .css file, and all the pages that reference that file will be updated automatically.

TIP 141 Placing Package Text as Images

Placing InDesign stories as text in GoLive is what you'll want to do most of the time, but there are always exceptions. For example, if a typographic or drop shadow effect on a headline cannot be reproduced with HTML and CSS, you may prefer to place that text as a graphic. You sacrifice some editability and download speed, but you can match the look and feel of the original print piece perfectly.

To place text or a table from an InDesign Package as a graphic, hold down the Shift key while you drag the text from the Package window to GoLive's Layout Editor. Instead of placing text, you see an image of the text converted in the Save For Web dialog (**Figure 141**). Adjust the optimization settings and image size as needed and save the final GIF into your Root folder.

Figure 141 If you can't reproduce the same effect with HTML and CSS, consider placing the text as an image.

TIP 142 Repackaging Print Layouts for GoLive

We think it's obvious that this new package feature connecting InDesign CS and GoLive CS integrates print and Web design in unprecedented ways, but what happens when your clients change their minds? Do you have to start all over again? Of course not!

Just make the changes to the print piece in InDesign CS and repackage the layout with the same filename and location as before with the File > Package For GoLive command (**Figure 142a**).

Figure 142a Repackage the InDesign layout to update the content in your Web pages.

Now switch to GoLive CS, select the updated InDesign package in the Site window, select Site > Update Files Dependent On > Selection, and watch GoLive update all the necessary Web pages with changes to the text and images (**Figure 142b**).

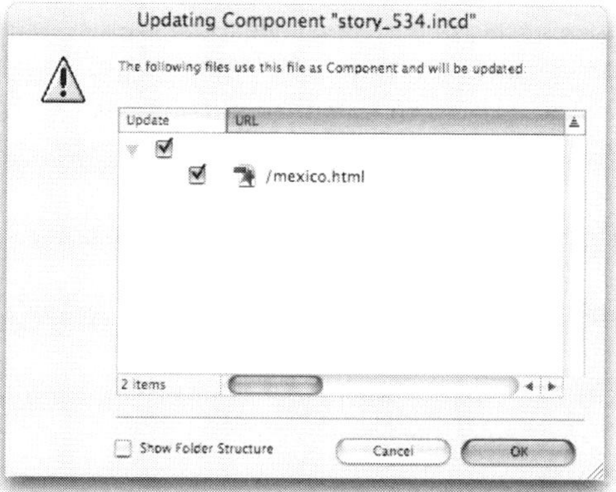

Figure 142b Update your Web site by repackaging in InDesign and updating files dependent on the package in GoLive.

TIP 143 Detaching Placed Text Components

When you place text from an InDesign package, the copy is used in GoLive as an XML component. This makes long-term content management and updates much easier, but it also makes it difficult to edit or stylize the text in GoLive.

To break the connection between the component and the InDesign package, select the component in the Layout Editor and choose Special > Detach Selected Component (**Figure 143**). Now you can edit and stylize the text in GoLive, but if you repackage the InDesign layout, this detached text doesn't update automatically.

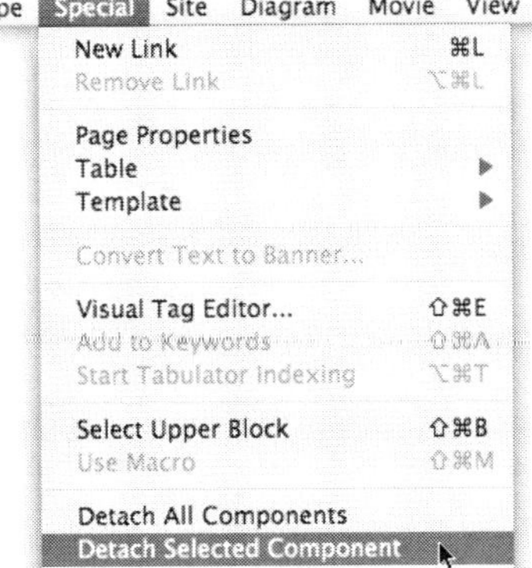

Figure 143 Detach a component, and you can edit and stylize the text as much as you want.

If you don't need or want the automatic updating of Package contents, select Special > Detach All Components to break the connection of every component on the open page.

CHAPTER EIGHT

Adding Interactivity

We adore clean-looking, well-organized Web sites that offer pertinent and timely information. We abhor gratuitous glitz used for no other reason than the designer felt like playing with cool software. That doesn't mean we are against interactivity on a Web site, though. Quite the contrary—a bit of well-thought-out interactivity can make the user's experience go from mundane to delightful.

In this chapter we take a look at various ways you can add interactivity to your Web site. We cover everything from rollovers and JavaScript Actions all the way to forms, QuickTime, Flash (SWF), and image maps. Just remember that interactivity used on a Web site should have a reason behind it. Simply sprinkling your page with flashing, flying, blinking goodies won't endear you to your audience. In fact, it may alienate them entirely. Use your judgment when adding interactivity. Ask yourself, "Does adding this animation/pop-up window/other-flashy-goodie make my visitor's experience better?" If the answer is no, or even maybe, then forget it. If the answer is yes, then GoLive's full collection of interactive tools is just what you need.

TIP 144 Creating Rollovers

Navigation Pizzazz

If you want to create a navigation bar that's more advanced than just rollover images, check out MenuMachine (see Tip 184) for building DHTML drop-down menus.

A very popular effect found on even the simplest Web sites is called a *rollover*. The name describes the effect itself, because as you *roll* your mouse *over* an image, the image's appearance is altered. But the effect can also be used when the mouse clicks the image or moves away from it.

Rollovers add subtle feedback to a page so visitors know what is clickable and what's important. Here's how to do it: Add an image to the page, open the Rollovers & Actions palette from the Window menu, select the Over state, and click the New icon near the bottom of the palette. Now use the Fetch URL tool to assign the rollover image in the URL field at the bottom of the palette. If you want to add other rollover states, such as a Click state, follow the same process.

When you assign an image to a rollover, make sure the Preload option is enabled, and GoLive will write JavaScript that automatically loads all the images when the page loads in a Web browser (**Figure 144**). If Preload is unchecked, the over state image won't download until the visitor moves his cursor over the image, where he'll probably see an undesirable delay while the second image downloads.

Figure 144 Edit your rollover states and status message in the Rollovers & Actions palette.

You can also add a status message that appears in the bottom-left corner of the browser window when a visitor hovers his cursor over the rollover image. With the Over state selected, click the Create new message icon and type the status message in the message field in the bottom of the Inspector.

TIP 145 Saving Time with Automatic Rollover Detection

Creating rollovers isn't very hard, but if you have to create lots of them for a site or a complex navigation bar it can become very tedious. GoLive makes this process easier than any other Web-authoring application in the world, and it happens to be one of our favorite features.

GoLive is one smart puppy. It can learn new tricks, such as recognizing how you name the image files that make up the multiple rollover states. When you train GoLive, it can sniff out all the required images and write all the JavaScript code, including the Preload option, automatically. To teach GoLive how you name your rollover images, choose Rollover Detection Settings from the Image Rollovers & Actions palette menu.

The rollover settings are case sensitive and support several unique naming patterns. The Rollover Detection Settings dialog includes a good explanation of how this feature works (**Figure 145a**). The default settings match the output defaults for Adobe ImageReady.

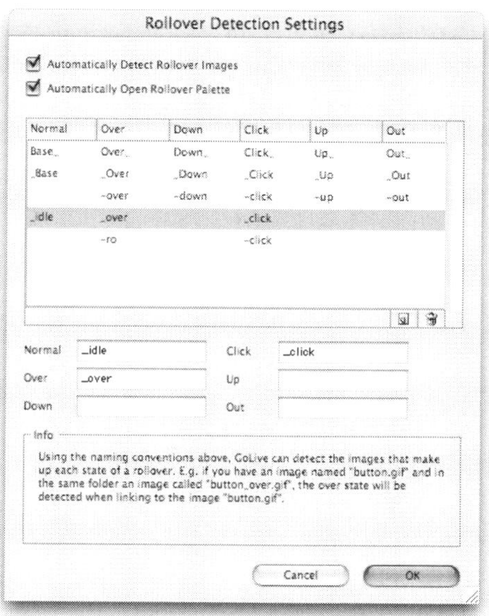

Figure 145a The Rollover Detection Settings dialog lets you tell GoLive how you name your rollover images.

After you specify how you name your rollover images, the rest is a piece of cake. Just drag and drop the Normal state image into the Layout Editor and watch in amazement as GoLive automagically finds all the images for multistate rollovers, writes all the JavaScript code, and includes preloading code. You can see all the new rollover states listed in the palette (**Figure 145b**).

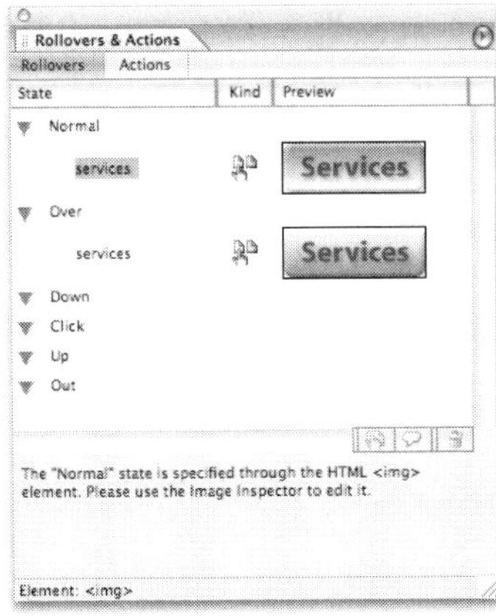

Figure 145b After GoLive detects your rollover images, you can see the results and customize the rollovers in the palette.

If you have already placed a Normal state image on your page, there's still an easy way to automatically detect the rest of the rollover images. Select the image in the layout and select Detect Rollover Images from the Rollovers & Actions palette. Voilà!

TIP 146 Finding and Installing New Actions

GoLive actions—pre-built JavaScripts that are configurable in the GoLive Interface—make building interactivity into your Web site simple and trouble free. GoLive ships with a number of actions pre-installed. The included actions perform tasks from the very simple (open a new window, set the status) to the relatively complex (write a cookie, create a password). You'll find the actions in the Adobe GoLive CS/Modules/Jscripts/Actions folder, and they are separated into subfolders related to the types of tasks they perform (**Figure 146**).

Figure 146 Actions are nestled in subfolders of the Actions folder.

When you download new third-party actions for GoLive, we recommend you install them in a subfolder called something like Third Party, because it will make it easy for you to migrate your actions the next time you upgrade GoLive to a new version. In that event, all you need to do is remove the Third Party subfolder from the Actions folder, install the upgrade, and then return the Third Party folder to the Actions folder.

Note

For a detailed look at how to install, use, troubleshoot, update, and organize GoLive actions, we highly recommend the excellent reference ebook by Mads Rasmussen called Adobe GoLive Actions for Newbies, *found at http://www.rasmussens.dk/newbies/redcross.html.*

Adobe Studio Exchange Web Site

A great place to find hundreds of actions from third-party developers is http://share.studio.adobe.com. Many actions are free, some are shareware, and some are paid commercial software.

Action! Action! Read All About It!

To learn more about some impressive third-party actions (and extensions, too), see Chapter 11. To see how GoLive's handling of JavaScript Actions stacks up against the competition, download the excellent GoLive JavaScript Actions white paper from adobe.com: http://www.adobe.com/products/golive/pdfs/gl_whtpr_js.pdf.

TIP 147 Using JavaScript Actions

Using GoLive's JavaScript Actions is quite simple. A JavaScript has to be attached to an event to run—an event such as a movement of the mouse, a keystroke on the keyboard, a browser window being opened, and so on. One of the most common triggers for a JavaScript Action is the click of a link.

Select the text or an image that will be the trigger and then open the Rollovers & Actions palette from the Window menu. Click the Actions tab, and on the left side appears a list of events to choose from. Select an event, click the New button on the right (**Figure 147a**), and then select an action from the Action pull-down menu (**Figure 147b**).

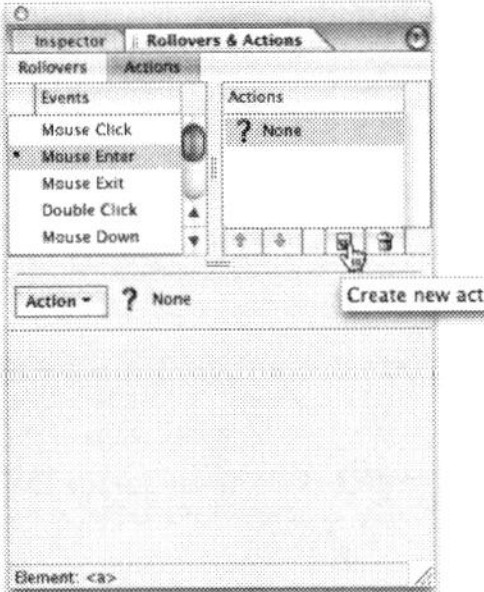

Figure 147a Select an event in the Actions palette and then click to add a new action.

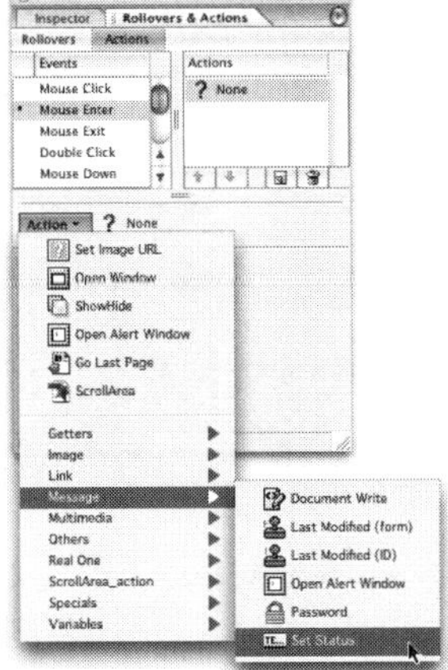

Figure 147b Choose an action from the Action pull-down list.

The numbers you see next to the action's name indicate what browsers that action is compatible with. If you want to limit the available actions to be compatible only with certain browser versions, then choose Set Action Filter in the flyout menu.

TIP 148 Creating Remote Rollovers

When visiting a Web site, you may roll your mouse pointer over a link or image and find that an image appears elsewhere on the page. This is referred to as a *remote rollover*, and in GoLive the effect is created with the Set Image URL action.

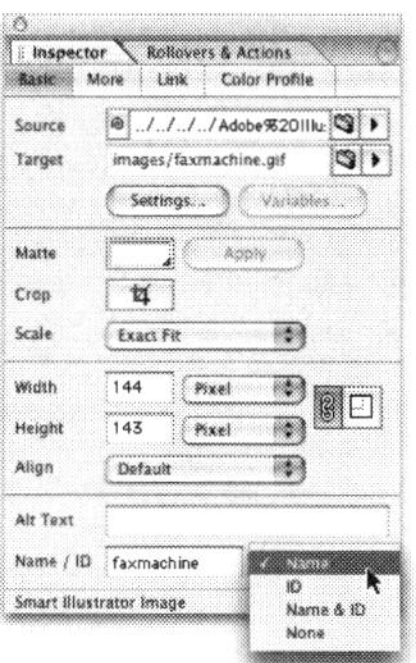

Figure 148a In the Inspector, assign a name to the image that will change.

To use Set Image URL, you'll need at least two images that are the same size. Put the one that will be swapped out on the page, select it, choose Name from the Name/ID pull-down list in the Basic tab of the Inspector, and give it a name (**Figure 148a**).

Next, select the image you want to use as the trigger and assign a Set Image URL action to the image on the Mouse Enter event using the Rollovers & Actions palette.

Note

You may also use a text link or any element that accepts the name attribute as the trigger for Set Image URL.

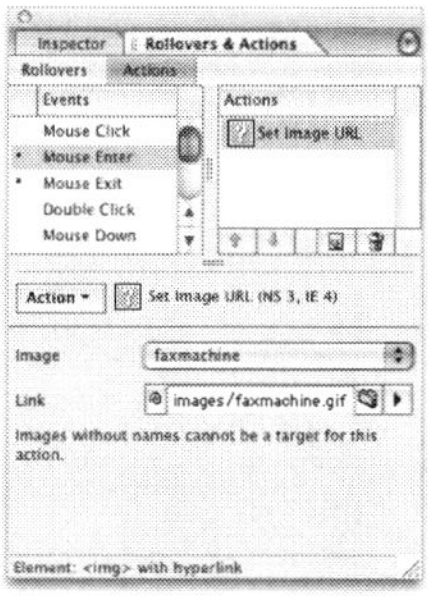

From the Image pull-down list, select the name you assigned to the first image you placed on the page and then use the Fetch URL tool to point to the image that will be used for the remote rollover (**Figure 148b**). Click Preview to test the action.

If desired, you can create another Set Image URL action and assign it to the MouseExit event. This controls what happens when you move the mouse away from the trigger. Choose the remote image by its name and reassign the image to the original state with the Fetch URL tool.

Figure 148b Choose the name of the image that will be swapped out in the Action Inspector and then choose the alternate image.

TIP 149 Flattening the JavaScript Library

The code for every action that you have installed in GoLive is stored in an external JavaScript library called CSScriptLib.js, and GoLive automatically creates the file when you use an action or a rollover in a Web site. This library file is placed into a folder called Generated Items and includes all the necessary JavaScript for the actions to function properly.

Since you're unlikely to use every single installed action in your Web sites, you won't need the library file to contain the code for all the actions, which can be quite large. You'll want to flatten it down so that it contains only the JavaScript for the actions you've used in the site. By default, the flattening process is handled by GoLive when the file is uploaded, but you can flatten it manually if you want to see what the file size will be. Choose Site > Flatten JavaScript Library or use the contextual menu to access the Flatten JavaScript Library command (**Figure 149**).

Figure 149 Flattening the CSScriptLib.js file reduces its size, sometimes dramatically.

Using an external JavaScript library means that the code for actions or rollovers used on multiple pages does not have to be reloaded with each and every page that utilizes the action. Instead, the library loads the code once, the browser caches it, and you'll get faster-loading pages. Not only that, but GoLive manages all URLs in the JavaScript library, so you can move pages around or even rename them, and all the referenced URLs will be updated as necessary by GoLive.

Creating Your Own Actions

If you are familiar with JavaScript, you may want to make GoLive actions of your own. To find instructions on how to do so, see the SDK Programmers Guide.pdf, part of the GoLive Software Development Kit (SDK) that ships with GoLive.

Trivia

The filename CSScriptLib.js has absolutely nothing to do with CSS. The CS stands for CyberStudio, which was the original name of the application before Adobe acquired it from the company named GoLive Systems.

TIP 150 Highlighting Actions

To get a quick idea of where actions are being used on your page, employ GoLive's ability to highlight actions. It's an easy way to get an overview of how many actions you're using and where they're located on the page. Select one of the following two methods to invoke highlighting:

- Choose Window > Highlight, click the Special button, and then choose JavaScript Actions (**Figure 150a**). Click Clear to turn off the highlighting.

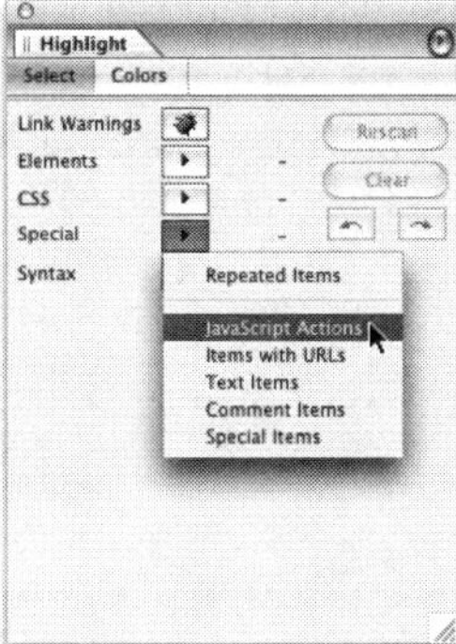

Figure 150a You can highlight actions on a page by using the Highlight palette.

- Choose Window > Rollovers & Actions, click Actions to access the Actions area, and then choose Highlight Actions in Document from the flyout menu (**Figure 150b**). This command is a toggle, so you'll need to select it again to turn the highlighting off.

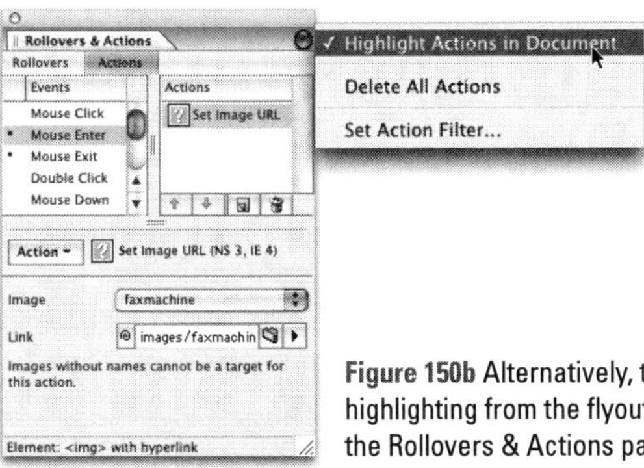

Figure 150b Alternatively, turn on highlighting from the flyout menu of the Rollovers & Actions palette.

Deleting Actions

You could locate and delete each action by hand, but that could take a long time on a complex page. Instead, just choose Delete All Actions in the flyout menu of the Rollovers & Actions palette.

TIP 151 Copying and Pasting Actions

GoLive actions are powerful, prebuilt JavaScript functions that make it easy to create interesting, useful, and interactive effects in your Web pages. With GoLive you can copy and paste actions from one link to another or from one event to another. For example, if you accidentally create an action for the wrong event, just cut and paste the action to the correct event. Also, if you create a sequence of complicated actions, you can copy and paste all those actions from one link to another.

To copy or cut an action, select it in the Actions list (the right side of the Actions palette) and then choose Edit > Copy or Edit > Cut (**Figure 151**). To paste the action onto a new link, select the link and then, in the Actions & Rollovers palette, click the Action button to enter the Actions area. Select an event from the list on the left, put your cursor into the Actions list, and choose Edit > Paste.

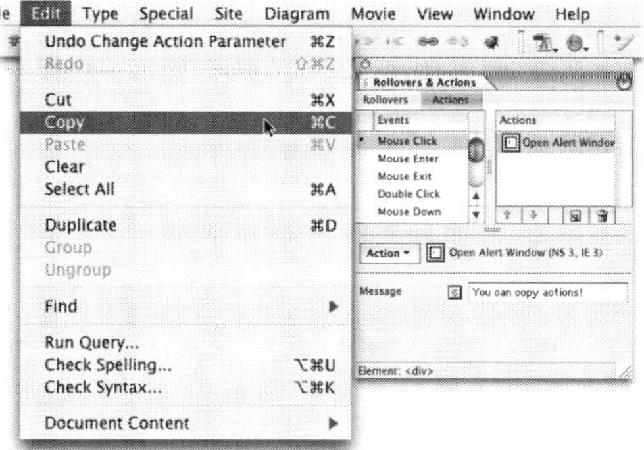

Figure 151 Copy and paste actions just like text.

Remembering Recently Used Actions

Ever notice that you seem to use a handful of actions more than others? GoLive helpfully adds recently used actions to the top of the Action pull-down menu in the Rollovers & Actions palette to make it easy to access those often-used actions.

TIP 152 Showing and Hiding Layers

A striking but easily accomplished effect created by GoLive actions is the ability to show or hide layers. For example, you may have a text link on a page that when clicked reveals a hidden layer with additional information in it. In this tip, we show you step by step how to set this up. Complete the following steps to create a ShowHide action:

1. Open a blank page and type **Hello**. Select it and type a pound sign (#) into the URL field of the Inspector.

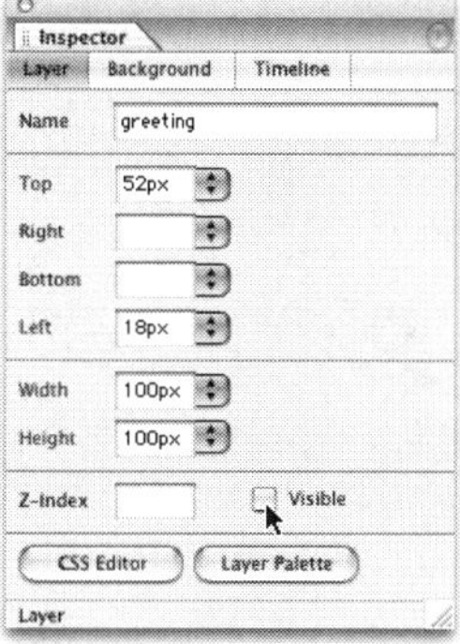

Figure 152a Name the layer and make it invisible in the Inspector palette.

2. Drag a layer onto the page and in the Layer tab of the Inspector palette name it **greeting**. Type **Hello to you, too!** inside the layer. In the Inspector palette, turn off the Visible check box. The layer will now be hidden (**Figure 152a**).

3. Select the linked word *Hello*. In the Actions area of the Rollovers & Actions palette, choose Mouse Click for the Event, click New to create a new action, and then select Multimedia > ShowHide from the Action pull-down menu.

4. Select greeting from the Layer and Show from the Mode pull-down menus (**Figure 152b**).

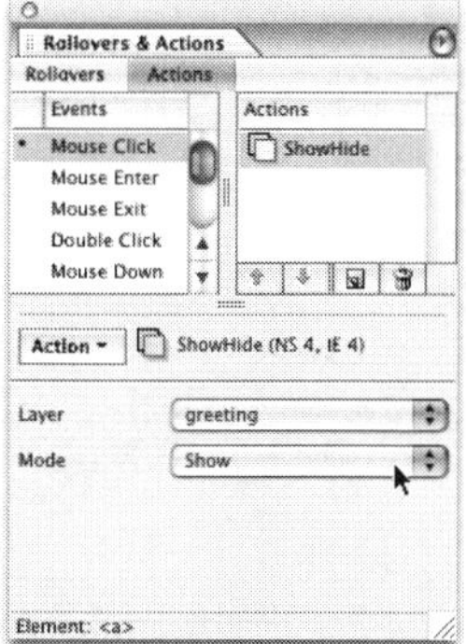

Figure 152b Choose a ShowHide action and designate the layer you want to show or hide.

Now click Preview at the top of the page and click the link. The hidden layer should appear, showing you the response. It's that easy. You may also choose Toggle as the mode, which would allow the layer to be shown and then hidden with each subsequent click of the link.

TIP 153 Opening New Windows

Little windows that pop up without warning are a nuisance, but a window that opens when a user needs more information can be an effective design solution. In this tip, we show how easy it is to create just such a new window. Follow these straightforward steps:

1. Select text and create a link by typing a pound sign (#) into the URL field of the Inspector palette. (You can also use an image for the link—just select the image and use the Link tab of the Inspector to create the link.)
2. In the Rollovers & Actions palette, select the event to use as a trigger. In this example we'll use Mouse Click.
3. Create a new action by clicking the New button on the right.
4. Select Link > Open Window from the Action pull-down menu.
5. In the Actions palette, choose the options for your window. In this example, we made a window 300x300 pixels in size and disabled the browser's Menu and Tools options (**Figure 153**).

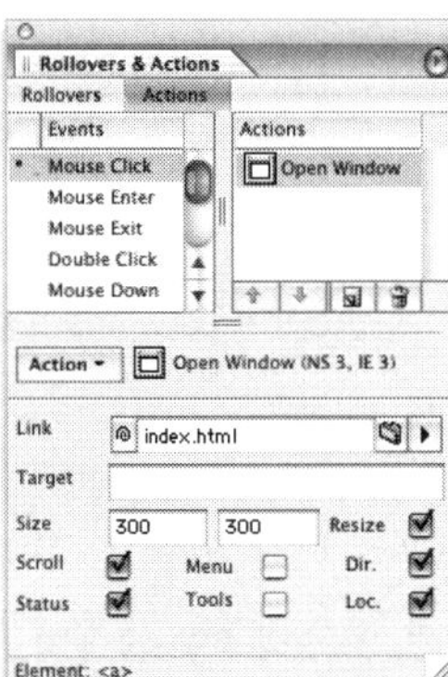

Figure 153 Set options for your window in the Actions palette.

6. Create a new window in any size and with or without the browser interface features such as scroll bars or menus. Use the Fetch URL tool to link to the page that will load into the new little window.

You'll need to preview this action in a browser, because GoLive's preview will not open a new window for you. Click the Preview in Browser icon on the toolbar and click the link to open the new window.

Closing Windows

This action is the simplest of all actions. To close a page, add a link saying something like "Close This Window." Then attach the Close Window action to the Mouse Click event. When the user clicks the link, the window goes buh-bye.

TIP 154 Randomizing Images

If a picture is worth a thousand words, what are three pictures worth? Six pictures? Instead of forcing yourself to pick that one perfect image for a Web page, you can choose from several images and let GoLive randomize the display every time a visitor loads the page. It's easy to set up with JavaScript Actions when you follow these steps:

1. Add the base image to the page just like a normal image. If all the images are the same dimensions, leave the dimensions as pixels in the Inspector. If the images are not the same size, then set the image dimensions to Image in the Inspector.

2. Select the image in the page and give the image a unique name in the Basic tab of the Inspector. Limit the name to letters and numbers to keep things simple (**Figure 154a**).

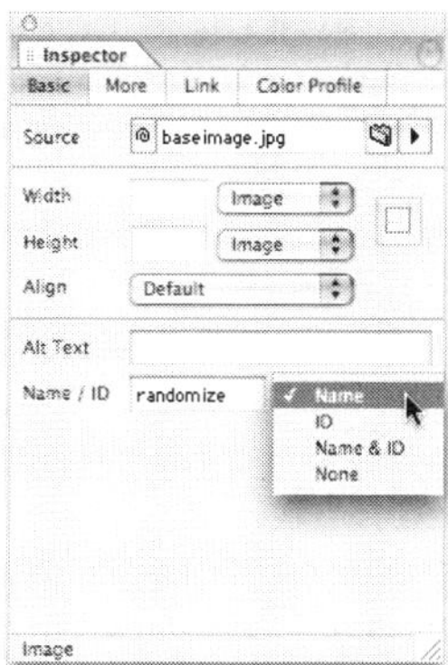

Figure 154a Name the image in the Inspector so you can control it with JavaScript Actions.

3. Add a head action (see Tip 147) to the page, open the Rollovers & Actions palette from the Window menu, and switch to the Actions tab.

(continued on next page)

4. With the head action still selected, choose On Load in the Events menu and pick Images > RandomImage from the Action pull-down menu (**Figure 154b**).

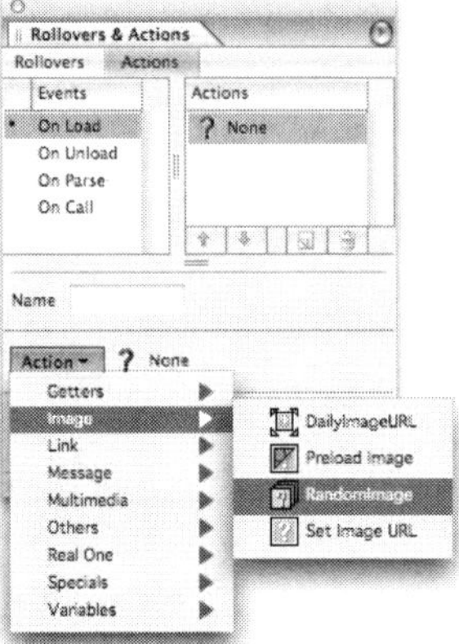

Figure 154b Set the Random Image action to occur when the page loads so the visitor instantly sees the random image.

5. Decide which three images you want to randomize and assign them in the bottom of the palette (**Figure 154c**).

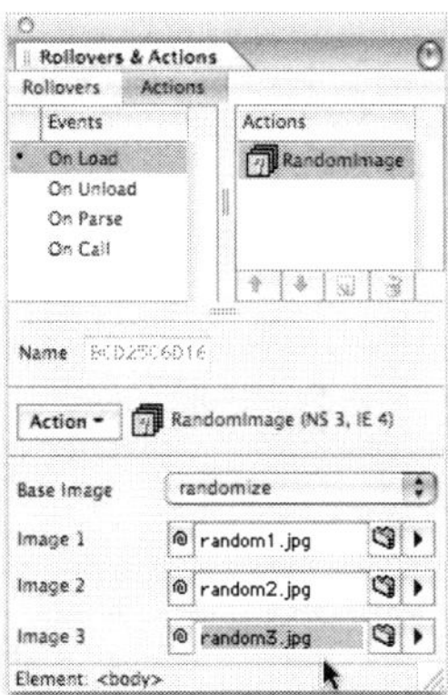

Figure 154c Assign the random images at the bottom of the palette.

6. To see the Random Image effect, preview the page in a Web browser (see Tip 83). Reload the page several times to see the image change.

Bonus Tip

If three images aren't enough, you can try the free 6 Random Images action from http://share.studio.adobe.com/axAssetDetailSubmit.asp?aID=3867. Make sure you remove the default Random Image action so they don't conflict.

TIP 155 Targeting Two Frames

When you create a link in a page of a frameset, you always assign a target to the link so the Web browser knows which frame to open the link into (See Tip 64). Usually this works fine, but what happens when you have a more complicated frames design? For example, maybe you need one link to change two frames to update a navigation frame and a content frame. Use the Target2Frames action to change two frames simultaneously with one link. Just follow these steps:

1. Create a frameset with at least three frames and make sure all the frames have unique names.
2. Select the text or image you want to use and assign the link by clicking the Link icon in the toolbar.
3. Open the Rollovers & Actions palette from the Window menu, select the Mouse Click event on the left, and click the New Action icon on the right. Then choose Link > Target2Frames from the Action pull-down menu. Notice GoLive automatically adds a pound sign (#) as the link destination in the Inspector. Leave this as is and don't add a custom link because the action will do all the linking for you.
4. Set the two frames and the pages you want to load into those frames at the bottom of the palette (**Figure 155**).

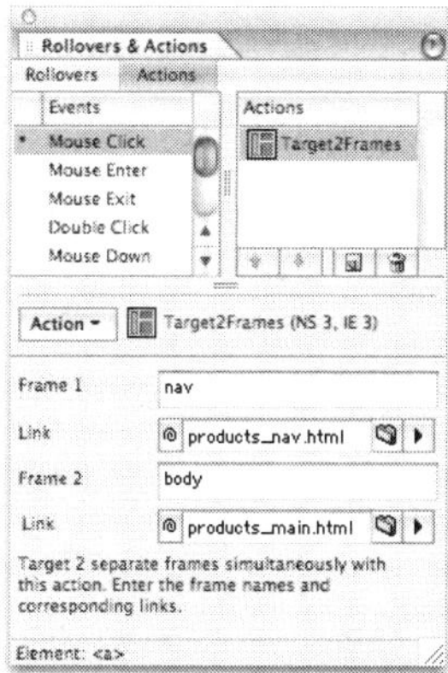

Figure 155 Set the action parameters in the palette and test in a Web browser.

5. Preview the frameset in a Web browser to check the results. Voilà!

TIP 156 Creating Forms

Forms are a great way to gather information and feedback (and maybe even orders) from your Web site visitors. To create a form, start by dragging a form container from the Forms section of the Objects palette into the Layout Editor.

You must place the rest of your Form objects inside the form container for them to work properly. Adding a table to the form container is generally a helpful way to organize all the form fields and their labels. There are more than a dozen different form elements you can use within GoLive. Here are descriptions of the items you'll use most frequently:

- Text Field —Use these for short text entry such as name, email, and street address.
- Passwords —This works the same as a text field except when the user enters text it is rendered as bullets or asterisks. This is an effective way to guard sensitive information such as passwords and credit card numbers from prying eyes.
- Text Area —This is like a special text field that can have multiple lines for longer entries. It's perfect for a comment or question field.
- Check Box —Use check boxes when more then one answer might be appropriate. For example, if your form asked us for our favorite flavor of ice cream, we'd want to check vanilla, strawberry, *and* chocolate.
- Radio Button —Use a radio button when asking an either/or question. For example, are you male or female?
- Popup —These are great when you want to ask your visitor to pick from a predetermined list of options. For example, what state are you from?

- Label —After you create all your form elements you should label each one with a label object.
- Submit Button —Every form needs a Submit button so the visitor can send a response.
- Reset Button —A reset button isn't necessary, but it's helpful if the visitor makes mistakes and wants to start over.
- Hidden —The visitor won't actually see hidden form fields (thus the name), but the values of hidden fields are stored in the code of the page and submitted with the rest of the form data. You may or may not need to use these fields, depending on how your hosting provider supports form submissions.

When you're done creating the form, select the form container again in the Layout Editor and give it a name in the Name/ID field in the Inspector (**Figure 156a**). You also need to set the form action in the Inspector according to the instructions you receive from your hosting provider or system administrator. Set the Method option to Post and you're pretty much done.

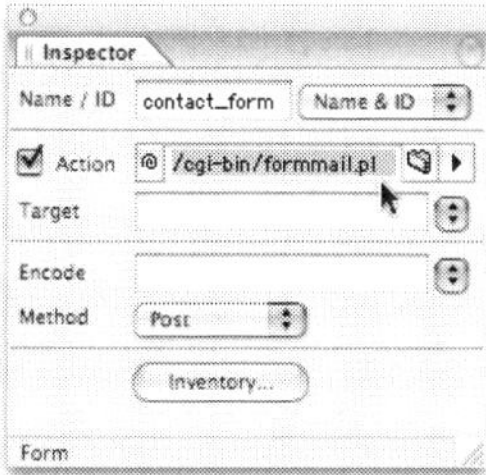

Figure 156a Set the form's name, action, and method in the Inspector.

Contact Your Hosting Provider

We wish there were an easy solution, a proverbial silver bullet, that we could tell you about to make your forms submit to a database or send to an email account. Unfortunately, there are so many different ways to do it (PHP, ASP, JSP, Lasso, Perl, and AppleScript, to name a few) that it depends in each case on the configuration at your hosting provider. Please contact your hosting company or server administrator, not us, for details.

Depending on how your hosting provider sets up its form-to-email solution, you might need a little configuration file listing all the fields in the form. Instead of retyping all these by hand, click the Inventory button in the Form Inspector to open the Form Inventory dialog (**Figure 156b**). Click the top Export button to export the form element names to a text file and click OK when you're done.

Figure 156b Export all the field names with the Form Inventory dialog.

There are also a few key form-related actions and extensions you should know about:

- Form Element Extractor—For an even better form inventory, check out the free extension from Ken Martin at http://www.kpmartin.com/Downloads/.
- Smart Forms—Save yourself tons of time creating repetitive form elements with this free extension (see Tip 189).
- VerifyForm—Use this powerful commercial action to verify and reformat forms data before your visitors click the Submit button (see Tip 199).

TIP 157 Placing QuickTime and SWF Objects

You can really go a long way with HTML, CSS, and images, but adding rich media content such as QuickTime movies and SWF animations can improve a site dramatically when done appropriately. The good news is that adding this multimedia content to a page with GoLive is as easy as drag and drop. Select the .mov or .swf in the Files tab of the Site window and drag it into the Layout Editor. GoLive will automatically add the correct height and width attributes, plug-in information, and the object and embed tags to make everything work smoothly in the browsers.

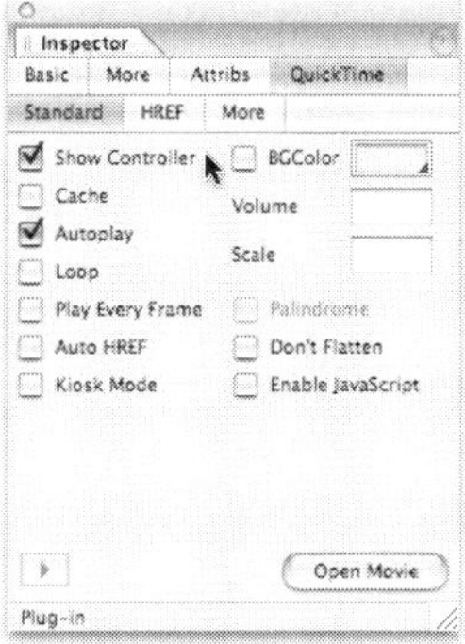

Figure 157a Adjust QuickTime-specific attributes in the QuickTime tab of the Inspector.

What's interesting about how GoLive handles multimedia content is the way the Inspector changes depending on the type of file you've placed. For example, when you place a QuickTime movie in a page, the Inspector includes a special QuickTime tab that gives you one-click access to options such as showing the controller, autoplaying the movie, and looping the video (**Figure 157a**).

When you place a Flash animation, the Inspector includes an SWF tab that lets you specify whether the movie autoplays, whether it loops, the quality of the playback, and how it scales when resized (**Figure 157b**).

Check out Tip 190 to learn how to add the Detect tab to the SWF Inspector and deploy intelligent plug-in detection code.

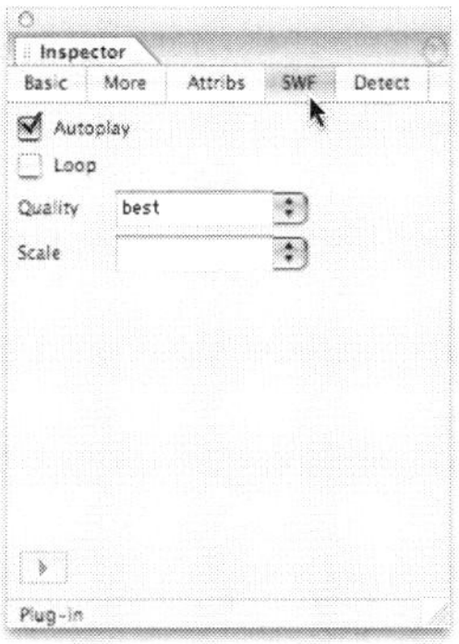

Figure 157b Control special SWF attributes in the Inspector.

TIP 158 Creating QuickTime Slideshows

GoLive includes an impressive QuickTime Web video editor, and one of its coolest features is the ability to easily create QuickTime slideshows. Follow the step-by-step instructions below and have fun!

1. Select File > New Special > QuickTime Movie and enter the dimensions of the QuickTime movie you want to create. Click OK (**Figure 158a**).

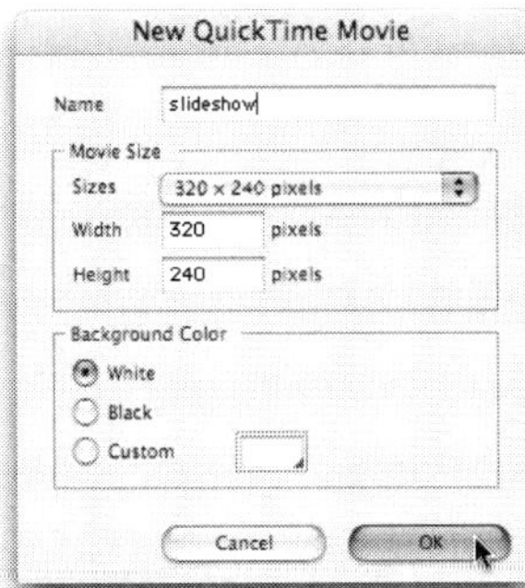

Figure 158a Create a new movie and specify the dimensions.

2. Choose Movie > Show Timeline Editor to reveal the Timeline window.

3. Drag a Picture Track from the QuickTime section of the Objects palette to the left side of the Timeline window. Change the dimensions of the Picture Track in the Inspector so they match the dimensions of the movie (**Figure 158b**).

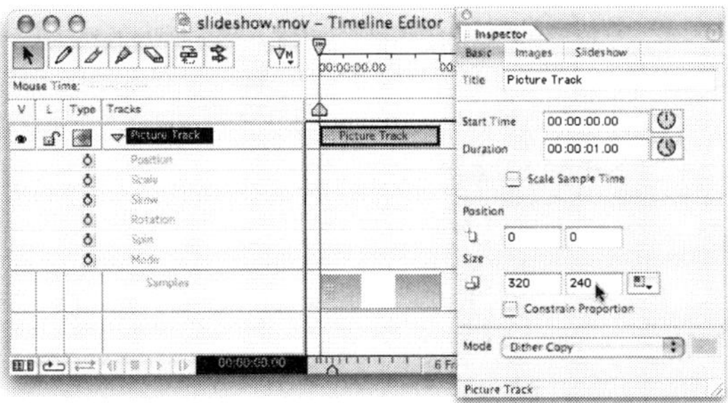

Figure 158b Match the dimensions of the Picture Track with the dimensions of the movie.

4. With the Picture Track still selected, look at the Slideshow tab of the Inspector palette. Use these options to control how long each image is visible and which transition effect, if any, you want to use (**Figure 158c**).

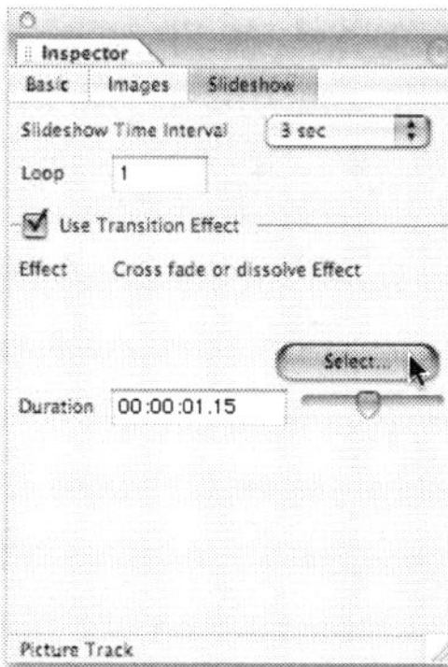

Figure 158c Adjust the slideshow delay, loop, and transition in the Inspector.

5. Now switch to the Images tab of the Inspector and prepare to import your still images. Before you click the Import button you have a few settings to check. GoLive will scale down images that are larger than your movie dimensions, so make sure the Images Constrain Proportion option is checked. If any of your images are not the same proportions or orientation as your movie, you may get a matting effect, which you can control by setting the Background Color option now (**Figure 158d**).

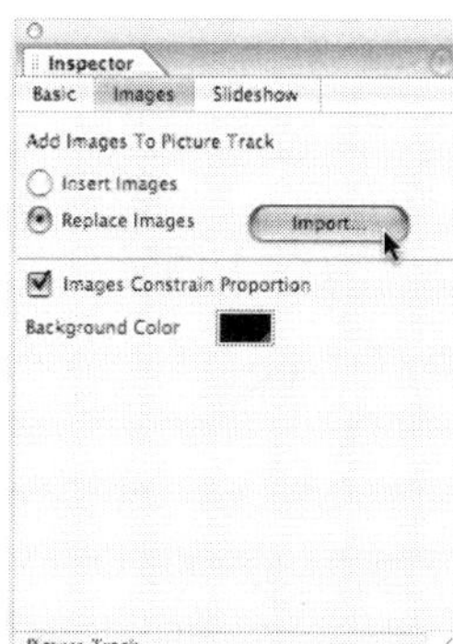

Figure 158d Adjust the image settings before you import the files.

(continued on next page)

6. Click the Import button and select the images you want in the slideshow. Because GoLive uses QuickTime technology, you can include images in many different formats (layered Photoshop, GIF, JPEG, PNG, Pict, BMP, Targa, TIFF, and so on), resolutions, and dimensions. You can even combine images from multiple folders and hard drives. When you are ready, click the Done button.

7. The next dialog prompts you to compress the images for the movie (**Figure 158e**). Because the slideshow consists of still images, we suggest using the Photo JPEG compressor as your preferred quality setting. Click OK, and GoLive will import, compress, and sequence your images with a transition.

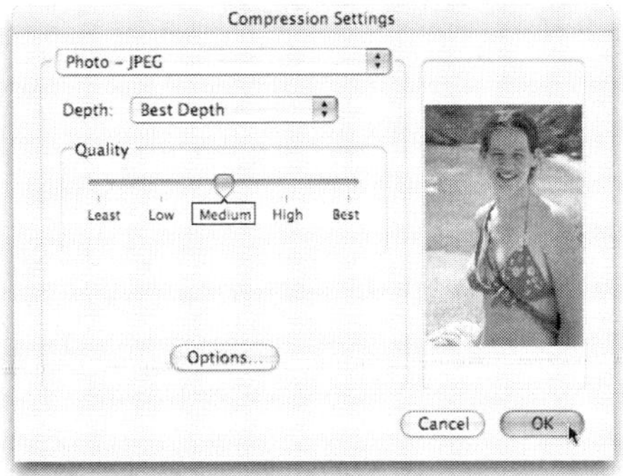

Figure 158e Choose Photo JPEG to compress the pictures in the slideshow.

8. When the slideshow is created, your Timeline window will be filled with all your still images, and a transition will be placed between each image (**Figure 158f**). To further customize your movie, double-click any of the A/B transition icons in the Timeline window to use a different transition.

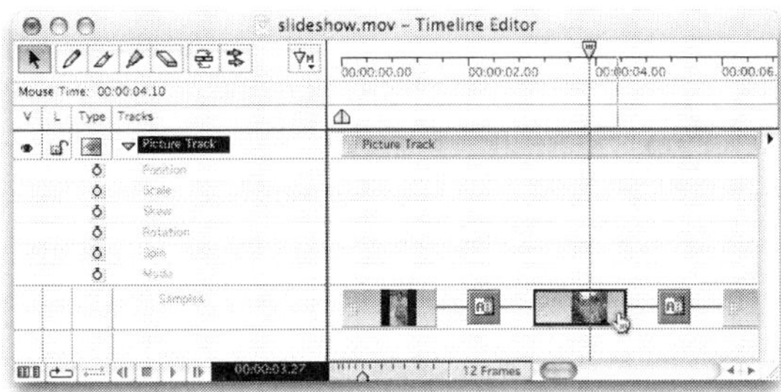

Figure 158f GoLive automatically sequences the still images and transitions for you.

9. When you're ready to save the movie, do not use the export commands because that would render each individual frame and cause the movie to have a much larger file size than necessary. Instead, choose Files > Save As and save the movie so it uses the native QuickTime transitions and minimizes the file size.

Now you can play the movie in the QuickTime Player or place it on a Web page (see Tip 157) for visitors to enjoy (**Figure 158g**).

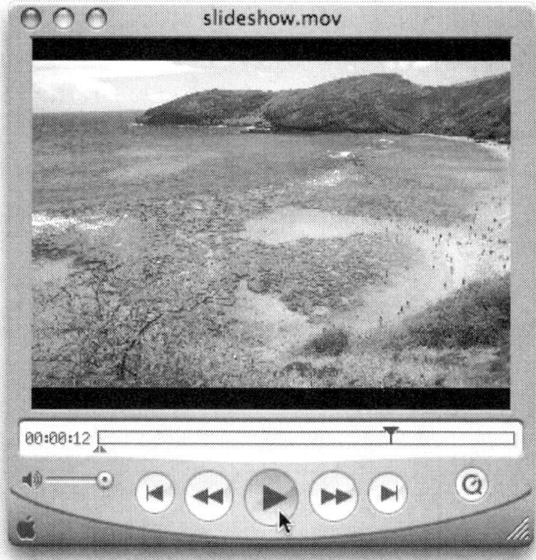

Figure 158g Anybody can view your slideshow with the free QuickTime Player from http://www.apple.com/quicktime.

TIP 159 Creating Image Maps

Image maps are just one more way to create interesting navigation bars in a page. Instead of slicing a design in Photoshop or creating a DHTML drop-down menu, image maps can be a simpler solution. Follow these easy steps:

1. Place an image in the Layout Editor and enable the Use Map check box in the More tab of the Inspector (**Figure 159a**). GoLive automatically adds a unique name for the map in the Name field, but you can customize this if you want. Also, notice the addition of a little yellow square with the letter M [M] in the Layout Editor. This is a visual indicator that there's an image map on the page.

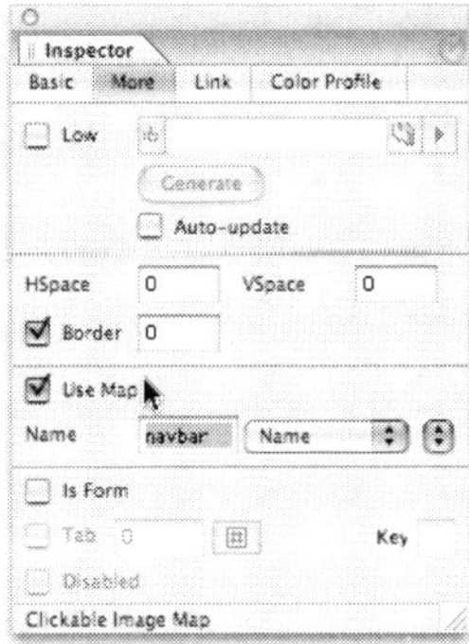

Figure 159a Turn a normal image into an image map by clicking the Use Map option in the Inspector.

2. Now look at the toolbar and see how it changed to offer the tools you need to draw hotspots (clickable areas) with hyperlinks (**Figure 159b**). To create a rectangular or circular hotspot, select the tools in the toolbar and click and drag on the image map in the Layout Editor. To create a polygonal hotspot, select the tool and click repeatedly with the mouse to create the corner points of the custom shape.

Figure 159b Use the tools in the toolbar to draw out the image map regions.

3. When you're done creating the map areas, select each one and assign a hyperlink in the URL field of the Inspector (**Figure 159c**).

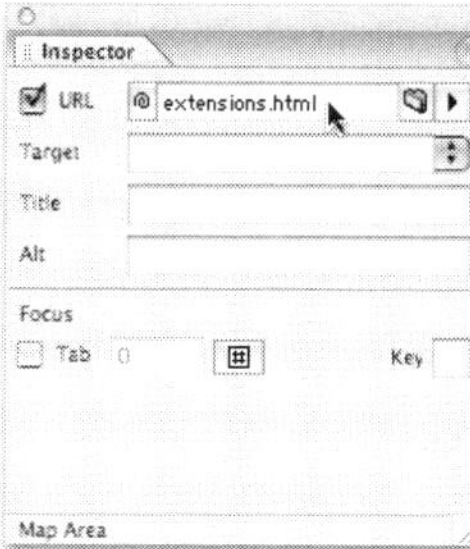

Figure 159c Assign hyperlinks to the hotspots just like a normal link.

Now that we have the basics out of the way, we want to show you a few power user tips you're going to love:

- To create several hotspots of the same size, as for a navigation bar, create one hotspot and copy and paste the rest. This will create multiple hotspots with the exact same dimensions.
- If you have a hard time positioning an image map hotspot exactly where you want it, select the hotspot and use the Transform palette to fine-tune its size and position.
- It can also be challenging to line up your hotspots evenly. Hold down the Shift key to select multiple hotspots and use the Align palette to tidy things up.
- You can zoom in on an image map without zooming the entire page. To get better control over very intricate image maps, hold down your Shift key and resize the image proportionally from the bottom-right corner so it's larger. Your image will get larger, and the hotspots will stretch accordingly. Now adjust the hotspots as required. Click the Set to original size icon ☐ in the Basic tab of the Clickable Image Map Inspector, and the hotspots will scale proportionally to fit.

CHAPTER NINE

Advanced Site Management

One of our favorite true stories happened the day Adam was finishing a huge 7,500-page site with GoLive. Two hours before the site was supposed to go live, the client called and asked for some "minor last-minute changes." Adam knew that no last-minute change was minor, but he listened to the requests anyway.

What would surely have been a real nightmare with other Web-design software turned out to be a quick two-minute change with GoLive. It took longer to upload the updated files than it did to make the actual changes. The project was on time to the day and 15 percent under budget, and we wouldn't have done the site with anything but GoLive.

There are so many cool things you can create with GoLive, but at the end of the day one of the most important factors to meeting (or even beating) a project deadline is powerful site management. We like the fact that GoLive CS can handle really large sites faster than ever before. We love the fact that we have multiple undos even with site-management tasks. And we appreciate that GoLive tracks hyperlinks in HTML, XHTML, CSS, JavaScript, PDF, QuickTime, and SWF.

Features like these allow you to work quickly and creatively, and you never have to worry about broken links or missing images. Even all the third-party actions and extensions (see Chapter 11) work seamlessly with the link-tracking features of the Site window.

TIP 160 Using Find and Replace in a Document

Situation: You've landed a job renovating the neglected Web site of a medium-sized business. None of the pages is currently based on a template, nor is data stored in a database. You have every intention of implementing both of those features in the future, but the task at hand is to immediately correct and update the information on the static pages.

Not that long ago such a scenario would cause the Web designer to openly weep, but these days we use Find and Replace to quickly handle these kinds of edits. The find commands are located in the Edit menu. A number of submenu items are nested under Find: Find Content, Find Next, Find Previous, Find Selection, Enter Find String, Replace, Replace & Find Next; some of these options will be grayed out until you've performed at least one find operation. Knowing when and how to use these commands is the key to successfully performing edits with ease.

Open the page where you want to perform a find operation, choose Edit > Find > Find Content, and click the In Current Document button. You can type, paste, or drag text or syntax into the input box at the top (**Figure 160**).

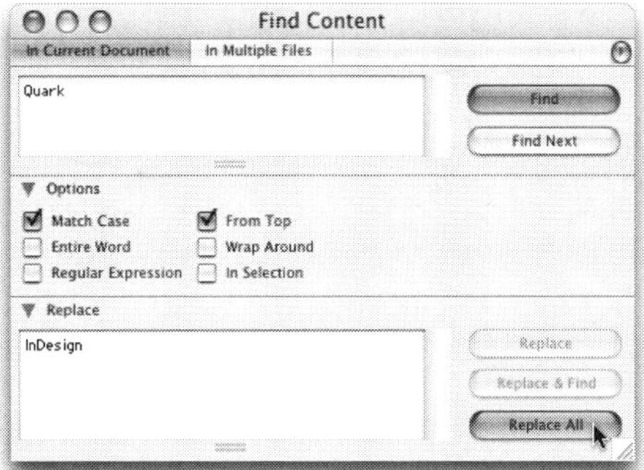

Figure 160 To run a find operation on a single page, click the In Current Document tab and select from the available options.

Toggle open the Options section to select options for your search:

- Match Case—Enable Match Case if you want the case of letters to be considered—for example, you want to find *web* but not *Web*.
- Entire Word—Select Entire Word if you want a word to be found only if it exists on its own—for example, to find *and* but not *handsome*.
- Regular Expression—Enable Regular Expression if you want to use wildcards in your search operation, but be careful! If you don't know what you're doing, you could wreak havoc on your pages.
- From Top—If you click From Top, the search will start at the top of the page. Otherwise it will begin at the location of the cursor.
- Wrap Around—Wrap Around will perform the search from the cursor to the end of the page and then go to the top and end up back at the cursor again.
- In Selection—To run the find operation on a selection only, enable In Selection.

Note
To search for text, run the find operation in the Layout, Source, or Outline Editor; to search for syntax, use the Source or Outline Editor.

To replace the found item with other text or syntax, type the replacement into the Replace input box. With your options selected and replacement specified, you're ready to run the search. To begin, click the Find button. If a match is found, it will be highlighted on the page. Click Find Next to move on to the next instance or click Replace to replace the found item with what you have in the Replace input box. Click Replace & Find to both replace the found item and move on to the next instance. If you want to replace all found instances, click Replace All.

Look What I Found!

GoLive has a clever feature that enables you to run additional searches without reopening or bringing the Find Content window back into focus. If you've previously run a search, you'll notice that additional Find commands such as Find Next become available in the Find submenu. Simply by using the associated keyboard shortcuts you can run find operations on your page without even using the Find Content window.

TIP 161 Using Find and Replace in Multiple Documents

The Find Content window has a tab labeled In Multiple Files that enables you to run searches on more than one document at a time on either text or HTML. Click this tab if you need to perform a global Find and Replace operation across multiple pages in a site. The options in this section are the same as those used in the In Current Document area (see the previous tip). The difference here is that you must specify whether to search for text in Layout Mode, Text in Source Mode, or Code Elements by selecting one of those choices from the pull-down menu (**Figure 161a**).

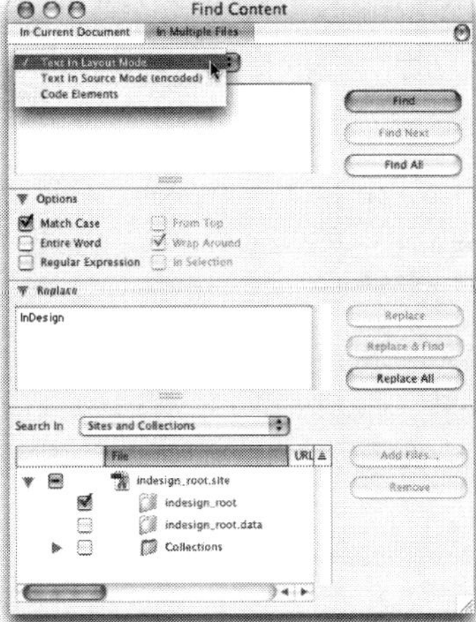

Figure 161a Select a search method from the pull-down menu in the In Multiple Files section of the Find Content window.

If you elect to search for text, you'll see the standard replace options in the input box below. However, if you choose Code Elements, the lower portion reads "Change" and offers an additional pull-down menu with options for how the found element should be treated (**Figure 161b**).

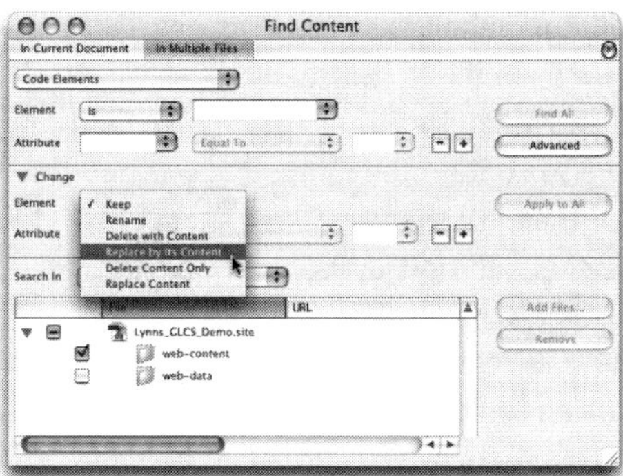

Figure 161b The Element pull-down offers six options for handling the found code.

The Search In pull-down menu offers three choices:

- Sites and Collections—Selecting this option puts all opened sites into the list. Enable the check box next to whichever one you want to search in. You can even toggle open the site and search only in the web-content or web-data folder of that site. You can select more than one by checking off more than one check box.
- Files—If you only need to search a particular set of files, choose this option and click the Add Files button to add files into the list.
- Results List—If you have previously run a search, you can use the results list that was returned as a basis for a new find operation.

Click Find All to find all matches. In the results window, the number in the Hits column indicates how many times the item was found in each searched document (**Figure 161c**). Double-click a file in the results list to open the file and see the first match highlighted.

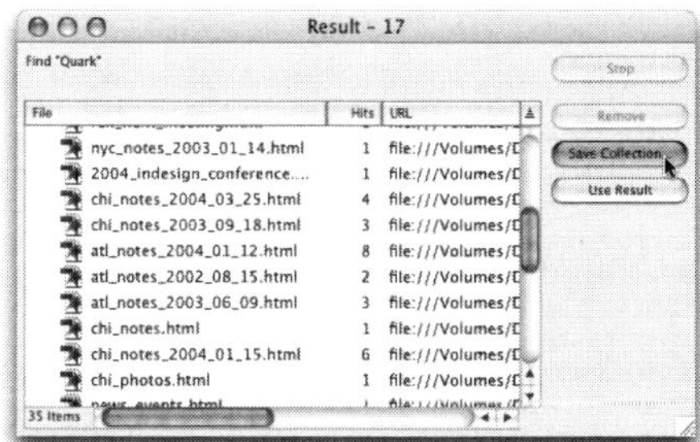

Figure 161c The results list not only shows which documents contain the found item, but also how many times the item was found within each page.

Drag and Drop Files into the Find Window

An easy way to add a group of files into the Find Content window is to select them in the Site window and drag them directly into the Search input box.

Using Regular Expressions

If you would like to use wildcard searching, also known as regular expressions or regex, GoLive gives you a head start by offering a number of frequently used search patterns that you can select from the Find Content flyout menu.

TIP 162 Saving and Loading Searches

If you need to get really granular when you run a search, you can take advantage of GoLive's ability to run searches on the results of previous searches. Say you want to find a set of files that contain the word *heartache* and also contain the word *backache*. You can first search for *heartache* and then use the results from that search to run another search for *backache*. Additionally, you can save the results as a collection for use in other ways (see Tip 163).

To use the results of one search as the basis of another search, click the Use Results button in the results list. The results will automatically be loaded into the Search In input box in the Find Content window. You can remove items from the list before using the results if you'd like.

To save the results as a collection, click the Save Collection button. The Create a New Collection dialog will open, enabling you to give a name to the collection (**Figure 162**). As with the Use Results option, you can delete files from the results list before saving it as a collection if necessary.

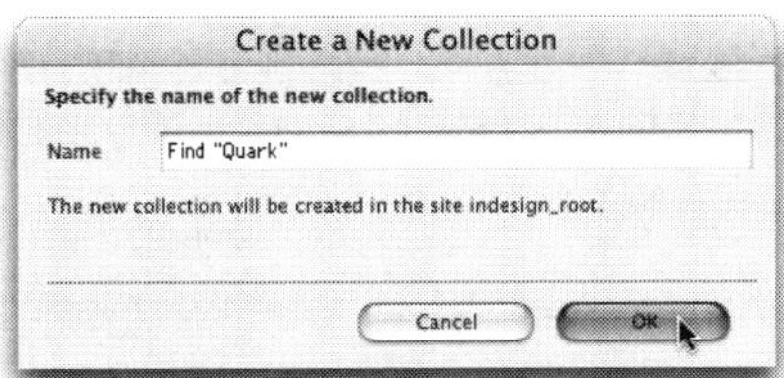

Figure 162 You can save the results of a find operation as a collection. See the next tip for more information.

Note

Remember that a collection can only be saved into one site. If you search in multiple sites, you can still create the collection but can only save it into one site.

TIP 163 Exploring Collections

Often there are files in your site that receive more edits than others. Wouldn't it be nice to be able to access only those pages without having to drill down into various folders to find them? Use GoLive's new collections feature, and the problem is solved.

To create a collection, follow these easy steps:

1. Click the Collections tab at the top of the Site window.
2. Click the Create New Collection button in the toolbar.
3. Name the collection.
4. Drag (or copy) files from the Site window into the new collection.

That's it. Now when you need to get to that collection of files, just open the collection and use the pages as usual (**Figure 163**).

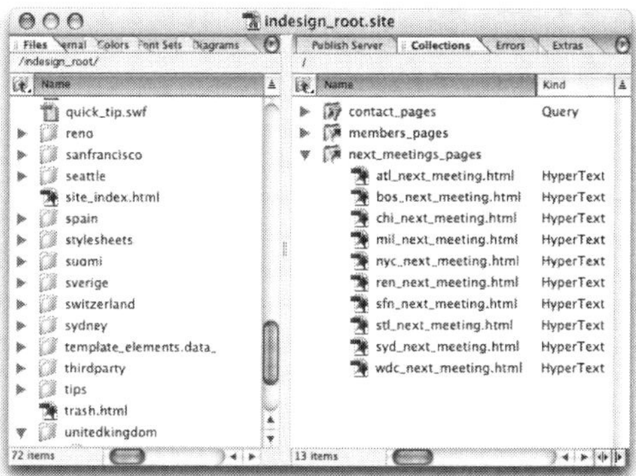

Figure 163 Collections are useful for grouping together sets of files that you often need to edit.

Binding Collections to Dynamic Queries

You can create a collection by saving the results of a find operation, the results of a syntax check, or the results of a query. In all three cases, the results window will have a button called Save Collection. You can also select a collection and then bind it to a query by enabling the Attach check box in the Inspector palette and then choosing the query from the list. To update your collection, click the Run button to rerun the query.

TIP 164 Diagramming New Sites

You're probably used to drawing out site maps (on paper or with the computer) and then regenerating the file structure in HTML. Put those late nights of confusion and chaos to an end with the powerful diagramming features in GoLive. Actually, GoLive offers three site-mapping modes, so let's start by explaining the different options.

Navigation View

Open the Navigation view of a site from the flyout menu in the top-right corner of the Site window. The Navigation view generates a visual site map for an existing site based on a combination of the folder structure and the hyperlinks between the pages (**Figure 164a**). To customize the orientation and presentation of the map, use the variety of options in the View palette. Using the Navigation, Display, and Filter options, you can modify the site map to look any way you want. To add pages to the site in this view, just drag pages from the Objects palette or templates from the Site window.

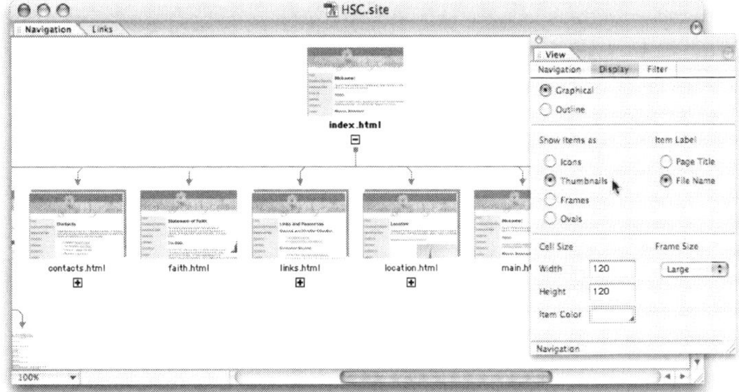

Figure 164a Use the Navigation view to get a hierarchical site map view of an existing site.

Bonus Tip

To create a linked site map with an outline structure, choose Diagram > Create Table of Contents when the Navigation view is open.

Links View

The Links view is grouped together with the Navigation view and is also accessed by using the flyout menu in the top-right corner of the Site window. The Links view is an interesting way of examining existing sites to better understand all the link relationships between various files (**Figure 164b**). It's sort of like the In & Out Links palette on steroids (see Tip 165). To customize the presentation and options for the Links view, you adjust the settings in the View palette. If the Links view starts to get unwieldy, turn on the Panorama pane so you can easily navigate around the site. Turn on the Reference pane to see which files a selected page references.

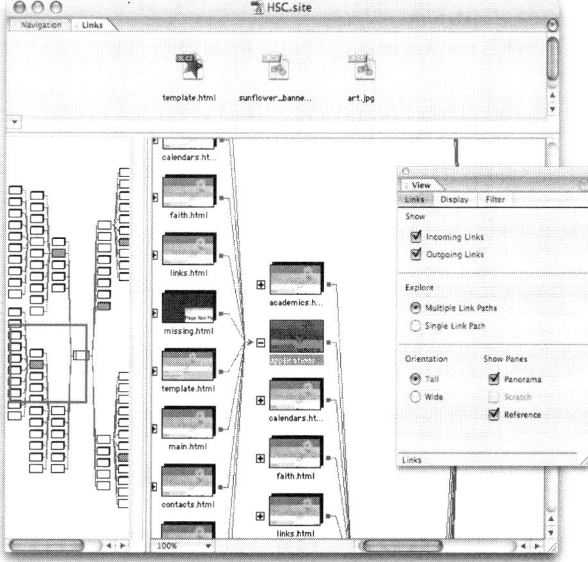

Figure 164b The Links view is like the In & Out Links palette on steroids.

Exporting Site Maps to PDF

Choose File > Export > Diagram, select PDF in the format pull-down menu, and click OK. This turns your diagram in an Adobe PDF that anybody can view with the free Adobe Reader. It's a great way to get feedback and approval on a project before it starts.

Diagrams

The first two views are for existing sites, but Diagrams are for mapping out new sites or new sections of existing sites.

1. To create a new diagram, switch to the Diagram tab of the Site window and choose Diagram > New Diagram. The new diagram will be added to the site, and you should give it a customized name (**Figure 164c**). Double-click the diagram to open its window and start editing it.

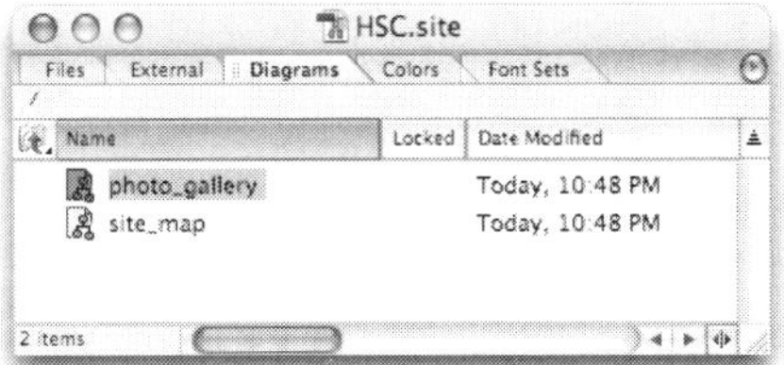

Figure 164c Create a new diagram and name it in the Diagrams tab.

2. So that GoLive knows how the new diagram fits in with the rest of the site, you need to add an anchor page to the diagram. To add an anchor page, just drag the home page, or any other page in the Files tab of the Site window, into the diagram window (**Figure 164d**). Notice the anchor page has the special anchor icon next to it in the diagram window.

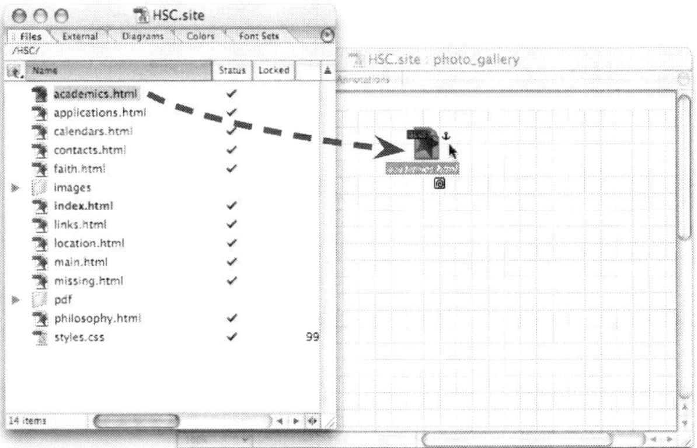

Figure 164d Drag and drop a page from the Site window to create an anchor page.

3. Now plan out the rest of the site map by dragging objects from the Diagram section of the Objects palette into the diagram window. You can add basic objects such as pages, sections, and groups as well as advanced objects, including references to wireless content, server-side scripts, and multimedia content (**Figure 164e**).

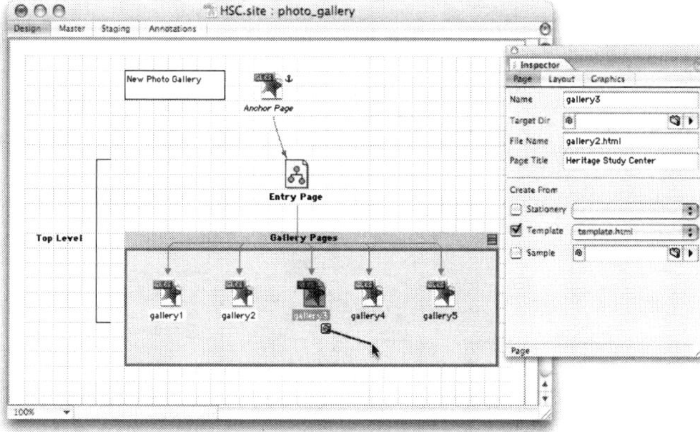

Figure 164e Use objects from the Diagram section of the Objects palette to build your site map.

4. Use the point and shoot (Fetch URL) tool next to any files in the diagram window to create link relationships between multiple files.

5. After the organization of the site map is complete, you can assign templates (see Tip 111) to the pages to accelerate the rest of the site-design process. Just select a page in the diagram, open the Page tab of the Inspector, and choose a template in the Template pull-down menu (**Figure 164f**).

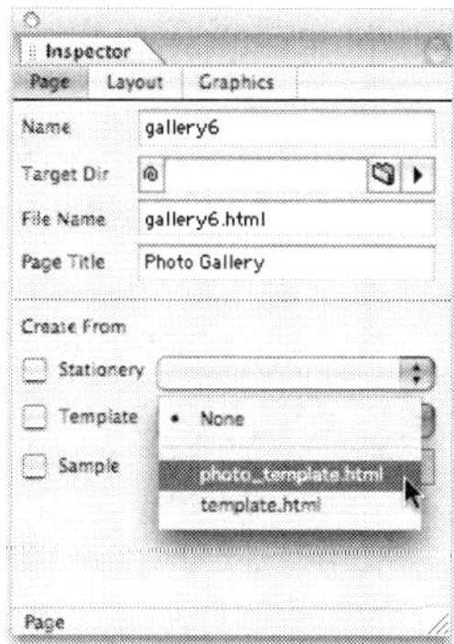

Figure 164f Assign a template to the pages in the diagram before submitting them into the site.

(continued on next page)

6. Before you're done with the site map, you can customize the presentation of the diagram using all the options in the View palette (**Figure 164g**). The variety of controls is amazing. You also might want to customize the diagram by putting your company logo or the name of the project on the diagram using the Master tab of the diagram window.

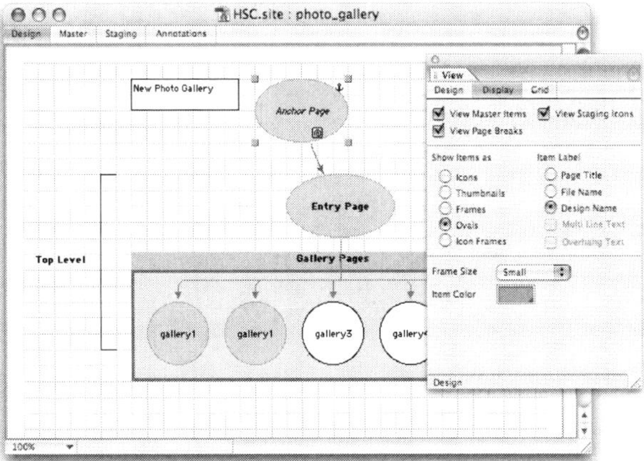

Figure 164g Adjust the Design and Display settings for the diagram in the View palette.

7. When you're ready to start adding content to the pages in your diagram, click Diagram > Staging> Submit All and watch GoLive move all the pages from the diagram into the Files tab of the Site window. It's incredible how much time this can save you, but even more impressive is the fact that all the links and references within all your pages and templates are updated perfectly by GoLive. By default, pages in a diagram are submitted to the top level of the Site window, but you can control this behavior. Before you submit a diagram, select files and sections in the diagram window and name a folder in the Folder or Target Dir(ectory) fields in the Inspector (**Figure 164h**).

Figure 164h Assign the target directories for the diagram pages in the Inspector palette.

8. If you change your mind after you submit a diagram and want to try a different design idea or navigation bar, you can recall all the pages of a diagram. Just select Diagram > Staging> Recall All and try a different approach.

TIP 165 Managing Files with the In & Out Links Palette

The In & Out Links palette in GoLive CS offers a unique way to view file relationships in your site and manage links. Open the In & Out Links palette in the Window menu and select a file in the Files tab of the Site window. The selected file is automatically positioned in the middle of the palette (**Figure 165a**). On the left are all the files that reference the selected file, so if you select a file such as the home page, an external CSS file, or a template, you'll probably have tons of referencing files on the left. On the right side of the palette you see all the files referenced by the selected file. If you select a JPEG, you should have no files on the right, but if you select the home page or a navigation component, you should have lots of files listed on the right.

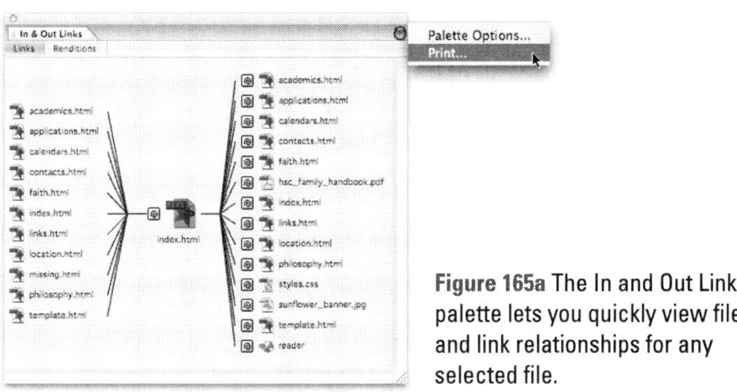

Figure 165a The In and Out Links palette lets you quickly view file and link relationships for any selected file.

To determine which file is which, position your mouse pointer over a file in the palette, and its file path, relative to the root level of the Web site, is displayed in the bottom-left corner of the palette. This is particularly helpful if you have multiple files with the same name, such as index.html, in the same site. If seeing the file relationships on paper is helpful, choose the Print command in the palette flyout menu.

The good news is that In & Out Links isn't just a pretty way to look at file links—it's also an easy way to redirect links and fix errors. If you want to change links from one file to another file, use the point and shoot (Fetch URL) tool next to the filename in the palette to point to a new file in the Files tab of the Site window (**Figure 165b**). If there's a broken link or missing file error in the palette, you can redirect the reference to the correct file.

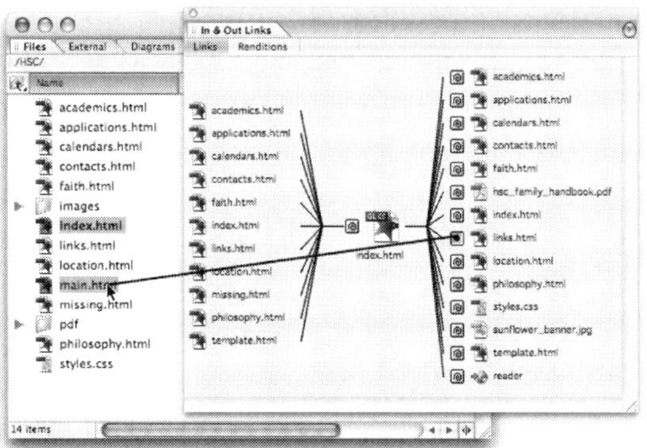

Figure 165b Use the In & Out Links palette to redirect links and fix errors.

The In & Out Links palette is one of the most powerful site-management features in GoLive, and it has a few hidden options many users are not aware of. When you look at the palette with a large site, it might be overwhelming based on how you need to use it. To control what is shown in the In & Out Links palette (**Figure 165c**), select Palette Options from the Palette menu in the top-right corner of the palette.

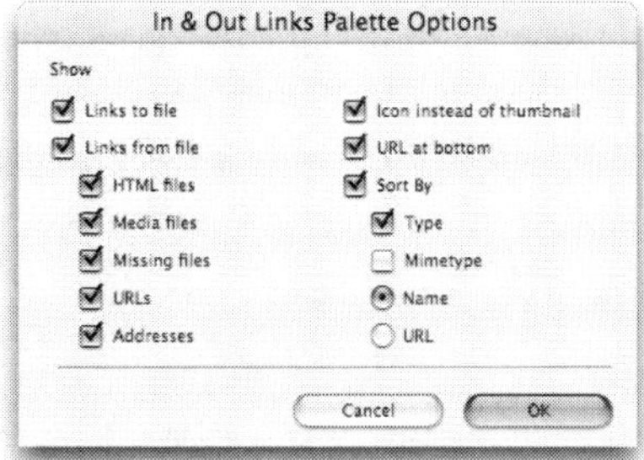

Figure 165c Control what you see and how it's sorted with the In & Out Links Palette Options window.

With these palette options you might choose to hide the links to the selected file and show only HTML files linked from the selected file. Select the filtering options you need from the options dialog and click OK.

TIP 166 Using the Errors Tab to Fix Problems

If you use the site-management features in GoLive, it's very unlikely that you'll see any errors in your site, but in the rare case you do, fixing them is easy. If you see any bug icons in the Files tab of the Site window or errors in the Errors tab of the Site window, you should refresh the Site window first before you panic. It's possible that you inadvertently moved or renamed some files in your operating system that GoLive doesn't know about yet. If that doesn't solve the problem, open the Errors tab of the Site window and read on for how to fix various common problems.

- Missing Files—Select the missing file error in the Site window and use the point and shoot tool in the Error Inspector to update the links to the correct file (**Figure 166a**). Confirm the warning dialog and you're done.

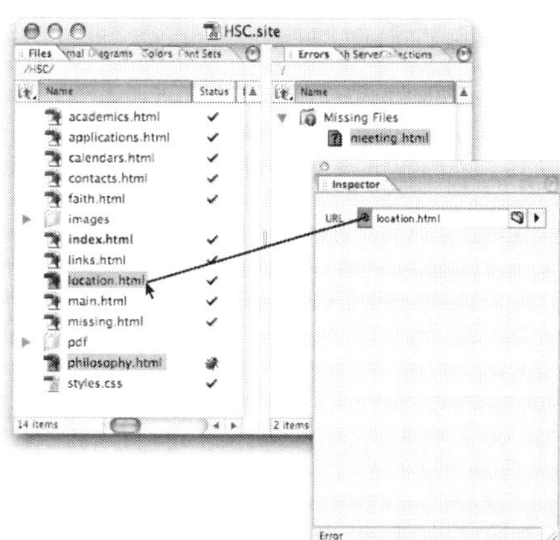

Figure 166a Point and shoot from the Error Inspector to fix missing files.

(continued on next page)

- Orphan Files—Orphan files are files that GoLive can find on your hard drive but that are not located in your web-content folder. This means that unless you fix these errors, the orphan files will not be uploaded to the server and will cause errors for your visitors. To fix an orphan file error, drag it from the Errors tab to the Files tab (**Figure 166b**). GoLive will copy the orphan file into the root folder and update all links throughout the site to the new location.

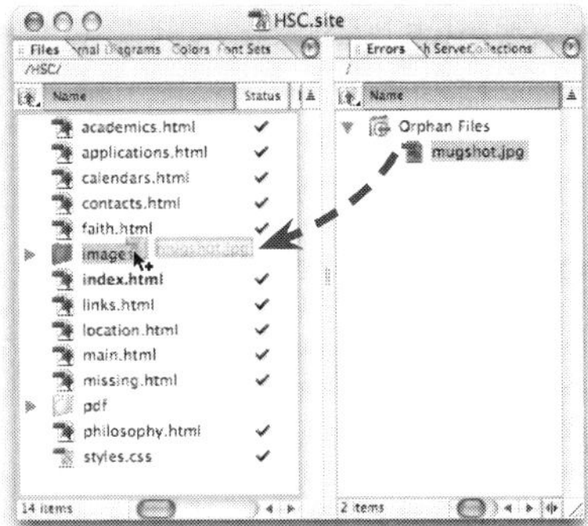

Figure 166b Drag and drop orphan file errors to copy the files to the site and update the necessary links.

- Filename Constraints—If there's a certain way you want to name all of the files and folders in a site, choose Site > Settings. Under Filename Constraints, click Site Specific Settings and select one of the presets (**Figure 166c**).

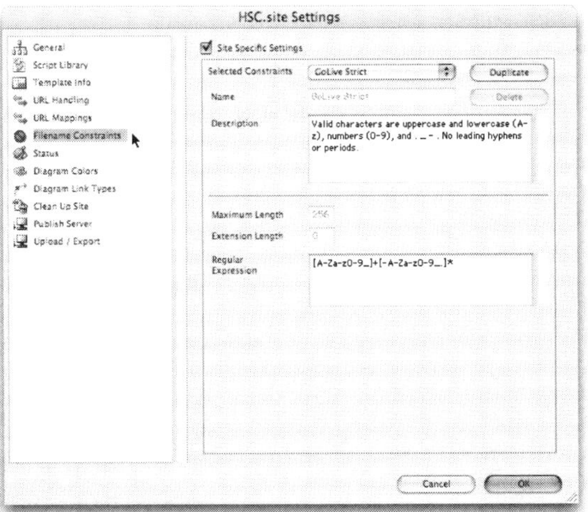

Figure 166c Customize the Filename Constraints for a site in the Site Settings dialog.

Now the Site window will warn you about file and folder names that violate this preference, but it won't automatically change filenames or prohibit you from creating new ones that don't follow the rules. The feature warns you, but you have to fix the error. You can easily do so by selecting the file in the Errors tab and changing the filename in the File Inspector (**Figure 166d**).

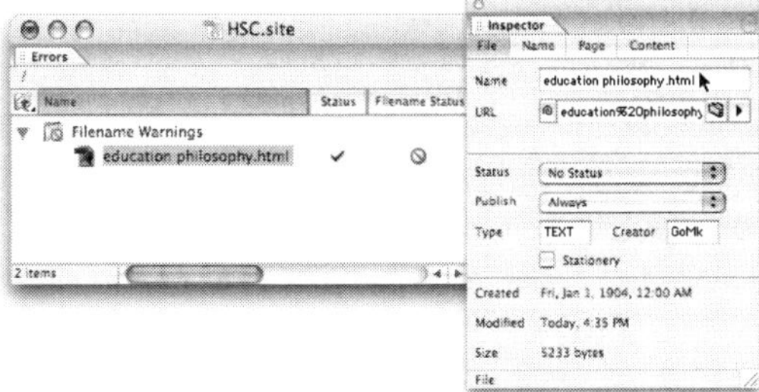

Figure 166d Select a Filename in the Errors tab and change the filename in the Inspector.

TIP 167 Changing References Across a Site

Sometimes you need to change references throughout a site from one file to a different file. You can try to make these changes with complicated find and replace sequences, but Change References makes it easy with just a few clicks.

Select a file in the Files tab of the Site window that needs to be redirected and select Site > Change References. The selected file is automatically added to the top field, so now all you have to do is tell GoLive what file you want to replace the links with. Use the point and shoot tool to locate the new file in the Site window and click OK when you're ready (**Figure 167**).

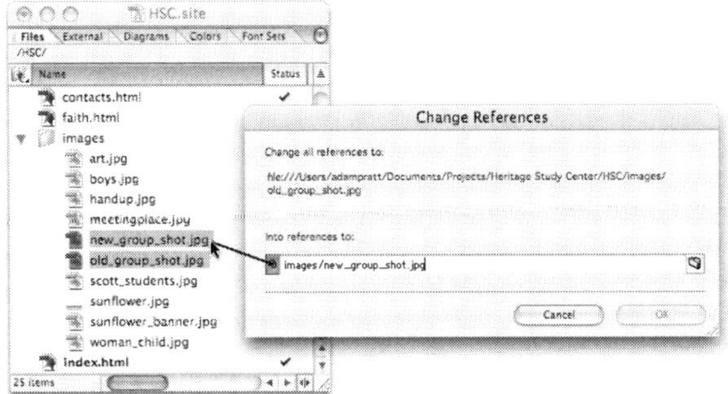

Figure 167 Assign the new and old references and click OK.

Confirm the changes in the Change References dialog and click OK. Kick back and watch as GoLive does all the heavy lifting and updates all the necessary pages.

Warning About Image Sizes

If you change references for an image, you should try to make sure the two images have the same pixel dimensions. The Change References command only updates the image reference, not the image dimensions. If the two images are different sizes, you should perform a quick site-wide Find and Replace (see Tip 161) to update the image dimensions.

TIP 168 Finding Site Assets

You know you have a file called red_car.jpg somewhere in your site, but you couldn't find it for a million bucks. Instead of wading through all the folders and subfolders in your site, choose Site > Find Site Assets. Type your search criteria in the Find Site Assets dialog and choose what part of the site you want to search in (**Figure 168**). Searching for assets in the Files tab is the most common use, but you can also search in the Collections, Colors, Errors, External, Extras, and Font Sets tabs of the Site window.

Enabling Instant Find

To see the results of your search as an instantaneous filter, make sure the Instant Find option is enabled and you don't even have to click the Find All button.

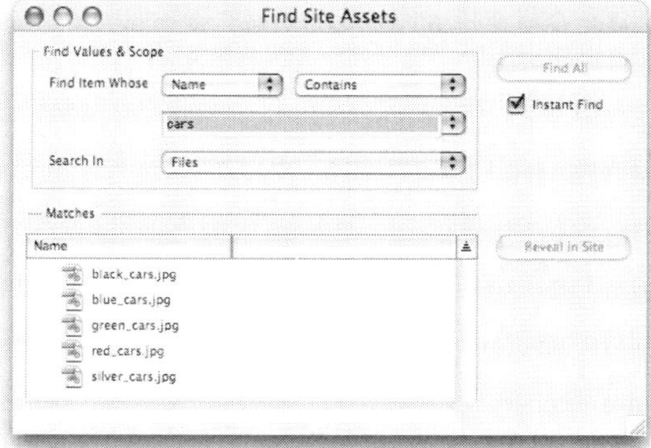

Figure 168 Enter your search criteria and click Find All to quickly locate site assets.

After you get the search results, you can select any file in the list of matches at the bottom and open the In & Out Links palette (see Tip 165) to see what files, if any, are referencing the found file. To see where a matching file is located in the Site window, select it in the list of matches and click the Reveal in Site button. To open a found file, just double-click it in the Find Site Assets dialog.

TIP 169 Cleaning Up a Site

Making a Backup First

As with any site-wide operation, be sure to back up your site first in the rare event you make a mistake or something goes wrong. Take our word for it—you'll thank us later.

GoLive offers a method for removing unused files and orphan file errors (see Tip 166). Open the Site window and choose Site > Clean Up Site to clean up these stray nuisances and get rid of unnecessary files. A dialog appears, offering options for removing and adding files to the site (**Figure 169a**).

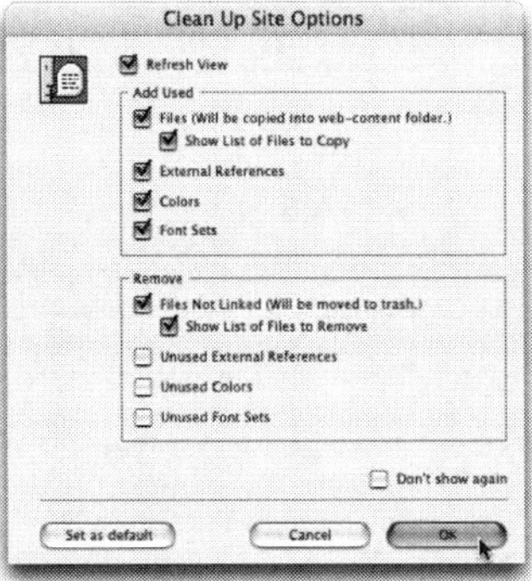

Figure 169a Choose the options you want in the Clean Up Site Options dialog.

Once you have made your selections, click the OK button. GoLive will cycle through the files and then display another dialog showing which files will be removed or added (**Figure 169b**).

Figure 169b GoLive shows you a list of the files that will be added or deleted before any operation is completed.

You can check or uncheck files in this list. When you have finished, click OK, and the process will be completed.

TIP 170 Finding File Differences

Whether you're troubleshooting an obscure coding problem or experimenting with different solutions to a CSS problem, the ability to compare the source code of two files side by side can be very helpful. GoLive CS adds a new file-differencing command that you can activate by selecting Site > Find Differences. Use the point and shoot tools in the Find Differences dialog to select the two files to compare and click OK (**Figure 170a**).

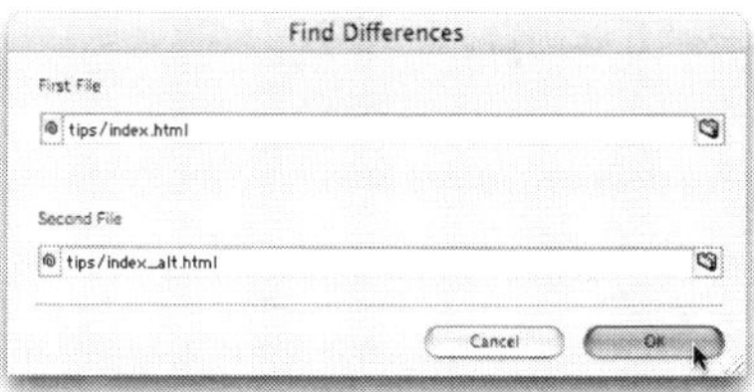

Figure 170a Select Site > Find Differences and choose two files to compare.

The next dialog shows you a side-by-side code view of the two files and highlights any differences for you (**Figure 170b**). To make sure the two files scroll together, leave the Synchronize Scrolling option enabled. All the differences between the two files are listed at the bottom of the dialog; you can click on an entry to jump to the correct part of the page.

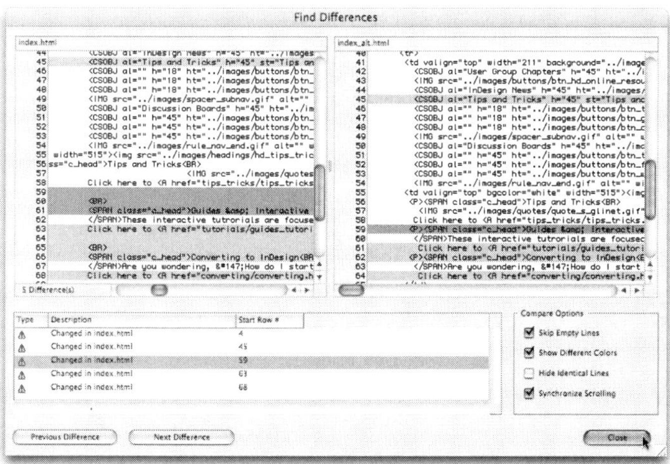

Figure 170b The Find Differences dialog lets you navigate and compare code differences between two files.

Hiding Identical Lines

If the differences between two files are very slight, you should turn on the Hide Identical Lines option. Now you see just the differences instead of wading through all the common lines of code.

What It Works On

The Find Differences command only works on markup files such as HTML and CSS. It doesn't work on binary files such as GIFs, JPEGs, or PDFs.

TIP 171 Running Site Reports with Queries

New in GoLive CS is a feature called queries, which give you the ability to search through your site for files based on a variety of criteria. A query can be run on a whole site, on selected files in a site, or on the results of another query.

You define queries in the Query Editor. To get to the Query Editor, first select Edit > Run Query to open the dialog shown in **Figure 171a.** Click the New Query button to define a brand-new query or select an existing query in the list and click the Edit Query button. Either way, the Query Editor will open (**Figure 171b**).

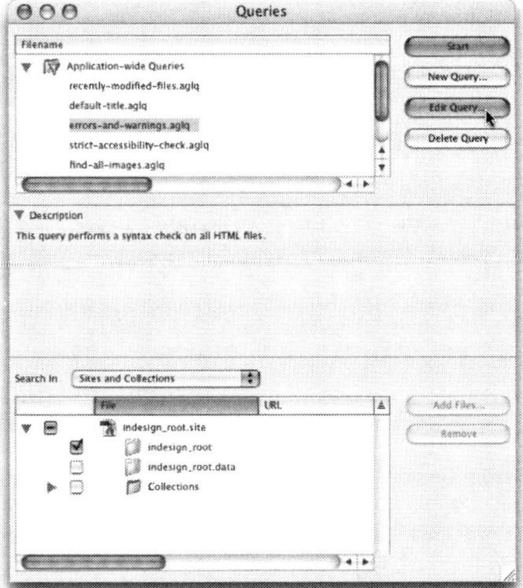

Figure 171a Choosing Run Query from the Edit menu opens the Query dialog.

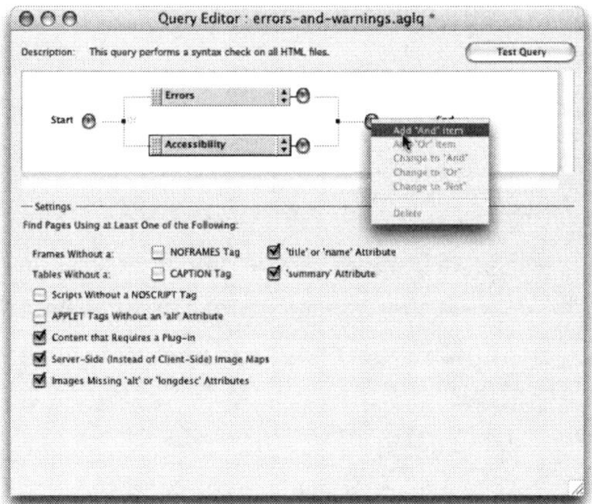

Figure 171b Choosing New Query or Edit Query opens the Query Editor.

Click the double-facing arrow next to a criterion to reveal a pull-down menu of other criteria. This menu is called the Find What menu. When a criterion is selected, its options are shown in the lower portion of the Query Editor. Make the appropriate selections for your search from those options.

To add additional criteria, click the arrow button to the left of the Find What menu. From there you can select an Add or Or criterion or change the current selection to an Add, Or, or Not criterion. Click the arrow button to the right of the Find What menu to delete a criterion.

When your query is ready to go, click the Text Query button to begin running it. After the query is complete, you can save the results as a collection or use them as the basis of another query, syntax check, or find operation. When you close the Query Editor, you'll be asked if you'd like to save your query. If you do, then go ahead and name and save it.

Finding Default Page Titles

Included with the built-in queries is a criterion for Errors, which includes an option to find any page that still has the default page title. Run this query to quickly gather up those pages and change their titles to something appropriate for your page. Remember, search engines rely on page titles to properly index Web pages. The more precise the page title, the better.

CHAPTER TEN

Publishing Your Site

You've learned a lot, put in a lot of hard work, and you're eager to share your Web site with the world. Before you upload it to a Web server, of course, you need to purchase a domain name and establish a hosting account if you haven't done so already. There are plenty of domain registrars, but www.godaddy.com and www.dotster.com are two of our favorites, and their prices are great. Whichever registrar you choose, make sure the company is approved at www.icann.org/registrars/accredited-list.html.

The next step is to find a hosting provider who can give you the service and support you need at a price you can afford. GoLive uses standard Internet protocols such as FTP and WebDAV, so you don't have to worry about finding a special company to host your GoLive sites. If you're looking for a particularly GoLive-savvy hosting company, we recommend you check out www.golivehost.com or www.mediatemple.net.

When you've got those two tasks squared away, it's time to upload. The first few tips in this chapter cover basic settings and uploads, but we quickly advance to some really cool power tips.

TIP 172 Managing Publish Server Settings

GoLive manages all your server settings in a centralized location instead of saving settings in each site and forcing you to enter the same options over and over again. Select GoLive > Server (Mac) or Edit > Server (Windows) and you see the Edit Publish Server dialog (**Figure 172**). Enter your settings here once, and they're instantly available to every site you work on, as well as to the FTP browser that's built in (see Tip 180).

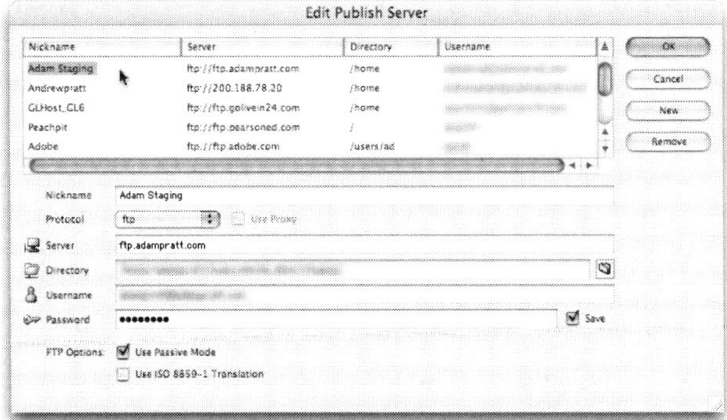

Figure 172 Manage all your publish server settings in one place.

Click the New button to create a new entry and give it a nickname in the first field. You'll probably select FTP for your protocol, but notice you can also pick from HTTP (WebDAV) and File for a local file server. Now enter the information for server address, directory, username, and password as provided by your hosting provider or server administrator. If you don't know the directory path, click the browse icon in the Directory field and let GoLive try to find it for you.

To create a new entry that's similar to an existing entry, select it in the list and click the New button to duplicate it. This is a great way to save time.

Save Password Now on by Default

Notice that the Save check box next to the Password field is on by default. If you're not worried about security on your computer, you can leave this option on and save yourself time and hassle every time you connect to a server. If you are worried about security, uncheck this box and don't include the password here. You'll be more secure if somebody gains unauthorized access to your computer, but you'll have to enter the password every time you connect.

TIP 173 Entering FTP Settings for Web Sites

After you've entered all your publish server settings as described in Tip 172, open your Site window and choose Site > Settings. Select Publish Server on the left and click Add to choose a server from the entries you've already entered (**Figure 173**). If you need to add a new publish server, you can do that now. If you're having trouble connecting to a publish server, click the Edit button and verify that the settings you entered match the account information from your hosting provider.

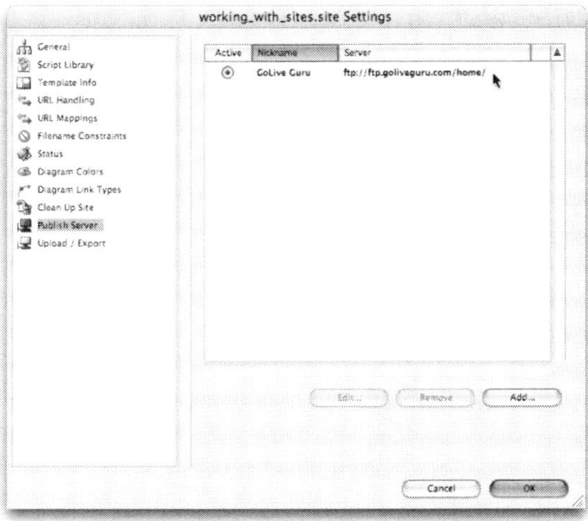

Figure 173 Open the Site Settings dialog and assign a publish server to your Web site.

The publish server settings you assign to a site are stored in the application preferences and in an encrypted format in the sitename/web-settings/siteServersettings.xml file. This means that if you deliver this site to a client or move the site to a different computer, all the login settings travel with the site, and you don't have to reenter any server settings. Just make sure to copy the entire project folder, including the Site file and the Root, Data, and Settings folders.

TIP 174 Connecting to the Publish Server

After you enter server settings and assign them to the site, you can connect to the publish server in a few different ways. The easiest method is to click the Connect to publish server icon in the toolbar (**Figure 174a**). You can also choose Site > Publish Server > Connect.

Figure 174a Connect to the Web server with this toolbar icon.

When you're connected, you can see your local files in the Files tab on the left and the server files in the Publish Server tab on the right (**Figure 174b**). This means you can connect to the server and do all your uploading and downloading right inside the GoLive Site window. There's no need to buy any shareware or launch any other utilities—it's all built in.

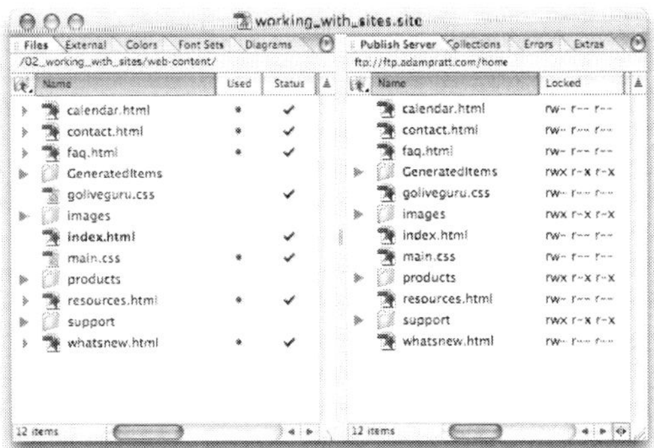

Figure 174b See your local and server files side by side in the Site window.

To disconnect from the server, click the Disconnect icon in the toolbar or Control-click (Mac) or right-click (Windows) in the Publish Server tab of the Site window and choose Disconnect from publish server (**Figure 174c**).

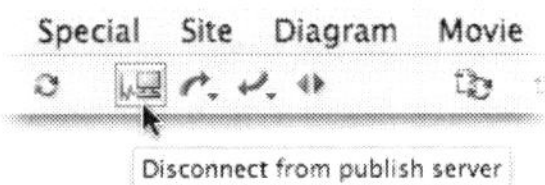

Figure 174c Disconnect from the server the same way you connected.

Troubleshooting FTP Connections

If you're having problems connecting to a server, make sure Passive Mode is turned on in the server settings. This frequently solves your connection woes, especially if you can connect to the server but can't see a files list.

TIP 175 Connecting to Multiple Servers

Let's face it: Connecting to an FTP server really isn't that big of a deal. Lots of people do it every day. However, one thing that makes GoLive's server connectivity really outstanding is the ability to connect to and synchronize with multiple servers at the same time. That's right—you can switch from one server to another with a single click. Make sure you have multiple servers assigned in the Publish Server pane of the Site Settings, as seen in **Figure 175a**.

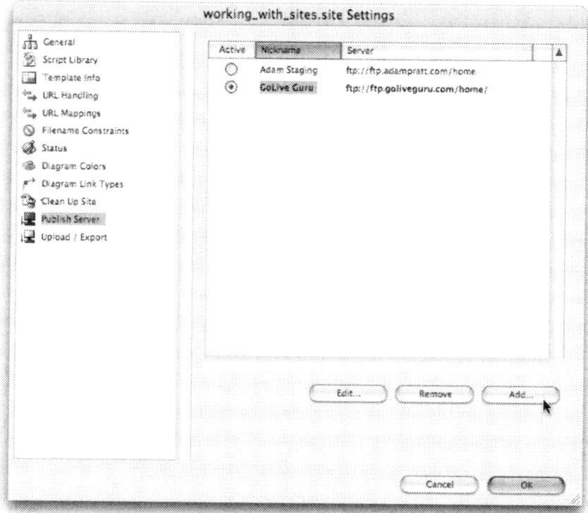

Figure 175a Add multiple servers to the Site Settings so you can switch between them later.

When you're connected to a server, you can easily switch to a different server by choosing a different server nickname from the list in the Site > Publish Server menu (**Figure 175b**).

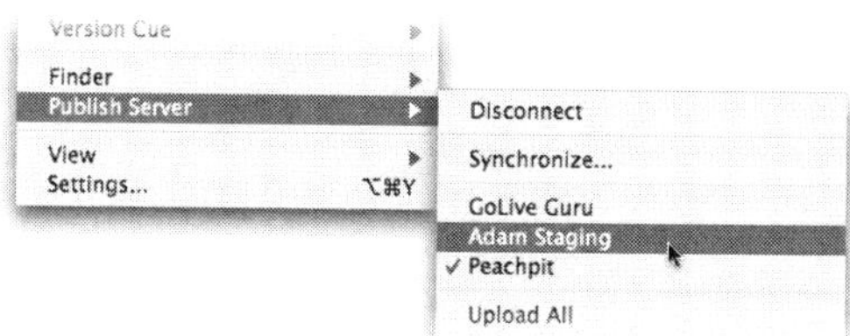

Figure 175b Switch between servers on the fly in the Site > Publish Server menu.

Managing Staging and Production Servers

Many Web designers upload their sites first to a staging server for review and then upload the same files to a production server after they've been approved. GoLive's ability to connect to multiple servers makes this workflow much less tedious.

TIP 176 Uploading Files

You can drag and drop files between the Files and Publish Server tabs of the Site window to upload and download files, but this process is prone to error. Instead, let GoLive keep track of the files you need to upload. There are three upload commands you need to learn (**Figure 176**):

- Upload All—You'll use this command the first time you upload a site because it uploads all the local files in your site to the Web server.
- Upload Selection—This uploads all selected files in the Files tab of the Site window to their correct location on the Web server. It's even smart enough to correctly upload multiple files that are selected in different folders, even multiple nested folders, to the appropriate locations on the Web server.
- Upload Modified—Uploads only the files on your hard drive that are newer than the ones on the server. A dialog lets you confirm exactly which files are uploaded before the process begins.

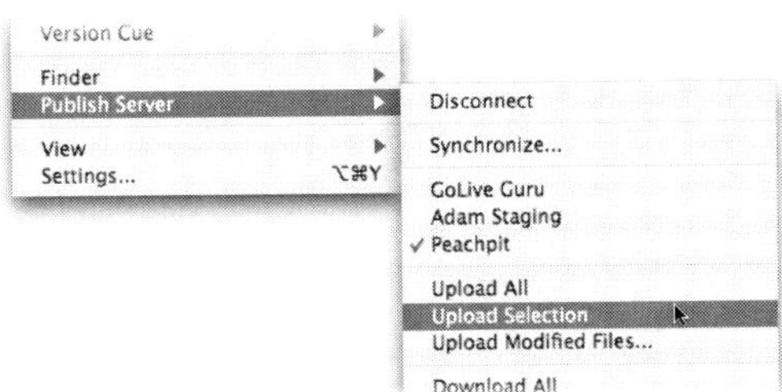

Figure 176 Three upload commands give you time-saving options for uploading.

Toolbar Shortcuts

The upload commands are powerful, but they can be difficult to access all the way at the bottom of the Site menu. You can access the same commands from the Upload icon in the toolbar. You can even change the default behavior of the button if you click and hold the icon and choose from the Change Button To menu.

TIP 177 Synchronizing Modification Times

Several things can cause the files in your Site window to get out of sync with your Web server, including

- Somebody else moving or updating files on the server.
- A corrupted or re-created GoLive Site file.
- Changes to server settings, including daylight savings time changes.

If the Site window insists on uploading files you know are up to date, open your Site window and choose Site > Publish Server > Sync Modification Times All (**Figure 177**). It might look like new files are uploading, but it's just synchronizing the modification times of the files on the remote server with those on your local computer.

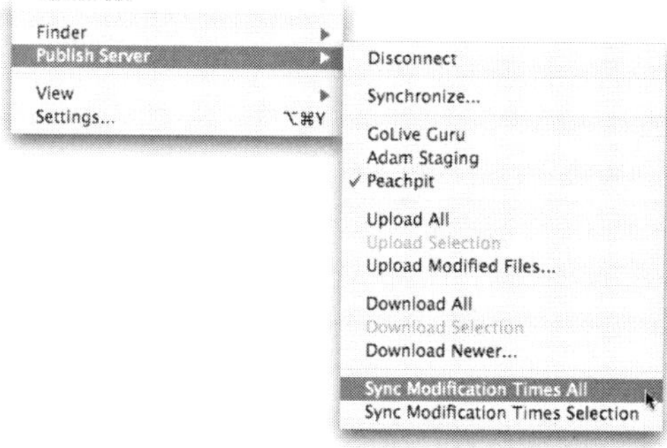

Figure 177 Sync modification times on the server when things get out of whack.

If you have a specific set of files that need to be synchronized, select the appropriate files and folders in the Files tab of the Site window and choose Site > Publish Server > Sync Modification Times Selection. This process can be helpful if you move large files such as videos on the server and don't want to have to unnecessarily upload the files again just to get the Site window synchronized.

TIP 178 Synchronizing Files and Deleting Server Extras

When you have multiple offices or several people working on the same site, it can be tricky to keep all the files synchronized and not accidentally copy over newer files. The new Synchronize command helps keep everything up to date and also satisfies a long-standing feature request from customers, making it easier to delete unnecessary files on the server.

To use the Synchronize command, open the Site window, connect to the publish server (see Tips 172–174), and choose Site > Publish Server > Synchronize. You can also click the Sync icon (◀▶) in the toolbar to open the Synchronize dialog. GoLive takes a moment to compare the local and remote files and shows a dialog with two side-by-side files lists (**Figure 178**).

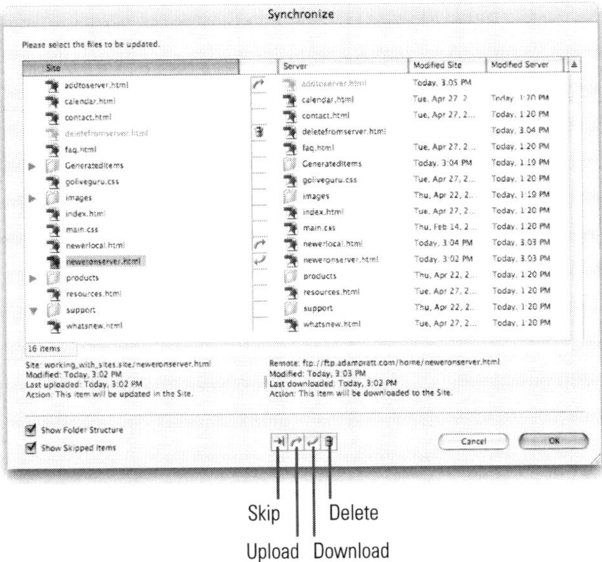

Figure 178 The Synchronize dialog lets you upload, download, and delete files so everything is synched up again.

Select files in the list and click the button at the bottom of the dialog that corresponds to the action you want to take. When you're ready to synchronize, click OK and let GoLive synchronize all the files.

- Skip—This is the default action and unless you have a lot of files out of sync this will apply for most files.
- Upload—If the local file is newer, choose Upload.
- Download—If the remote file is newer, choose Download.
- Delete—If the remote file is unnecessary, you can delete it, but be careful to not accidentally delete server files such as scripts and databases.

TIP 179 Stripping Extra Code

GoLive offers powerful authoring tools that can save you a lot of development time, but often the trade-off is a bit of extra source code. For example, if you use templates, some comment tags are inserted in the source code, and if you want your source code formatted nicely, some space characters are added.

If you're really picky about your source code or need it to validate perfectly against certain standards, GoLive can strip out these extra tidbits and upload the most pristine code you've ever seen. To enable code stripping, choose Site > Settings and select the Upload/Export pane on the left. Enable the Site Specific Settings check box at the top of the dialog and look at the Cleanups section (**Figure 179**). You can tell GoLive to strip the following code every time you upload or export your site:

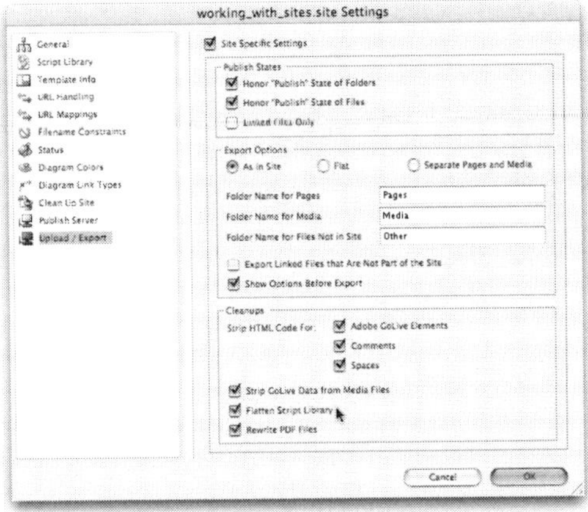

Figure 179 Enable code stripping in the Site Settings dialog to control the final output.

- Adobe GoLive Elements—Special tags for features such as JavaScript Actions and components.
- Comments—Any source code comments, including those used to manage templates.
- Spaces—Any extra spaces for formatting your source code.

Stripping extra code doesn't affect how the pages work in a Web browser, but removing spaces reduces the readability of the code. If you strip GoLive elements, it will be all but impossible to reedit advanced Go-Live features such as JavaScript Actions and components.

Automatically Flattening the JavaScript Library

Check the Flatten Script Library option to optimize the site-wide JavaScript library (GeneratedItems/CSScriptLib.js) every time you upload files from your site. When the library is flattened, it uses only the functions necessary for your site and will optimize overall download time of your site.

TIP 180 Using the Built-in FTP Client

Most of the time you'll just use the FTP tools that are integrated with GoLive's Site window and the Publish Server tab. However, every once in a while you'll need to quickly upload something to an FTP server that might not be associated with a site you're editing. For example, while we've been writing this book we've uploaded many screenshots and PDF files to our project server. Instead of launching a separate FTP client, we use the one built into GoLive, which you can open with the File > Connect to FTP/WebDAV command (**Figure 180**).

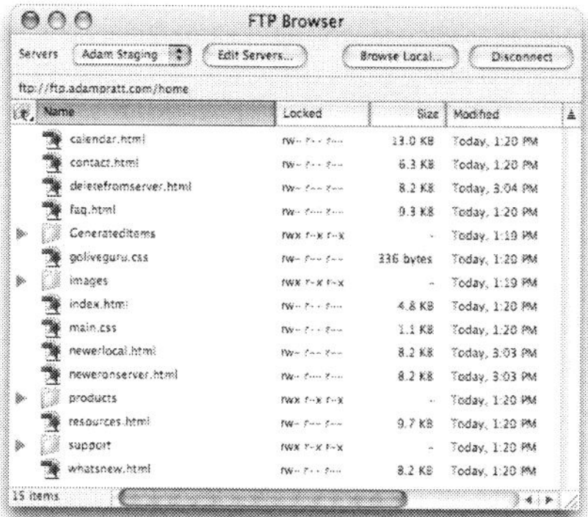

Figure 180 Use the FTP client in GoLive for all your file transfer needs.

From here you can enter server settings, select the server you need to connect to, and click the Connect button. After you connect, you can create new folders and delete files with the buttons in the toolbar, and you can upload files by dragging them into the window. When you're done, click Disconnect.

Downloading a Page

Surfing the Web for design inspiration is a great way to get your creative juices flowing. When you find a cool design or technique, you can learn from the example by choosing File > Download Page in GoLive and pasting the URL into the dialog that opens. GoLive will download the page and render it in the Layout Editor, where you can deconstruct the design. Remember: Learn, don't steal.

TIP 181 Browsing Local Files

Adding Files to the Site Window

You can drag and drop files from the local file browser in GoLive directly to the Files tab in the Site window. This is a convenient way to add files to the site. If you've ever thought about purchasing a second monitor and video card, now's the time!

If you think the Site window is as close as GoLive gets to the cool Photoshop File Browser, then here's a great tip you're really gonna love. First, open the FTP Browser with the File > Connect to FTP/WebDAV command. Next, click the Browse Local button at the top of the window and select a local folder to browse.

A Local File Browser window opens and displays all the files in the selected folder in a simple list view. If you Control-click (Mac) or right-click (Windows), you can select three other views (Icons, Thumbnails, and Tiles) from the View menu. Switch to the Thumbnails option to see a preview of your files (**Figure 181**). You can even change the sort order with the Arrange by contextual menu.

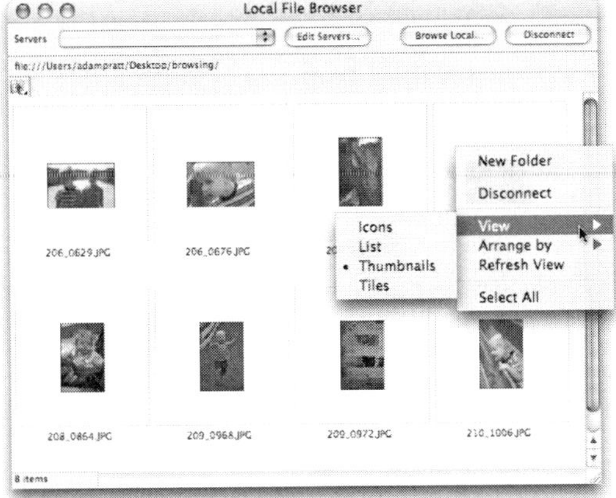

Figure 181 You can browse local files and even make it look like the Photoshop File Browser.

TIP 182 Troubleshooting Server Connections with the Server Log

If you've ever tried to connect to a server, you've probably at some point encountered an error. Did you type the wrong password? Maybe the server timed out? Whatever the cause, you know there are a lot of reasons why server connections can be a problem. Fortunately, GoLive includes diagnostic tools to help you troubleshoot these annoyances.

If you have server connection problems, choose File > Log. The Log window opens to show you any recent errors (**Figure 182a**). Use the information tracked here to diagnose connection problems with your hosting provider. To make the logging more verbose, choose the Log pane in the application preferences and turn on the Warnings and Status Messages options. You can even control how many log sessions are stored (**Figure 182b**).

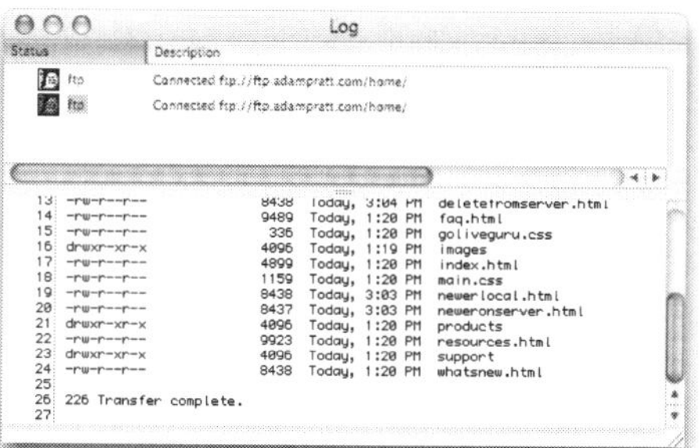

Figure 182a Open the Log window to troubleshoot recent connection errors.

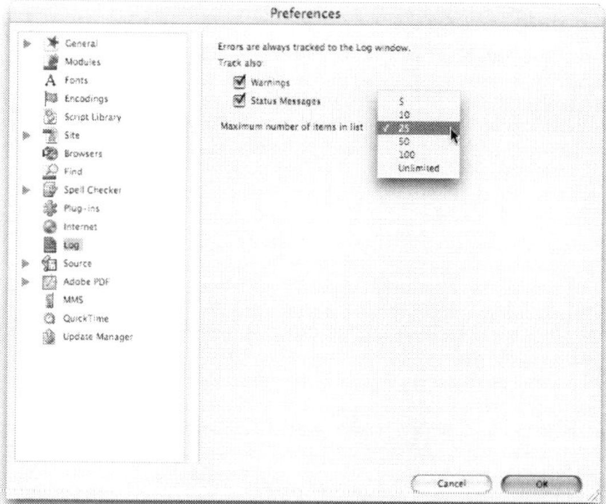

Figure 182b Use the Log preferences to control how much detail is recorded in the log.

Saving as a Text File

If your hosting provider or server administrator wants a copy of your log file, open the Log window and Control-click (Mac) or right-click (Windows) on the log entry. Choose Save As to save a text file you can print or email.

CHAPTER ELEVEN

Third-Party Actions and Extensions

Hundreds of third-party actions and extensions are available for GoLive. *Actions* are prebuilt JavaScript functions that add powerful interactivity to your Web site with the ease of point and click, meaning you don't have to know how to program or understand source code to add great features to your Web sites. Verifying forms data entry and creating interactive slide shows are two examples of what third-party actions can add to your Web sites.

Extensions are different from actions in that they add features, such as new menus and palettes, to the GoLive authoring environment. GoLive comes with a few extensions to get you started, and you'll find many more at Adobe's Action Exchange at http://share.studio.adobe.com.

Most serious Photoshop users enhance their digital toolbox with third-party plug-ins that add specialized features. GoLive actions and extensions work in a similar way to increase your productivity, enable your creativity, and expand the possibilities. The first tip in this chapter shows you how to install new extensions. Then we introduce you to 16 of our favorite actions and extensions, many from trusted Adobe partners.

TIP 183 Installing Extensions

A few extensions might include their own installers, but most will require you copy them to the correct location in the GoLive application folder. Follow these instructions to install extensions:

1. Install GoLive CS if you haven't done so already.
2. Copy the folder for the new extension, such as Smart Forms 2.0, into the Adobe GoLive CS/Modules/Extend Scripts folder (**Figure 183**). If you look inside an extension folder you'll notice there's always a file called Main.html; there might also be a few other script or image files. Don't copy these individual files—always install the entire extension folder.

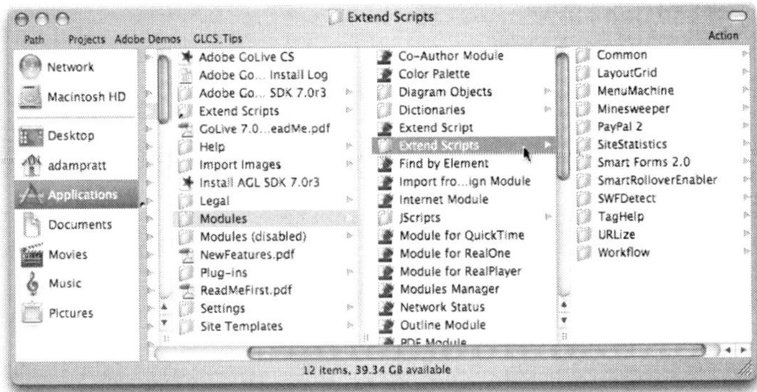

Figure 183 Copy the new extension folder into the Extend Scripts folder and relaunch GoLive.

3. Quit and relaunch GoLive to enable the new extension.

To temporarily disable an extension, open the application preferences, select Modules on the left, and in the list of extensions on the right uncheck the ones you want to disable. Your new configuration will be active after you quit and relaunch GoLive.

Most extensions add new commands to the Special, Extensions, or Window menu, but consult the instructions that accompany your new extension for details.

Cross-Reference

See Tip 148 for step-by-step instructions on installing new JavaScript Actions.

TIP 184 Building DHTML Drop-down Menus

Name: MenuMachine

Developer: Big Bang Software

Source: http://www.menumachine.com

Cost: $45 US

MenuMachine adds a new DHTML drop-down menu object to the Basic section of the Objects palette that makes creating complex navigation bars a piece of cake. The code created by MenuMachine is the most reliable and compatible of any DHTML menu system we've ever seen, and we recommend it highly.

Drag the MenuMachine object into the Layout Editor to create the beginnings of a new DHTML navigation menu. Create the menu using the Inspector palette, which lets you use images or text and colors to achieve the desired rollover effects (**Figure 184**). You'll probably want to use the same DHTML menu on several pages, so the fact that MenuMachine works flawlessly in GoLive components (see Tip 109) and templates (see Tip 111) is a huge time-saver.

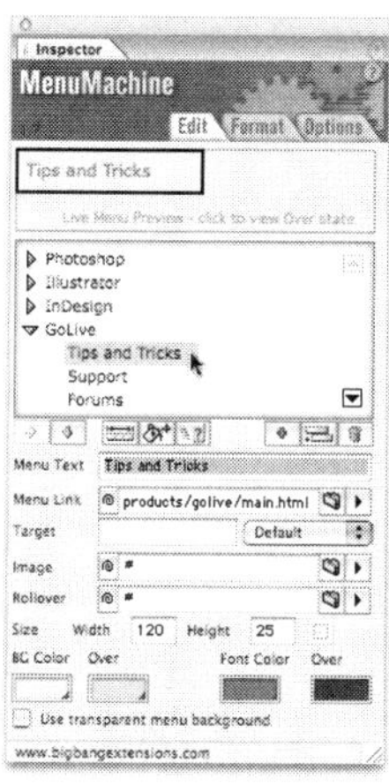

Figure 184 MenuMachine uses the familiar GoLive interface and integrates flawlessly with the power site management to keep everything up to date.

There are tons of cool features we don't have space to cover here, so make sure you check out the great documentation that comes with MenuMachine. Select Help > MenuMachine Help in GoLive for complete instructions and documentation.

MenuMachine has been updated frequently to add features and improve compatibility with the latest browsers, so keep your eyes open for new developments from Big Bang.

TIP 185 Importing Text and Styling Tables

Name: Super Importer

Developer: Ken Martin

Source: http://www.kpmartin.com/Downloads/

Cost: $10 US Shareware

GoLive CS can open text documents, but to get the text onto a Web page you have to use either copy and paste or select the text and drag it onto the page. The results could be, shall we say, less than beautiful. Special characters often appear as little boxes or strange-looking glyphs. Until now there was no way to simply put your cursor where you want the text and import a text document directly onto a page.

Enter Super Importer. Ken Marin's small but mighty extension gives GoLive users the ability to place text documents directly into their GoLive pages. On top of that, it also gives a faster, more elegant way to import tab- or comma-delimited text (**Figure 185**).

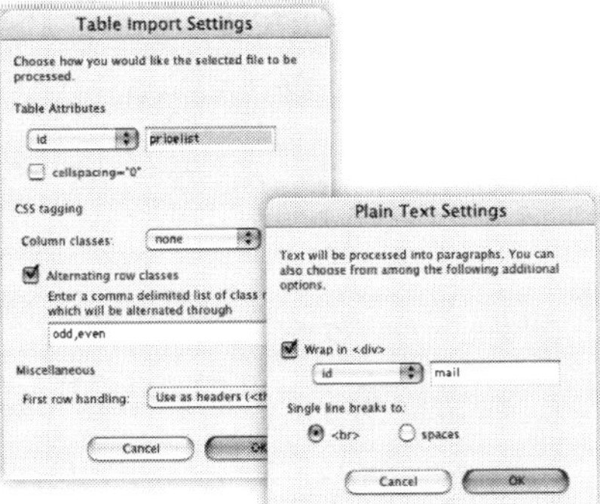

Figure 185 Super Importer imports text quickly and properly encodes special characters as HTML.

Although GoLive has the ability to import delimited text into tables, it requires you to first place a Table object onto the page and to select a cell. Super Importer has no such requirements. Simply choose File > Import > Tab Separated text (or Comma Separated text), and a table will be created at the cursor insertion point with all the necessary rows and columns intact. You can also easily style the new table with CSS classes as part of the import process. As with the plain text, Super Importer does a fabulous job of encoding all special HTML characters so they appear correctly in a Web browser. Another highlight of Super Importer is that it allows you to use a plain-text or delimited text document as a GoLive component.

TIP 186 Adding a Secure Shopping Cart

Name: CatalogIntegrator Cart

Developer: eCatalogBuilders

Source: http://www.catalogintegrator.com

Cost: Free–$1,995 US

Building an online storefront has never been easier. Install Catalog-Integrator Cart into GoLive and you'll get a full set of BuyObjects in your Objects palette that you can simply drag and drop onto your GoLive pages to set up a store.

After installing the extension, restart GoLive and in the Objects palette click the BuyObjects button. There are quite a few objects there, so it's helpful to use the Toggle Orientation button in the lower left of the Objects palette and then widen the palette a bit to get a full view of the available BuyObjects (**Figure 186**).

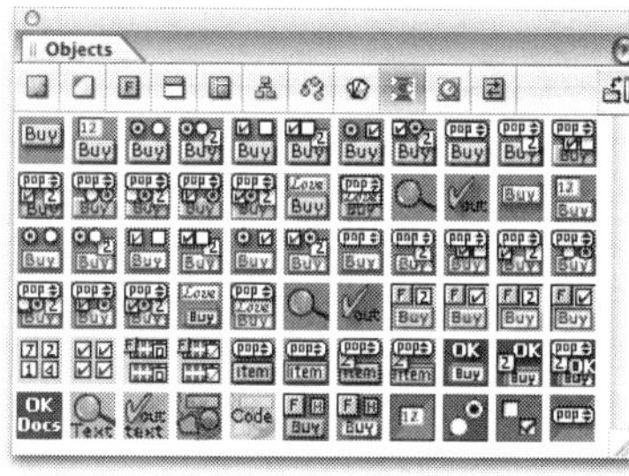

Figure 186 The CatalogIntegrator Cart BuyObjects.

Each BuyObject is a fully contained HTML form object. After you've dropped one onto a page, use the Inspector palette to configure fields such as SKU number, product name/description, price, size, and color. The CatalogIntegrator Cart is a free download and comes in two varieties: one version for Windows servers and one for Unix and Mac OS X servers. Whether you build the site on Windows or Mac makes no difference—it's only the type of server that will be used to host the site that matters when deciding which version to choose.

Once you have created the shopping cart pages, you'll need to hook up to a server in order to receive the store's orders. To that end, CatalogIntegrator offers a full line of products to meet your needs, everything from a small-scale PayPal interface to a hosted cart to a full-blown, real-time merchant account.

TIP 187 Cleaning Up Garbage Code

Name: DocCleaner

Developer: Oliver Michalak

Source: http://golive.werk01.de/DocCleaner

Cost: $15 US

This is an extension that we simply cannot do without. In fact, we might even get physical if someone tried to take DocCleaner away from us. For cleaning documents of unwanted fonts tags or nonbreaking spaces, for removing width or height attributes of a table, for getting rid of tag attributes or even tags themselves, your best friend is DocCleaner (**Figure 187**).

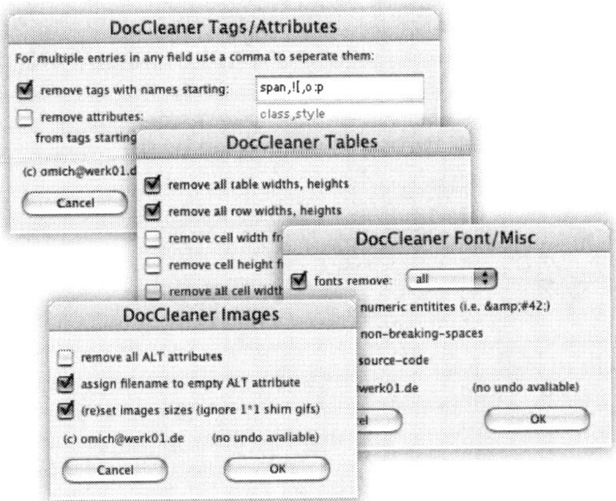

Figure 187 DocCleaner handles a variety of cleaning tasks quickly and efficiently.

If you need to clean legacy HTML pages that are riddled with <font> tags in order to use CSS to style text on pages, you will find this extension indispensable. Conversions of multiple documents can be time consuming and challenging, but DocCleaner makes this and similar tasks a breeze. You can run DocCleaner on one page, a selection of pages, or on an entire site.

TIP 188 Adding PayPal eCommerce

Name: PayPal eCommerce Extension

Developer: Transmit Media

Source: http://www.transmitmedia.com/golive/paypal/

Cost: Free

The PayPal eCommerce Extension allows you to add e-commerce to your Web sites by creating payment buttons and basic shopping-cart functionality. It enables you to accept credit card payments for items or services that you sell on your site. To receive payments, you will need to open up a free PayPal business account (unless you already have one). Customers making payments to you need not have a PayPal account, only a valid credit card. Payments made to you will be credited to your PayPal business account. PayPal even supports payments in several currencies, including US dollars, Canadian dollars, euros, British pounds, and Japanese yen.

The extension consists of four new objects that are added to the Objects palette. When you drag any of the objects onto a page, a helpful wizard pops up, asks you a few questions, and writes all the necessary PayPal code for you (**Figure 188**).

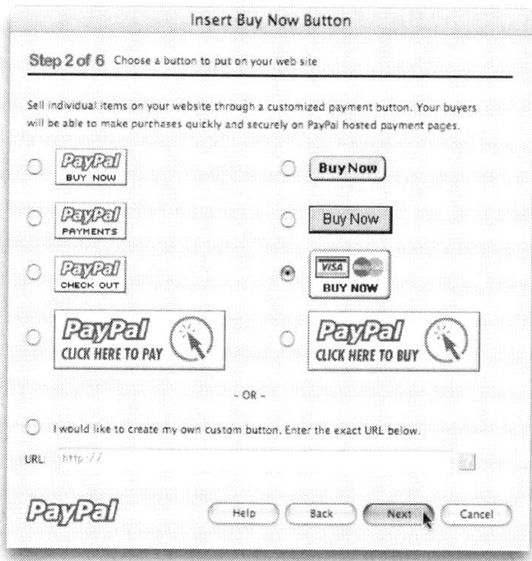

Figure 188 Add one of the four PayPal objects to a page, and the wizard gathers all the required information.

The palette objects are

- Buy Now—Inserts a PayPal button that visitors can click to pay you with any major credit card. Visitors will be taken to the PayPal Web site, where they can then enter payment information, which will be credited to your PayPal account.
- Add to Cart—This button allows visitors to add multiple products or services on your site to their personal shopping cart.
- View Cart—This button allows visitors to view the contents of their shopping carts without having to add a new item.
- Subscription—Recurring payments can be used to set up an ongoing charge or payment plan for customers—for example, a monthly or quarterly fee instead of a onetime charge.

TIP 189 Using Common Form Elements

Name: Smart Forms 2.0

Developer: Adam Pratt

Source: http://www.golivein24.com/resources

Cost: Free

The handy Smart Forms extension adds dozens of the most common, prebuilt form elements in a new section of the Objects palette (**Figure 189**). The feedback regarding Smart Forms has always been positive, and we've heard stories of Web designers completing a new form design before their managers were even done making the request. It could save you a lot of time, too.

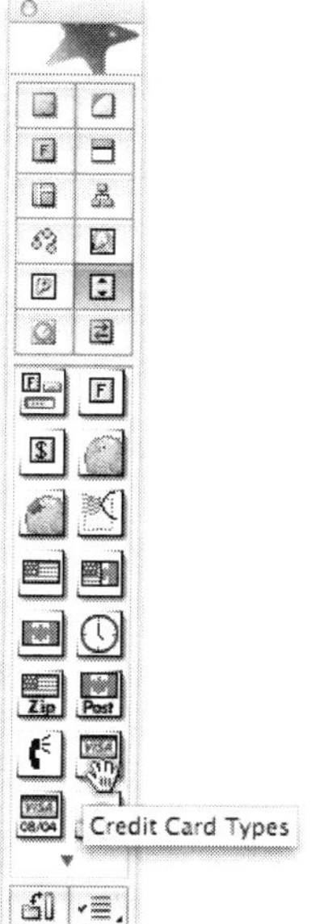

Figure 189 Smart Forms will save you time and eliminate typing mistakes.

First, create a form on your Web page. Now when you need a common form element, such as countries of the world, states in the US, or credit card types, just grab it from the new Smart Forms section of the Objects palette. There are 35 prebuilt form elements, including

Form Starter

Ecommerce Form Starter

Countries

US Postal

States and Provinces

Canadian Provinces and Territories

US Timezones

9-digit US Zip Code

10-digit US Phone Number

Credit Card Types

Credit Card Expiration

Delivery Methods

Gender

Marital Status

Age Groups

Education Level

Household Income

Bonus Tip

There's also an international version of Smart Forms available that includes 13 prebuilt form elements that might be helpful to users outside North America.

TIP 190 Detecting SWF Plug-in Compatibility

Name: Advanced SWF Authoring

Developer: GoLive product team

Source: http://share.studio.adobe.com/axAssetDetailSubmit.asp?aID=8802

Cost: Free

The GoLive product team put together a nifty extension that sniffs out whether a visitor to your page has the proper SWF plug-in needed to see Flash animations. This is a very cool extension because it offers a lot of flexibility as to how the detection happens, and it creates the necessary code in your page.

After installing the extension, you'll notice a new section in the Inspector palette when a SWF is placed onto a page. The section, called Detect, offers three detection methods: You can create a page that will direct the user to the Flash page if the plug-in is detected or to an alternate page if the plug-in is not installed (**Figure 190**); you can specify a GIF or JPEG that will replace the SWF if the plug-in is not detected; or you can specify HTML to replace the SWF if the plug-in is not detected.

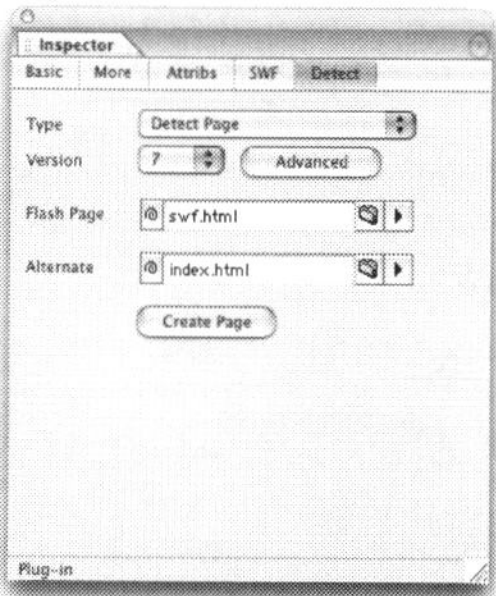

Figure 190 This extension adds a new Detect section to the SWF Inspector.

In all three cases, you simply choose a detection method from the Type pull-down in the Inspector palette and then click the Create Page button, which creates a new detection page, or click the Insert Detect button to insert the code into the current page.

In our tests we got an alert when using the image-replacement method. The alert is to let you know that you need to enter the pixel dimensions of the GIF or JPEG into the inspector because the extension doesn't automatically do so itself, but its wording is a little unclear and even a bit scary. Don't let it throw you, though. Just click the OK button and enter the width and height of the image into the Inspector palette. It works like a charm!

TIP 191 Finding Source Code Help

Name: Tag Help

Developer: GoLive product team

Source: Installed by default

Cost: Free

Have you memorized the correct syntax for every single HTML element and attribute? If you have, then you're probably too smart to be reading this book. If, on the other hand, you haven't memorized all of the World Wide Web Consortium W3C specifications, the TagHelp extension in GoLive will help you along. Think of it as a free HTML training tool built right in to GoLive.

Open the Tag Help palette in the Help menu and select an object in the Layout Editor. The Tag Help palette should refresh with an explanation directly from the W3C Web site explaining how to use the tag you have selected (**Figure 191**). Click the hyperlinks in the Tag Help palette to follow the links and learn more.

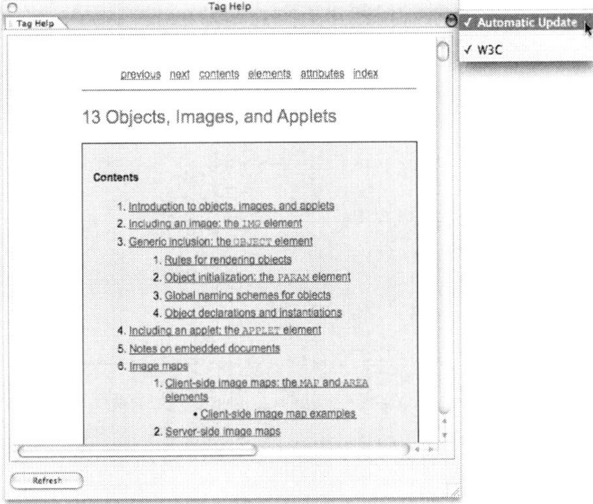

Figure 191 You can get help for all your HTML tags in the Tag Help palette.

If you have a mixed selection in the Layout Editor, the Tag Help palette can get confused and won't know which part of the HTML specification to show you. You can make a more specific selection by selecting a single tag in the markup tree at the bottom of the document window (see Tip 52). Tag Help also works when you're working in the Outline Editor (see Tip 74).

If the Tag Help palette doesn't update when you make a new selection, make sure that

- Automatic Update is enabled in the palette menu.
- You try clicking the Refresh button in the bottom-left corner of the palette.

TIP 192 Adding a Search Engine

Name: Atomz Search

Developer: Atomz

Source: http://www.atomz.com/golive/

Cost: Free for sites up to 500 pages

Atomz Search is an easy way to add search capabilities to your site. The service is free for sites up to 500 pages, but you should contact Atomz directly for pricing for larger site installations. With the Atomz extension for GoLive, you can quickly and easily insert the Atomz Search form into your Web pages. The extension supports multiple Atomz Search accounts and multiple Atomz customer logins so a Webmaster can easily manage multiple sites and accounts all from within GoLive. If you don't already have an Atomz account, then sign up at http://www.atomz.com.

Once you've installed the extension, be sure to quit and restart GoLive. Then select Special > Insert Atomz Search to insert the search form into the current document. You can also drag and drop the Atomz Search object from the Atomz section of the Objects palette in the Layout Editor.

You'll be asked for your email address, password, and site name, and the extension instantly writes all the code you need for a fully functional search engine (**Figure 192**). It really is that easy!

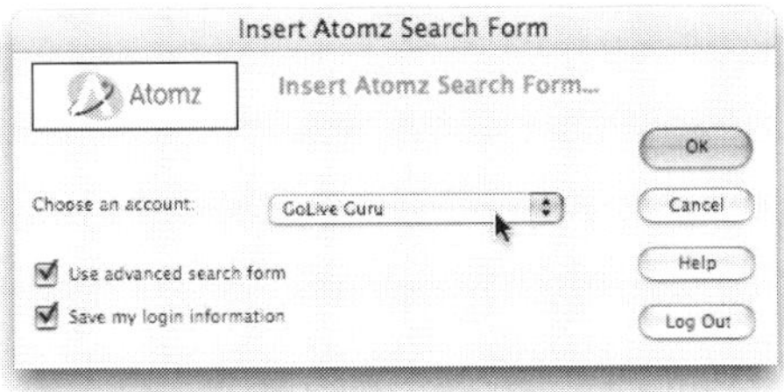

Figure 192 If you can drag and drop, you can add a search engine with Atomz.

TIP 193 Automatically Converting Hyperlinks

Name: URLize

Developer: GoLive product team

Source: SDK Samples folder

Cost: Free

If you have a bunch of email addresses or Web site URLs in a page that you need to convert to hyperlinks, it can be a really tedious task. Links pages and employee directories are perfect examples of Web pages with lots of hyperlinks or email addresses. It's not a hard task, but it's really boring and error prone.

The URLize extension automates hyperlinking and is included for free as a sample extension with GoLive. If you don't have the Adobe GoLive SDK/Samples folder in your GoLive application folder you can always download the latest version of the SDK and the Sample extension at http://partners.adobe.com/asn/golive/download.jsp.

To convert a link, select the email address or URL in the Layout Editor and choose Extensions > URLize text > Convert a selected URL or email text to a link (**Figure 193**). GoLive instantly converts the selected text, such as http://www.adobe.com, into a link to itself.

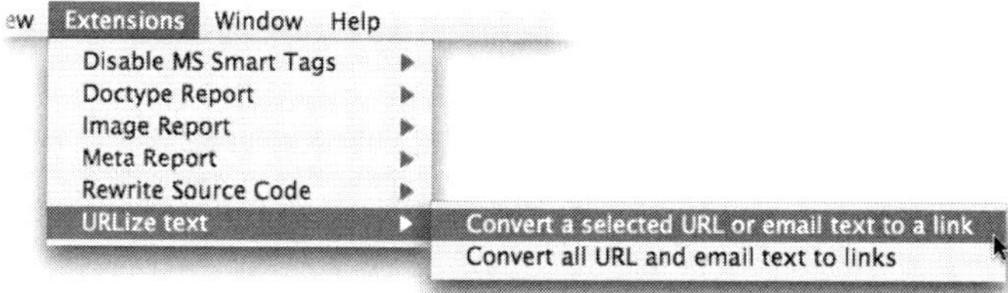

Figure 193 Select one of the URLize commands to automatically convert hyperlinks.

You can also convert the entire page at once. If you have several URLs and email addresses to convert in a page, select Extensions > URLize text > Convert all URL or email text to links. What a time-saver!

TIP 194 Developing Data-Driven Web Apps with Blue World Lasso

Name: Lasso Studio 7 for GoLive

Developer: Blue World Communications

Source: http://www.lassostudio.com/

Cost: $299 US

Lasso Studio enables Web developers to build visually rich, powerful, data-driven Web applications using the familiar GoLive interface (**Figure 194**). Solutions built using Lasso Studio can be deployed on any server running Lasso Professional 7 on any platform. Lasso Studio can connect to a variety of databases, including FileMaker Pro, MySQL, Microsoft SQL Server 2000, FrontBase, Sybase, OpenBase, PostgreSQL, Oracle, and hundreds more.

Figure 194 Lasso Studio adds dozens of new objects to the Objects palette, a Lasso Studio menu, and three new palettes in the Window menu.

Here are some of the features Lasso Studio adds to GoLive:

- You can display database tables and fields right within GoLive.
- Lasso Studio lets you preview data live from your database right within GoLive.
- You can use syntax coloring for LDML code, including tags, keywords, strings, and expressions.
- There is a code-completion feature for all LDML tags.
- You can quickly build an entire data-driven Web site using the Site Builder wizard.
- Lasso tags are represented as icons to minimize visual disruption of your layout while designing.
- You can instantly change the active database via the Database Selector.
- The visual editing environment provides more than a thousand Lasso tags.
- You can build and edit robust programming expressions with guided ease.
- Workgroup editing is allowed on a shared database without requiring direct access to databases.
- You can instantly convert your existing Lasso solution to LDML 7 syntax.
- A single-user version of Lasso Professional 7 server software is available for development and testing.

TIP 195 Running Search Engine Optimization Reports

Name: Meta Report

Developer: OUTActions

Source: http://www.outactions.com

Price: Check site for details

Oliver Zahorka of OUTActions is well known for the dozens of high-quality JavaScript actions he's created for GoLive. New from OUTActions is a collection of powerful reporting extensions that help you assess and troubleshoot different aspects of your Web site, including actions, CSS, DOCTYPEs, images, and metatags.

Building Web sites can be very satisfying work, but we all know how important it is to drive traffic through optimized search engine results. One key factor of search engine rankings is metatags, such as keywords and descriptions, and this is why you'll want to use the Meta Report extension.

To help you inventory your use of metatags in a page or site, select Extensions > Meta Report and choose the appropriate command:

- On This Page—Runs a report on a single page, which must be open.
- On Selected Pages—Runs a report on all the selected pages in the Files tab of the Site window. This is ideal for checking just one section of a site at a time.
- All Pages in Site—Runs a report on every page in the site regardless of how many files are selected or open.
- On Selected Extras Files—Select templates or stationery in the Extras tab of the Site window to report on the building blocks of the rest of the site.

When the report is complete, a new page is generated that shows you a summary of all the metatags used, their values, how many times each tag is used, and on which pages the tags are used (**Figure 195**).

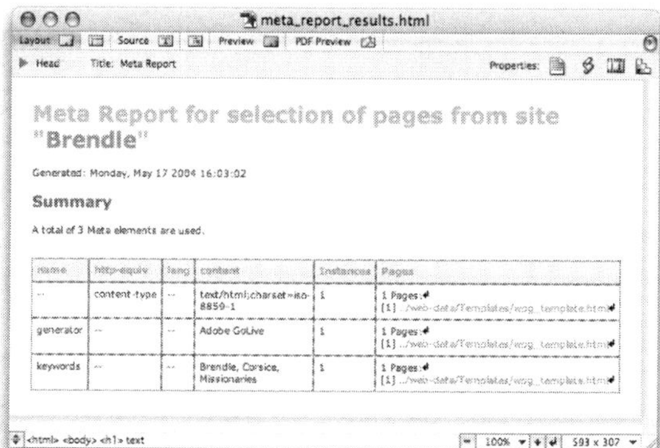

Figure 195 A metatag report can give you a reality check on the search-engine readiness of your site.

TIP 196 Adding a Tell a Friend Link

Name: Tell a Friend

Developer: Rasmussens Design

Source: http://www.rasmussens.dk/action

Cost: $10 US

GoLive users ask us all the time how to put a link on their Web sites that functions as a "tell a friend" feature. The aptly named Tell a Friend action from Rasmussens Design does exactly that, without the complexity of server-side scripting or difficult configurations.

This action launches most email clients and automatically puts the window title in the email subject line and the URL of the page in the email body. All the visitor has to do is click the link text, write the recipient email address, and send the message. You can also have text before and after the actual link text so it's completely customizable.

To use the Tell a Friend action, follow these steps:

1. Drop a body action from the Smart section of the Objects palette into the body of a Web page.
2. With the action placeholder still selected, choose the Tell a Friend action in the Actions section of the Rollovers & Actions palette.
3. Customize all the action parameters in the Rollovers & Actions palette (**Figure 196**). Make sure you resize the palette to be very tall so you can see all the options.

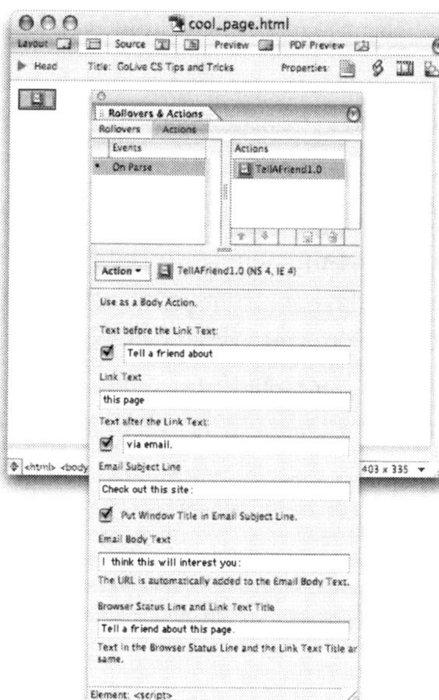

Figure 196 Experiment with the settings for the Tell a Friend action and test the results by previewing in a Web browser.

Bonus Tip

Configure the action once and then drag and drop it into the Snippets tab of the Library palette so that you can use it over and over again on other pages and sites.

TIP 197 Creating Interactive Slideshows

Name: SlideShowKit

Developer: MindPalette

Source: http://www.mindpalette.com/actions

Cost: $15 US

There are several ways to create interesting slideshows, but many of them require browser plug-ins, which can complicate the issue. Nate Baldwin of MindPalette has written dozens of amazing actions. One of our favorites is his SlideShowKit action set. This powerful action is actually eight actions combined together to perform some impressive slideshow effects, without the need for any plug-ins or special viewer software (**Figure 197**).

Figure 197 Just one example of what can be achieved with the SlideShowKit actions.

The SlideShowKit actions are very flexible and can be configured in a variety of ways, such as:

- Adding unlimited slideshows (user triggered or automatic) to your page, each with unlimited images.
- Toggling Play/Pause button option for autoplaying slideshows.
- Adding a link for each image in your slideshow to either open a new page or a pop-up window.
- Automatically generating a dynamic form selection menu for easy navigation through images.

- Automatically generating a count sequence as the slide show progresses (1 of 20, 2 of 20, and so on).
- Assigning a text caption or description that is automatically displayed with the corresponding image.

The actions come with a detailed PDF manual explaining all the options and there's a demo page at http://www.mindpalette.com/actions/natebaldwin/slideshow_kit/Examples. If you have questions about any of the MindPalette actions, they have great support forums at http://www.mindpalette.com/forum.

TIP 198 Adding a Scrollable Area to a Page

Name: ScrollArea 1.1

Developer: Ahgren's Actions

Source: http://www.golivecentral.com/pages/ahgren.shtml

Cost: Free

Michael Ahgren's ScrollArea action enables you to easily build attractive scrolling areas on your page. The action combines GoLive layers, which act as the container that scrolls, and either text or images that trigger the scrolling effects. Behind the scenes, the ScrollArea action writes the necessary JavaScript that makes the scrolling happen. All you need to do is use the GoLive Inspector, the CSS Editor, and the Rollovers & Actions palette to click your way to happy scrolling (**Figure 198**).

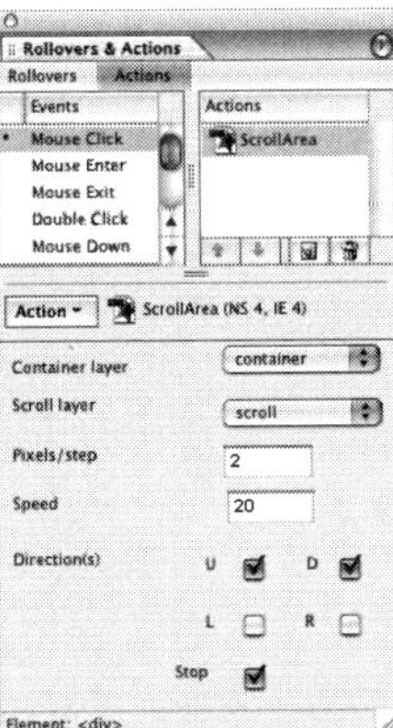

Figure 198 Set the options for your scrolling area in the Rollovers & Actions palette.

It's simple to do. Place a layer on the page called "container" and put another layer inside of that called "scroll." Next, select the text or image that will be the trigger, make it a link, and add the ScrollArea action. Selecting a Mouse Enter event will cause the scroll to begin when the user hovers over the link, which is a nice effect. In the Action palette, match up the layer names in the pull-down menus, designate the direction of the scroll, and you're pretty much done. There's an input field where you can control the speed of the scroll and a place to assign how much of the area should scroll, which is called the step size.

The ScrollArea action also includes great PDF documentation with directions on how to add text and images to the layer, how to set the options for step size and scroll speed, and how to scroll the area in as many as eight directions.

TIP 199 Verifying Form Field Entries

Name: VerifyForm

Developer: Walter Blady's Actions

Source: http://www.actionscafe.com

Cost: $45 US

If you have any forms on your Web site, you've probably wasted a lot of time correcting or reformatting some of the submitted data. Walter Blady of Actions Café has developed a commercial-grade product that verifies and reformats up to 15 selected fields in a single form (**Figure 199**) so the data you receive is complete, verified, and formatted just how you need it.

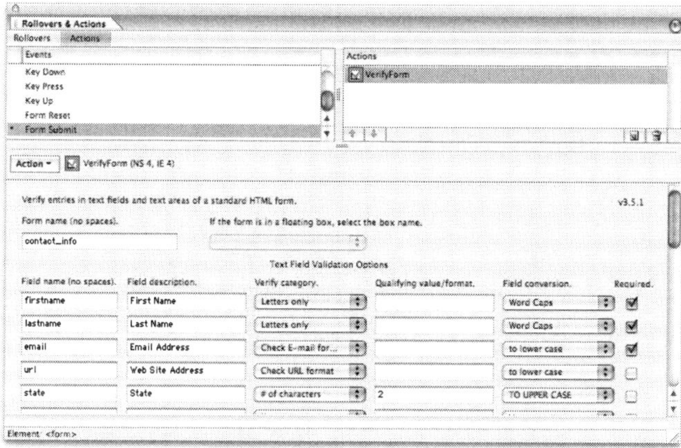

Figure 199 Set the VerifyForm action to work on the FormSubmit event so it can verify the data before it's submitted.

The VerifyForm action goes to work as soon as the visitor clicks the Submit button. All data-entry errors are displayed to the visitor and must be corrected before the form is submitted. VerifyForm can also block blank and duplicate forms from being submitted as well as guard against profanities or other inappropriate entries. Walter's actions include exhaustive documentation to get you started.

Some other benefits of using the VerifyForm action are these:

- Relieves server load by checking forms before they are sent.
- Offers great features for Web site owners who don't have access to CGI form handlers.
- Provides a comprehensive set of form-checking and field-formatting features.
- Checks text fields, radio buttons, and single- and multiple-select lists.
- Lets users send the form data as a delimited string ready for importing into a database.
- Allows users to design their own error message window to match the look of their Web site.
- Provides customizable form entry error messages.
- Uses cookie technology to repopulate forms if a user revisits the form page.

TIP 200 DJ Design Actions

Name: 20 Actions Collection

Developer: DJ Design

Source: http://actions.golivetutor.com

Cost: Free

Dave Jones at DJ Design packages all 20 of his free actions together in one zip file so users can download them all and use the ones they want. Some of his actions offer general-purpose features, such as printing pages (**Figure 200**) and custom window opening, as well as some very advanced JavaScript variable and code snippet actions.

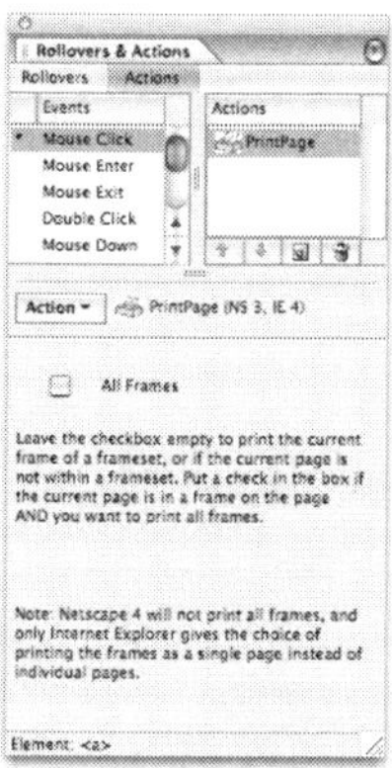

Figure 200 The Print Page action is helpful and easy to use.

All 20 actions are useful, but here are a few of our favorites:

- AutoFrameset and IntoFrameset—Use these two actions together to force a page into a frameset. This is useful when a page is linked via a search engine, because the search engines tend to index the individual pages, without the frameset.
- PrintPage—This action will print the current page, even if it's a frames page.
- Current Date—This action displays the current date on the page. You can even customize the font, size, and color of the type or apply a CSS class style.
- Open Window 1.2—This action is based on the original GoLive Open Window action and adds a new check box to force the new window to fill the entire screen. It also leaves all the check boxes unchecked by default, because most people seem to prefer that in their new windows.

APPENDIX A

Hidden Keyboard Shortcuts

GoLive CS has shortcuts that are not documented in the Help files. This appendix lists those shortcuts on both the Mac and Windows platforms for your GoLiving pleasure. Special thanks to Heiko Hahn for documenting these shortcuts and to all the GoLive engineers who implemented them.

Wherever two keyboard commands are separated by a slash (/), such as Command/Ctrl or Option/Alt, the first command is for Macintosh and the second for Windows. If only one shortcut, such as Shift or Control, is listed, then it's the same shortcut for both platforms.

General

Press this...	...when you do this...	...to this...	...and this happens
Shift (Mac only)	Close window	Welcome Screen	Documents that were open last time you quit GoLive open automatically
Option/Alt	Select Split Source	Document window	The orientation of the Split Source View rotates
Option/Alt	Click Open in the Open dialog	A document	The encoding dialog opens
Control-Option/ Ctrl-Alt	Click and drag	Layout Editor	Pan around the page with the Hand tool
Control (Mac only)	Select View > Show/Hide Rulers	Layout Editor	Rulers appear faster and without sound
Option-Shift/ Alt-Shift	Move mouse over objects	Layout Editor	The element source shows as a tool tip
Shift	Paste styled text from Microsoft Word	Layout Editor	Styles such as font-size, font-family, and margin are retained
Option/Alt	Click	Link Warnings icon in the toolbar	The selected state becomes the default
Option (Mac)/ Click and press Alt (Windows)	Select element	Markup tree in the status bar	A child element pull-down menu instantly displays
Shift	Select page properties	Page property icon	The <body> element is selected (in Split Source View)
Shift	Click	Zoom display in document status bar	The Zoom value toggle is reset to 400%
Control/Alt	Click	Marker pull-down menu in Source Editor	Functions are sorted alphabetically
Option/Alt	Click	Optimize Size button in Layout Grid Inspector	Only the height is optimized

Press this...	...when you do this...	...to this...	...and this happens
Shift	Click	Optimize Size button in Layout Grid Inspector	Only the width is optimized
Shift	Drag	Layer	The layer is restricted to horizontal or vertical movement
Shift	Use cursor keys	Layer	The layer is resized instead of moved
Command (Mac only)	Double-click	An external CSS or @import rule in the CSS Editor	The current CSS Editor is closed before the other CSS Editor is opened
Option/Alt	Edit element or class name	CSS Editor	You can change an element to a class style, or vice versa
Option/Alt	Click	Create a new font family icon in the CSS Editor	Existing fonts are replaced with the new ones
Shift	Click	Create a New font icon in the CSS Editor	The new font is added to the top of the list
Option/Alt	Click Selector and the Properties tab	CSS Editor	A preference is set to remember the last open tab
Shift/Alt	Select a value in a pop-up list	CSS Editor	The !important state is toggled on or off for the property
Option/Alt	Click	Browse button of the link field	The Edit URL dialog opens
Option (Mac only)	Press Return/Enter	Link input field	The URL is completed with http.//, even if there is no www
Option (Mac only)	Open recent file	Menu	The Select Encoding dialog opens
Option/Alt	Select Type > Fonts	Menu	All font names in font family are shown: Font1, Font2, Font3, etc.

(continued on next page)

Press this...	...when you do this...	...to this...	...and this happens
Option/ Alt-Shift	Select Type > Fonts	Menu	The font family and all font names are shown: Font Set (Font1, Font2, Font3)
Option/ Alt-Shift	Select File > Download Page	Menu	GoLive attempts to get references from URLs in JavaScript
Option/Alt-OK	Select Edit > Document Content > Change Doctype	Menu	The URL is written into the DOCTYPE
Option/Alt-OK	Choose Doctype	Flyout	The URL is written into the DOCTYPE
Shift	Undefine a region	Special > Template	ALL region definitions are removed
Shift	Detach from a Template	Special > Template	Regions in the page are retained
Option/Alt	Click Use Results	Find & Replace - Results	The Result window closes
Shift	Add a font to a family	Font Editor (Default Fonts)	The new font is added to the top of the list (the font family must be selected)
Shift	Select Edit > Document Content > Rewrite Source Code	Rewrite Source for a document	Rewrites source code according to Web Settings as in GoLive 6 instead of with the New Options dialog in GoLive CS
Option (Mac only)	Delete markup, characters, or browser profile	Web Settings	The confirmation dialog is suppressed
Option/Alt	Close the Web Settings	Web Settings	The changes are not saved
Option/Alt	Change a name	Web Settings: Tag- / Attr-Inspector	There is no conversion to lower case
Option/Alt	Move an item	Web Settings: Markup/ Characters	The item is copied

Palettes

Press this...	...when you do this...	...to this...	...and this happens
Option/Alt	Open/close folder	CSS palette, Style Info	All of the folders will toggle opened or closed.
Option/Alt	Show Apply Information	CSS palette, flyout menu	All three flyout options (Apply Information, Cascaded Preview, Cascaded Properties) are toggled on or off
Option/Alt	Select Element > CSS > Special	Highlight palette	The new selection replaces the previous selection instead of adding to it
Shift	Select Syntax Check	Highlight palette	The syntax check runs without first showing the Option window
Command/Ctrl	Click on a style	HTML Style palette	The Edit Style window opens
Command/Ctrl	Click a hide or lock icon	Layer palette	The command is applied to all layers
Option (Mac only)	Select User Profile	View palette	All selected profiles will be deselected
Option/Alt	Deselect Display Images	View palette	Both image and media files are hidden from view
Command/Ctrl	Click and drag a table icon	Objects palette	A custom-sized table is drawn
Option (Mac only)	Select (or Deselect) Addition	Syntax Checker	All additions are deselected
Option/Alt	Click on Display	Table palette	The parent table is selected

Images/Media

Press this...	...when you do this...	...to this...	...and this happens
Command + . (Mac only)	Crop an image	Smart Object	The crop is canceled
Control	Adjust crop with cursor keys	Smart Object	The crop rectangle is moved by 10 pixels
Option/Alt	Select a new source file	Smart Image	The settings dialogs are suppressed (, Save For Web, existing settings (if any) are retained, and existing target file(s) are kept if possible
Control	Define tracing image cut out with cursor keys	Tracing image	The tracing rectangle is moved by 10 pixels
Command/ Alt-Shift	Point and shoot from image	Image in Layout Editor	A lowsrc image is assigned
Shift	Set width or height of an image, layer, or plug-in content	Layout Editor or Inspector	The proportions are retained
Option/Alt	Click Send Area to Back/ Front in the toolbar	Image map area	The area is sent backward or forward one level
Option (Mac only)	Move area with cursor keys	Image map area	The area is moved by 10 pixels
Command/Alt	Click on area	Image map area	The point and shoot tool (Fetch URL) is invoked
Shift	Move area with cursor keys	Image map area	The area is resized by one pixel
Shift-Option/ Shift-Ctrl-Alt-	Move area with cursor keys	Image map area	The area is resized by 10 pixels
Command/Ctrl	Drag file into layout	SVG image	An SVG plug-in is created instead of a Smart Object
Option (Mac only)	Select File > Import > Photoshop Layers	Import Photoshop Layers	The first Photoshop layer becomes the background image of the page
Control	Save/cancel a layer	Import Photoshop Layers dialog	All remaining layers are canceled or saved

Site

Press this...	...when you do this...	...to this...	...and this happens
Option/Ctrl	Delete file	Site window (Files, External, Colors, Font Sets, Collections)	The Deletion confirmation dialog is suppressed
Shift-Control	Save	Site window	A force save is performed
Control	Click on a radio button	Site wizard	The next screen is loaded
Control, as you click the next buttons (Mac only)	Enter an already used site name	Site wizard	GoLive assigns the site a unique name instead of displaying a warning that a site with that name already exists
Control, as you click the Next buttons (Mac only)	Select an already taken site location	Site wizard	GoLive assigns the site a unique name instead of displaying a warning that a site in that location already exists
Command/Ctrl	Click on a file	Errors tab	Invokes the point and shoot tool as you click on the missing file error
Option/Alt	Add a new font family	Font Set Inspector	Existing fonts are replaced with the new ones
Shift	Add a new font	Font Set Inspector	The new font is added to the top of the list
Option/Alt	Select Site > Refresh View	Site menu	All references are reparsed
Command-Option/ Alt-Shift	Select Site > Refresh View	Site menu	Thumbnails are generated or updated
Shift	Open the site	Site file	Link checking and file verification are skipped

Import from InDesign

Press this...	...when you do this...	...to this...	...and this happens
Shift	Drag text items from the package window	Into the Layout Editor	The selection is placed as a Smart Object instead of text
Shift	Point and shoot source to a page item	Smart Object (layout)	The selection is placed as a Smart Object instead of text
Shift-Control-Option/Ctrl-Alt	Drag	Page Items view of the package window	The visible area is panned
	Double-click	Page Items View (outside page bounds)	The previous or next page is shown
	Double-click	Page item	The page is zoomed in
	Double-click	Asset	The page item is zoomed in
	Double-click	Page Items View (inside page bounds)	The page is zoomed out
Option/Alt	Click OK	Object Generator Settings dialog	The selected settings are used package-wide for all page items that have no custom settings

Outline Editor

Press this...	...when you do this...	...to this...	...and this happens
Alt (Mac only)	Click on color icon	Color attribute	The color picker opens
Command/Ctrl	Click on a link icon	Link attribute	The point and shoot (Fetch URL) becomes available
Command/Ctrl	Click on an element name	Element	A pop-up list appears containing all allowed element names for the present DOCTYPE

PDF Integration

Press this...	...when you do this...	...to this...	...and this happens
Control	Move or size a link region with the cursor keys	PDF Link Editing mode	The link region is moved or sized by 10 points
Shift-Command/ Shift-Ctrl	Open or import	A site with secured PDFs	PDFs are not parsed during importation or opening of the site

APPENDIX B

Objects Palette Descriptions

Experienced GoLive users are probably familiar with most of the objects in the Objects palette, but we frequently hear from new users that understanding all the icons in this palette can be confusing and overwhelming at first. This appendix defines the most used objects found in the palette. Special thanks to Bettina Reinemann and the rest of the GoLive UI team for creating these beautiful icons and helping us put together this list.

Basic

Drag these objects and drop them into a page to lay out a design or double-click them to insert them at the cursor location:

Layout Grid—Creates a grid for precisely placing design elements on a page (see Tip 33).

Layout Text Box—Creates a text area on a Layout Grid (see Tip 33).

Layer—Use to contain objects such as images or text; layers can be moved around the page, stacked, animated, and styled using CSS (see Tip 35).

Table—Use to display tabular data or to contain design elements (see Tip 36).

Image—Use as a placeholder for an image.

Plug-in—Use this when no other plug-in object is the correct choice.

SWF

SWF—Use as a placeholder for Flash content or link to the SWF file from the Inspector (see Tip 157).

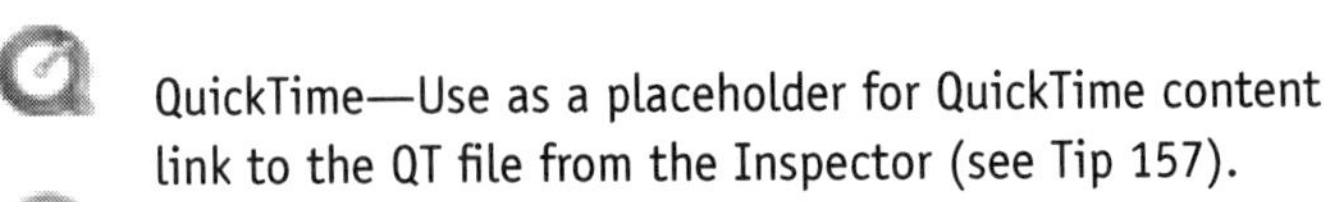
QuickTime—Use as a placeholder for QuickTime content or link to the QT file from the Inspector (see Tip 157).

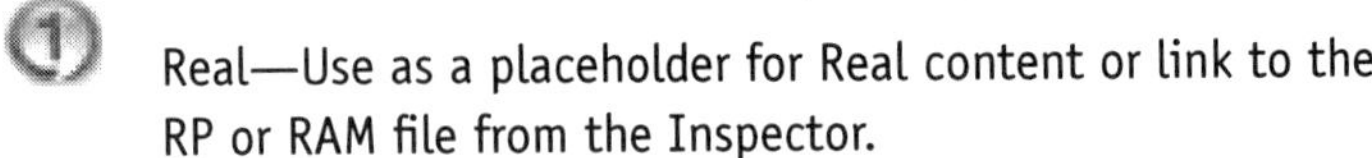
Real—Use as a placeholder for Real content or link to the RP or RAM file from the Inspector.

SVG—Use as a placeholder for SVG content or link to the SVG file from the Inspector.

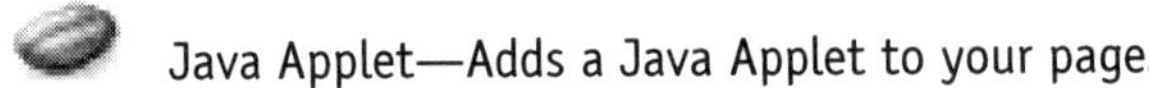
Java Applet—Adds a Java Applet to your page.

Object—Use this when no other object is the correct choice.

Line—Creates a horizontal rule in your page.

Horizontal Spacer—Adds a horizontal spacer to your page (Netscape only).

JavaScript—Use to add JavaScript to your page.

Marquee—Creates a scrolling marquee (Internet Explorer only).

Comment—Writes a comment into the page.

Anchor—Creates an anchor destination.

Line Break—Adds a line break in text.

Tag—Adds a tag element to your page; set its attributes in the Inspector.

Smart

These objects have additional functionality beyond those in the Basic set. Some of them use JavaScript, some are dragged into the body of the page, and some are dragged into the head of the page. All are configured in the Inspector palette (see Tip 118).

Smart Photoshop—Allows you to link to a native Photoshop file (see Tip 121).

Smart Illustrator—Allows you to link to a native Illustrator file (see Tip 127).

Smart PDF—Allows you to link to a native Acrobat PDF file (see Tip 128).

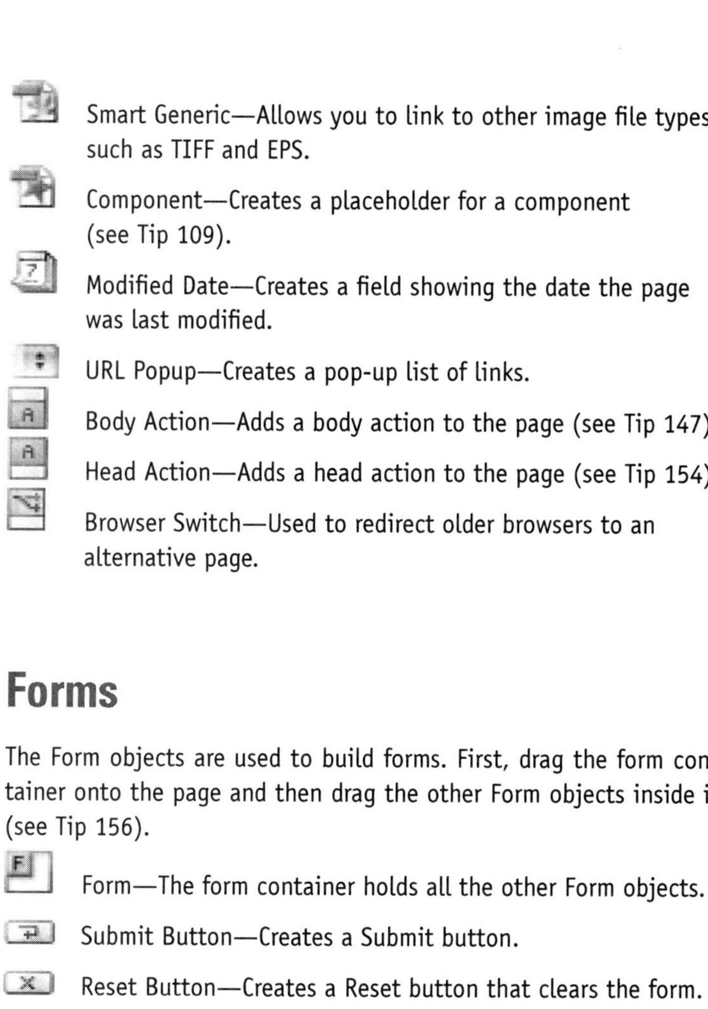

Smart Generic—Allows you to link to other image file types such as TIFF and EPS.

Component—Creates a placeholder for a component (see Tip 109).

Modified Date—Creates a field showing the date the page was last modified.

URL Popup—Creates a pop-up list of links.

Body Action—Adds a body action to the page (see Tip 147).

Head Action—Adds a head action to the page (see Tip 154).

Browser Switch—Used to redirect older browsers to an alternative page.

Forms

The Form objects are used to build forms. First, drag the form container onto the page and then drag the other Form objects inside it (see Tip 156).

Form—The form container holds all the other Form objects.

Submit Button—Creates a Submit button.

Reset Button—Creates a Reset button that clears the form.

Button—Creates a generic button; label it and set its function in the Inspector.

Form Input Image—Lets you use an image as a form input button.

Label—Lets you label a form element.

Text Field—Creates a text input field.

Password—Creates a password input field.

Text Area—Creates a text input area.

Check Box—Creates a check box.

Radio Button—Creates a radio button; may be used in a group so the user is limited to only one choice.

Popup—Creates a pop-up list of choices.

List Box—Creates an input field that contains a selectable list.

File Browser—Creates a browse button for the form to attach a file to the form submission.

Hidden—Creates a hidden element that contains information used when the form is submitted.

Key Generator—Creates access keys that let users navigate the form with keyboard commands.

Fieldset—Visually groups elements of a form together.

Head

Drag these objects into the head portion of a page to create tags that send information to the browser (see Tip 24).

IsIndex—Tells browsers the page is searchable via keywords. (This element is now outdated.)

Base—Tells the browser the original URL of the Web page.

Keywords—Lets you create keywords for searching (see Tip 26).

Link—Lets you specify an association between the current page and other pages.

Meta—Used to include information about your Web page (see Tip 26).

Refresh—Tells the browser to reload the page after a certain interval.

Element—Adds a <no edit> element to the head section.

Comment—Lets you add a comment in the head section.

Encode—Defines the character encoding for the document (see Tip 32).

Script—Lets you add JavaScript to the head section.

Frames

Drag these objects into the Frame Editor of an open Web page to create frames-based designs (see Tip 64).

Inline Frame—Creates an inline frame in a page for the effect of a virtual window (see Tip 65).

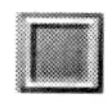

Frame—Adds a single frame to a frameset, whose options can be adjusted in the Inspector.

Frame Sets—More than a dozen predesigned frameset combinations are included; adjust the options in the Inspector.

Site

Drag these objects directly into the Site window to create new pages, external references, and other site assets (see Tip 16).

Generic Page—Adds a new generic page to the site.

URL—Creates a new external reference in the Externals tab of the Site window; customize in the Inspector.

Address—Creates an email address to the External tab of the Site window; customize in the Inspector.

Color—Creates a color swatch in the Colors tab of the Site window; can be accessed by all pages with the Swatches palette.

Font Set—Creates a new set of fonts in the Font Sets tab of the Site window that you can use to style text or assign to a CSS rule.

Collection—Creates a collection of assets in the Collections tab of the Site window (see Tip 163).

Folder—Creates a folder in the Files tab of the Site window so you can organize your files in a larger site.

URL Group—Creates a folder in the External tab of the Site window for organizing external URL references.

 Address Group—Creates a folder in the External tab of the Site window for organizing email addresses.

 Color Group—Creates a folder in the Colors tab of the Site window for organizing colors.

 Font Set Group—Creates a folder in the Font Sets tab of the Site window for organizing font sets.

Diagram

Drag and drop the Diagram objects into a diagram window to create site maps for new sites or new sections of existing sites (see Tip 164).

 Page—Adds a generic blank page to the diagram; you can assign a template or stationery to pages with the Inspector.

 Section—Use a section to quickly add multiple pages to a diagram that are grouped together.

 Group—Adds a rectangular box to the diagram so you can group multiple diagram objects into a logical collection.

 Annotation—Adds an Acrobat-style note comment to the diagram, a link, or an individual object in the diagram.

 Box—Adds a text box to the diagram where you can add customized text labels, notes, and a legend to the map.

 Level—Adds a vertical bracket to the diagram that you can resize and use to label the structure of the site map.

All the other objects represent other items that might be a part of a Web site, including a Java Applet, a PDF, or a QuickTime movie.

QuickTime

All the objects in the QuickTime section are added to a QuickTime movie in the QuickTime Editor. Don't get confused and try to drag these objects into the Layout Editor, because they won't work there.

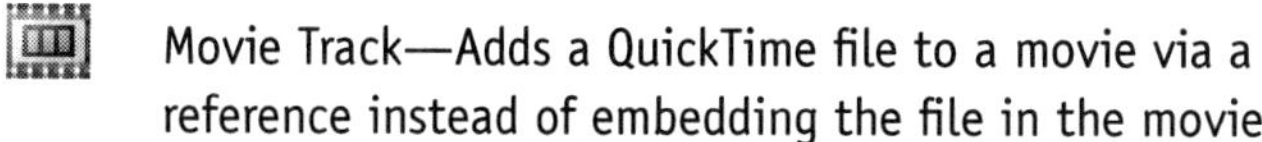

Movie Track—Adds a QuickTime file to a movie via a reference instead of embedding the file in the movie.

Video Track—Embeds a video into a movie.

Color Track—Adds a field of flat color to a movie; ideal for a matte or frame effect.

Picture Track—Adds a still picture or a slideshow of images to a movie (see Tip 158).

Generic Filter Track—Adds a cloud, fire, or ripple effect to a movie with a dynamic filter.

One Source Filter Track—Applies filters including blur, sharpen, color correction, and various special effects to a single video track.

Two Source Filter Track—Creates a transition between two video tracks.

Three Source Filter Track—Uses the luminosity of one track to affect the blending between two other tracks; useful for masking effects.

MPEG Track—Adds an MPEG-1 video track to the video; you'll also have to use a sound track for audio.

Sprite Track—Add this to a movie so you can add interactive sprite objects.

Sprite Object—Adds interactive sprite objects to a sprite track.

SWF Track—Adds SWF files to a movie.

HREF Track—Adds hyperlinks to a movie that can load other Web pages or frames.

Chapter Track—Adds a navigation pull-down menu to the player control for navigating to different sections of a long movie, similar to the scene selection feature on a DVD player.

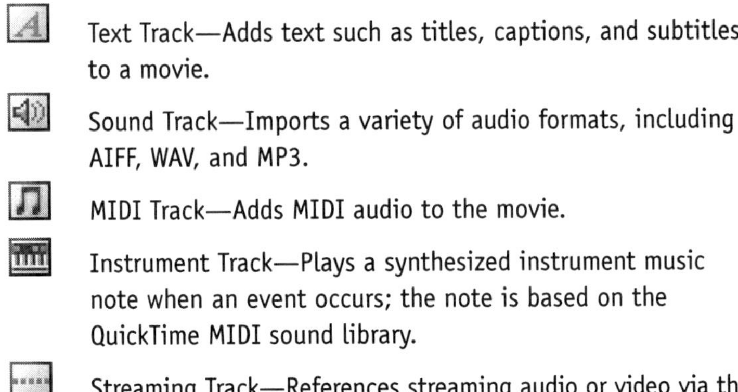

Text Track—Adds text such as titles, captions, and subtitles to a movie.

Sound Track—Imports a variety of audio formats, including AIFF, WAV, and MP3.

MIDI Track—Adds MIDI audio to the movie.

Instrument Track—Plays a synthesized instrument music note when an event occurs; the note is based on the QuickTime MIDI sound library.

Streaming Track—References streaming audio or video via the Runtime Streaming Protocol (RTSP); allows you to play live video sources inside a prebuilt QuickTime player interface.

Folder Track—If you use several tracks in a movie, use folder tracks to organize other tracks into groups.

APPENDIX C

GoLive Resources on the Web

Adobe Resources

GoLive Product Page
http://www.adobe.com/golive

GoLive Tryout Page
http://www.adobe.com/products/tryadobe/main.jsp#product=26

GoLive Tips
http://www.adobe.com/products/tips/golive.html

Adobe Studio
http://studio.adobe.com

Adobe Studio Exchange
http://share.studio.adobe.com/

GoLive Top Issues (Adobe Technical Support)
http://www.adobe.com/support/techdocs/topissuesgl.htm

Tips and Tutorials Sites

GoLive Central
http://www.golivecentral.com/

GoLive in 24
http://www.golivein24.com

GoLive 911
http://www.futurastudios.com/golive911/

GoLive Basics
http://www.golivebasics.com/

GoLive Tutor
http://www.golivetutor.com/

GoLive After Hours
http://www.afterhours.org.uk/

Sad Ark Tutorials
http://www.stochasticaphelion.com/Tutorials

MindPalette Tutorials
http://www.mindpalette.com/tutorials/index.php

Rasmussens Design
http://www.rasmussens.dk/tut/

Lists and Communities

Adobe User to User Forums
http://www.adobeforums.com/

Blueworld GoLive TalkList
http://www.blueworld.com/blueworld/lists/golive.html

GoLive Mod
http://groups.yahoo.com/group/golivemod/

Adobe-GoLive
http://groups.yahoo.com/group/Adobe-GoLive/

Actions and Extensions

Adobe Studio Exchange
http://share.studio.adobe.com

Good collection of third-party actions, extensions, and modules
http://www.actionext.com

Index

D

E

F

G

H

I

J

K

L

M

Q

R

S

V

W

X

Z